THE PRESS OF AFRICA

THE PRESS OF AFRICA

Persecution and Perseverance

FRANK BARTON

AFRICANA PUBLISHING COMPANY
A division of
Holmes & Meier Publishers, Inc.
New York

First published in the United States of America 1979 by

AFRICANA PUBLISHING COMPANY

A division of Holmes & Meier Publishers, Inc.

30 Irving Place, New York, N.Y. 10003

Library of Congress Cataloging in Publication Data

Barton, Frank.
   The Press of Africa: persecution and perseverance.

   Bibliography: p.
   Includes index.
   1. Press—Africa—History.   I. Title.
PN5450.B38   079′.6   78-7363
ISBN 0-8419-0393-X

PRINTED IN GREAT BRITAIN

To Africa's smallest tribe, its newspapermen

An endangered species

Contents

Preface: The Paradox of the Press in Africa

As political freedom came to the Continent, so did press freedom disappear. This is the paradox of the press of Africa: nobody should have been surprised at this, much less dismayed. Nothing that has happened or is happening to the press in Africa has not occurred in many countries which today claim some sort of press freedom. Despite the persecution, frustration and political control to which the press of virtually every state in Africa is subject it is still less corrupt than the press of Britain, the United States, France and most other Western countries in the early days of their newspapers.

The conventional view—that is the White view—of the press in Africa, like so many other White views of the non-White world, is that all is pretty well lost. The decay started, so the consensus goes, when the Union Jack, the Tricolour, the Belgian and even the Portuguese flags were run down for the last time.

Nothing changes. The same sort of views were expressed by Rome when their legions withdrew from ancient Britain and Western Europe. And, judged by the standards of the latter-day colonialists, many of those fears were realised.

The prophets of doom about the press of Africa could yet be right. It is much too early to be sure, and the greatest fallacy about Africa, perpetrated by Africans themselves quite as much as by White Westerners or Yellow Easterners, is that Africa is one great homogeneous whole, almost one country with one pattern and one inevitable destiny.

Africa is nothing of the sort. It is some fifty different countries, with perhaps a thousand different languages. And even if you hive off great sections to make cases—as I have dangerously done in this book—there are so many differences within those sections that any generalisations are fraught with danger.

Africa, the great Continent for the trigger-happy hunters of yore, is now an even bigger hunting-ground for a breed of mankind which is arguably doing infinitely more harm than merely decimating wild life—the researchers coming up with definitive answers.

Nigeria is as different from, say, Tanzania, as Germany is from Spain. Botswana has fewer links with Ghana than the Finns have with the Italians. Zambia's Kenneth Kaunda has about as much in common with Uganda's Idi Amin as Jimmy Carter has with Rumania's Nicolae Ceausescu—less.

And so it is with the press of Africa. Only the hand of officialdom which controls it—sometimes mail-fisted, sometimes velvet clad—is the common denominator.

There has not been a book from Britain about the press in Africa for ten years. There have been only two in that time from the United States. They are both sound, thorough studies, full of facts and figures. But in Africa the facts are always less than what has happened. I have tried to capture something of the feel of things. Although I became a research fellow at the School of African Studies at Sussex University in order to write this book, it is in no sense an academic work. It is a book about newspapermen in Africa. For if geography is about maps, history is about chaps, and ultimately this book is the story of the Black and White newspapermen who were or still are there—and some who hope to return some day.

Any book about contemporary Africa is out of date before it gets through the printer. This one will be no exception. And yet this may be an appropriate time to set down something of what has happened and what is happening to the press in Africa. Though the pattern is likely to change and change again as the old leaders die off and the young captains and majors eagerly wrest power from the corpulent generals, a generation of independence in many states, and at least a decade for the newest, has set the Continent on a path which is clearer to assess than ever before. It is a good time, or as good a time as there is ever likely to be, to take stock and make a record.

There are three colours to the colours of Africa: Black, White and Brown. This book looks at the press of the principal areas of the predominant two, Black and White, for the Brown of Arab Africa is another world from Black Africa, a place apart from the great heart of the Continent, with a culture, a religion and a civilization which has only touched Black Africa on the fringes where the two meet. So this study draws a line across the Sahara from East to West and looks South.

There are 38 states there with nearly 300,000,000 people—and not nearly enough newspapers.

****

I am indebted to the Ford Foundation and to the International Press Institute for their assistance in the research and preparation of this study.

1 The Expanding Continent with the Shrinking Press

Black Africa's best newspaperman lives among the Surrey hills of suburban London and commutes to the city every day. He says he will never go back to editing the biggest newspaper in Africa's biggest state.

The only African to hold a staff job in Fleet Street—on *The Times*—lives on the other side of London overlooking the River Thames. He would like to go back, but doubts he ever will.

After a year of penny-pinching in Britain, the editor of the only daily newspaper in one of Central Africa's smallest states has gone to Botswana to train government information officers. He will go home—along with those other newspapermen lucky enough to have got out of the country—when Hastings Banda of Malawi is no longer president, unless his successor is of the same ilk.

It has been too long away for the most experienced journalist from the tiny West African republic where Black Africa's press was born, and he will almost certainly live out the rest of his life as a Black Englishman, dealing in diamonds from his native Sierra Leone.

Not all the African newspapermen who have left home are Black. There are the White Africans of Rhodesia, Moçambique, Angola and South Africa. They have found it easier to adapt to the sub-editor's desk of the *Daily Mirror*, the news room of *The Guardian*, the press attaché's desk of a Portuguese embassy or to kick their heels and hope for something to turn up in London or Lisbon.

There are not a lot of them, Black or White, these newspaper-

men of Africa who have packed their bags, or had them packed
for them, and left for Europe. Many more have crossed Africa's
many borders to wait for things to change at home. They feel as
foreign as any African in the West. It may be the same sun that
shines on the exiled Liberian newspaperman in the Ivory Coast,
the Rhodesian in Zambia, the Somali in Tanzania, the Ugandan
in Kenya, but there is precious little else that is familiar or
warming.

From the Sahara to the Cape, the total out of the Continent
or exiled within it is probably less than a hundred. But they
represent more than just some of the best. They are the last
generation of a press that was born and developed under
imperialism, a press moulded in the Western tradition, and which
for the best part of two centuries followed a close parallel with
the press of Europe and North America, adopting all the best
and all the worst of journalism in those societies.

Now it has changed. Not yet completely, not yet irrevocably.
But undeniably changed. Only in the Southernmost tip of the
Continent, where the White man's roots are deepest and where
the struggle to uproot them will be hardest, has the press maintained its Western pattern. But as the portents for stark change
grow stronger, so does the certainty that there, too, the press is
in its last generation as a European model.

This is far from saying that the African press does not owe a
great deal to European influence, though there are plenty of
African politicians who constantly assert otherwise. They might
just as well say that the introduction of paper and ink was a
bad thing.

It was inevitable that this purging of the press of Black Africa
should have taken place; just as it was inevitable that the
Westminster-style parliaments established in the nineteen-fifties
and sixties, with their knee-breeched serjeants-at-arms and their
silver maces resting below Mr Speaker's chair, should have given
way to one-party or military rule. For the press was not merely
a foreign importation into what is still very largely a society where
people get their news from talking to their neighbours, but at
best an irritant and often a danger in the early years of nationhood.

If this is a paradox, then it is an easily understood one. For
the whole of its history, the press of Africa had been used by both
Black nationalists and White settlers to noisily assert their very

different viewpoints. When the Nkrumahs, the Kenyattas, the Nyereres, the Kaundas and the score of other African leaders took control of their nations from the colonialists, they considered they had enough trouble getting their new ships of state launched without any of the ships' company arguing with the captain.

And more significantly still, all those African leaders and most of the others had in one way or the other used the press in their fight against colonialism, by editing their own little back-room papers to be slipped surreptitiously under doorways in the urban shanty towns of the capital cities, making speeches and staging demonstrations which found space in the local press and unsettled the settlers, or forming close connections with the increasing number of foreign correspondents from the West who in the early postwar years began to ferret out the first stirrings of *uhuru*, to send the message back home to the metropolitan centres of power.

Africa's leaders recognise only too well the power of the press as an instrument of change. On very rare occasions, one of them will acknowledge the part some sections of it are playing in trying to bring about change in Black Africa's great enemy, South Africa. Zambia's Kenneth Kaunda has personal friends among leading South African journalists. 'They are fighting a battle which is morally justified on behalf of a decent society', he told an international gathering of newspapermen meeting in Kenya in 1968. 'I believe they belong to us. It is our duty to support them in everything they do.'

And yet Kaunda, one of the greatest and most humane statesmen on the Continent, cannot be said to have shown very much regard for the journalists of his own country. He has seized control of the newspapers and sacked editors and reporters who displeased him.

Alhadji Babatunde Jose, for many years chairman and editorial director of the *Daily Times*, Nigeria, raised distinguished eyebrows at a gathering of the prestigious Royal African Society in London when, in an address in April 1975, he said: 'In the name of press freedom and nationalism, we deliberately wrote seditious and criminally libellous articles against colonial governments.'

And though there were no African presidents in the audience they would have known only too well what he meant when he went on: 'Today, at least ten years after independence, many African journalists still believe that a good press is one that is in a constant state of war with the government; that a "progressive" journalist is one who writes anti-government articles every day, and a leading journalist is one who is in and out of prison for sedition.'

The newspapers of Africa, certainly of Black Africa, are not the true mass media. That role, such as it is, belongs to the radio. Millions of Africa's peoples, who will live out their lives as illiterates, get their local news from their friends, and what the government wants them to hear of the national and international news from the radio.

Nobody knows how many newspapers there are in Africa. Every time a count is made, which is not very often, the figures differ. But they are always less than the last count. Like everything else in Africa, the mortality rate among newspapers is much higher than anywhere else. Yet the press of Africa is important. Though it is not the mass medium of other societies, it is much the most important since it reaches that relative handful of people in every state who really matter—the politicians, the urban elite, the rising tide of well educated students, the businessmen and, possibly the most important of all, the officer corp of Africa's armies.

Almost two centuries old it may be, but the press of Africa still has a mystique which the greater marvels of radio and television do not rival. It is the power of the printed word. If something is 'in the paper', it has a status of its own—a condition still largely true even in much more sophisticated societies.

As Alhadji Jose told the Royal African Society: 'Many people believe whatever and anything they read in the newspaper as gospel truth. Such is the almost gospel belief in newspapers in certain countries that you cannot afford humour lest you be taken seriously. Therein lies the problem of newspapers and governments.'

It is this mystique for the printed word which gives the greatest hope for the press of Africa, and if it can survive these still early days of nation-building as the hands of the politicians reach for its throat and the bayonets of the soldiers' rifles nudge its ribs, it can come through to a maturity founded on its own values and beliefs, as different from the Western press as yams from potatoes, but as different, too, from the Communist press as palm wine from vodka.

It is a curious irony that while today it is fashionable for the West to condemn the many persecutions of the African press by Africa's new leaders, the first recorded note on the press of the Continent was its destruction by Europeans before it had managed to produce a single issue. Freed slaves from North America were settled in Freetown, Sierra Leone, in 1792. Two years later a printing press was imported and plans were made to produce a newspaper. But even as the first type was being hand-set, a French raiding party sailed in, looted, raped and sacked the settlement, slaughtered the livestock, desecrated the church and destroyed the press.

It was an inauspicious start to the newspaper industry in Africa and nothing quite so bad has ever happened to the press of the Continent since. If that little press in Freetown had not been wrecked then, remarkably, Black Africa would have been the first place on the Continent to have had a newspaper. Though Europeans had already been at the Cape for almost 150 years, it was not until 1800 that they got around to a newspaper of their own with the production of the *Cape Town Gazette*. As it was, the Whites only beat the Blacks to it by a year, for in 1801 Sierra Leone had either picked up the pieces of their old press, or, more likely, started a new one, and tropical Africa's first newspaper, the *Royal Gazette and Sierra Leone Advertiser*, was born.

Curiously, the Egyptians, with a civilisation much more advanced than anything else in the rest of Africa and with centuries of contact with Europe, did not have a newspaper until Napoleon occupied the country in 1797.

As one surveys the history of Africa's press from those early colonial gazettes through all the dozens of variations of publications serving Black nationalism, White imperialism, straight capitalism, sometimes sheer idealism and one or two imported gods like Jesus Christ and the Prophet Mohammed, the conclusion is that the end result is not very different from the beginning. The Adam and Eve of Africa's newspapers were the government gazettes. It is no accident that the Swahili word for newspapers is *gazeti*. They were produced by authority to tell the people what the rulers wanted them to know.

When the African peoples threw up their own leaders who did not like what the rulers were doing to them, the Black nationalist press was born. For more than a century and a half this press played an important part in the struggle against colonialism.

When that struggle was won, the press of Black nationalism withered away or, in a few cases where it survived, was suppressed by Black leaders who saw in it the same threat to their own rule as it had been to White rule.

With rare exceptions, even where the press had been run by the politicians who became their country's new leaders when independence from colonialism was achieved, it was discarded as having served its purpose.

Tom Hopkinson, editor in chief of *Drum*, the Continent's biggest magazine in the sixties, was in Leopoldville when the Congo became independent. One of the principal papers there had been run by Patrice Lumumba, the first prime minister. Hopkinson wanted to see Lumumba and having failed to get him at his office went to the newspaper. The offices were locked. He wandered all round trying to get in and eventually, in a back room, found a boozy caretaker sitting with his feet on a desk drinking a brandy and Coke.

Hopkinson asked: 'What's going on? Why isn't the paper coming out? Where's Lumumba?'

The caretaker was nonchalant. 'He's got what he wanted', he said, taking another swig. 'He's the prime minister. What's he need a newspaper for?'

The same sort of thing happened in territory after territory as Africa became independent. The press of Black Nationalism always had to struggle to keep alive, daily facing the threat of banning orders from the colonial authority or the demands of creditors. None were economically viable and most were kept going by the political party they served or well-to-do African traders with an eye on the future.

When independence was won, the party bosses had other things to do than produce newspapers and the traders were busy preparing for the spoils of victory. This is the sad story of much of the African press. In many other countries, although the press had started in much the same way, it produced a breed of men who became passionate about newspapers for their own sakes. This has not yet happened in Africa. But that may not be the final conclusion. There is some hope—no stronger than that, but one that African newspapermen all over the Continent cling to—that with the spread of education and the inch by inch economic progress of Black Africa, authoritarian rule will slacken. It is significant that in a continent where mass poverty makes socialism in all its various forms the natural political choice, those few states which are essentially capitalistic in outlook have a press which is able to exercise much greater independence than the others.

It is a bitter pill for Black Africa to swallow but despite the abuses of human dignity which have made South Africa the racial pariah of the world, the press there day after day is able to say things which if emulated by almost any editor in Black Africa would lead not merely to the end of the paper but the end of him.

This has very little to do with South Africa's Afrikaner government; it has a great deal more to do with the fact that the only comparable attraction to racialism for White South Africans is capitalism. If an intrinsic element of capitalism is the right to operate with minimal restrictions—if you are White—then that has rubbed off on the South African press.

The two States of Black Africa which are the most capitalistic, Kenya and Nigeria, are also the ones with the greatest degree of press freedom. Though there are careful limits to Kenya's press freedom, its biggest daily, *The Nation*, has probably more influence on the government of the country than any Fleet Street newspaper has over political life in Britain. The entire editorial staff of *The Nation* group of newspapers went *en bloc* to see the film of the Watergate story, *All the President's Men*, centred round the unearthing of the story by the *Washington Post*. The management paid for the tickets.

Even with a military junta which always has to look over its shoulder to see if any young major is coming up from behind, Nigeria, where the national press is now virtually government-owned, has developed a breed of very independent newspapermen.

The African revolution is far from over. It is not merely the young army officers who are flexing their muscles and biding their time. Though poverty, ignorance and disease are still rampant over most of the Continent, enough education is getting through to enable more and more people to understand how many beans make five—and that four and a half in the pockets of a tiny urban elite, and the bit left over spread among the masses, is not going to go on for ever.

The press in those societies, even when it is owned by the government, is not going to be able to play the adversary role of the West, but within limits that will range from straight-jacket to loose reins it may well become more than a muffled drum.

Though the declared policy of few—indeed none—of the Black
states of Africa is one of capitalism, because capitalism is seen to
equal imperialism, the tradition of millions of ordinary Africans
from peasant farmer to prosperous city businessman is based on
individual possession, even though these are often shared with the
'extended family'. Thus, in spite of all the attempts at collectivism,
it seems likely that this capitalistic strain in Africa will survive
and flourish. And if it does, then the press is more likely to
benefit.

The second greatest hope for a press that is not entirely
subservient is that Africans are the most natural politicians in
the world. They are intrigued by the political process, the
wheeling and dealing of politicians, the machinations of party
politics. This interest was born out of their colonial past when
the early African nationalists began the slow process that was
eventually to lead them to freedom. And after freedom came,
the habit was so ingrained, almost like a vice, that the present
generation of free-nation Africans continues with the political
intrigue. The newspapers of both Black and White Africa reflect
this, even the government owned ones. What appears to an outsider to be an inordinate amount of space given to political
speeches and political activity is only reflecting reader demand.

There are many abuses of political coverage in the African
press, but they are almost always the turgid over-exposure of the
national leaders' speeches, not the pure politics or the inter-play of
personalities and policies.

Even in one-party states, or military regimes, there will always
be rival factions, power groups, sections, insiders and outsiders.
It will not be so much a question of playing off one against the
other for African editors as picking their way through a mine-
field. They will sometimes be used by one faction against the
other; at other times, as the political dice come up with different
numbers, the outsiders will become the insiders. There is nothing
exclusively African about this sort of journalism. It still goes on
in many countries which claim a free press.

It is difficult to imagine that a press reflecting this African
obsession with politics and the people involved in the political
process will be able to resist sticking its nose in here, pointing a
finger there, occasionally raising its voice for or against something.
It is already happening. Zambia's Kenneth Kaunda has done
his utmost to bring the country's two dailies to heel. His govern-

ment owns one and controls the other. And yet in July 1976 Vincent Mijoni, editor of the wholly owned government *Daily Mail*, was putting up a two-inch high headline over a parliamentary story which read 'MPs Boob!' The story beneath said members of parliament 'acted sourly' and 'have put the clock back'. When he was summoned to appear before Parliament to apologise, Mijoni published his front page reply to the Speaker in which he said that '. . . democracy is a two-way traffic between leaders and the people' and that 'freedom of expression has many tongues, the strongest of which is Truth'.

Vincent Mijoni lived to see another day, and though his fingers must have sorely ached from the parliamentary rapping they received, his paper is a long way from being just the mouthpiece of the one-party state which owns it.

Africa's newspapermen require more than just courage to survive as individual voices ready to speak out when they are so moved; they require professionalism and skill to enable them to know how far they can go, what they can and what they cannot get away with.

Hilary Ng'weno, who resigned as editor-in-chief of Kenya's *Nation* Group in the mid sixties to become later one of Africa's few owner-editors, creating two thriving magazines which breathe independence in every issue, summed up the quest of the African newsman for some sort of freedom when he spoke to a gathering of newspapermen from all over the world: 'The only way we can do it is for newspapermen to keep poking their necks as far as they can go without being chopped', he said. 'That is the only way we can find out how much freedom we have.'

There are numerous difficulties in trying to count anything in Africa—even the number of countries. For where does Africa begin and end? Mauritius and the Malagasy Republic are generally included as being within the African orbit, but why not the Seychelles, which never is? Is Namibia a separate state? The United Nations says it is—but it has no government or parliament and to all intents and purposes is part of South Africa. If it is to be counted as a separate state, is it Black Africa or White Africa? And when you start trying to count newspapers, how do you define one? Is a stencilled hand-out delivered by a messenger on his bicycle to half a dozen government offices in the capital, plus the foreign embassies, a newspaper? And if it is not, then is a properly printed sheet folded

to make it into four pages, and sent to half a dozen government
outstations a newspaper?

And as for circulations, you can be not merely a few hundred
per cent wrong if you accept a lot of the figures given by
governments, but several thousand per cent out. It may be
politically expedient for a ministry of information to claim that
the circulation of its newspaper is ten thousand. Such a figure
may even have come off the press. But it is common for someone
who treads the corridors of such ministries to have to pick his way
between innumerable bundles of back copies that have never been
distributed.

In 1974 the circulation of Uganda's daily, the *Voice of Uganda*,
had the sort of increase in circulation that would have brought
joy to the heart of any ordinary circulation manager. But it
turned out that as there was virtually no other paper available
in the country, the market traders were buying up many
thousands each morning to wrap up their customers' produce.
President Idi Amin issued a decree making this a criminal
offence.

When in 1964 the United Nations made a count of the number
of dailies in Africa—including Mauritius and Malagasy—they
came up with 220, with a combined circulation of about
3 million. When these figures were broken down to show how
Black Africa fared—that is, without Arab Africa and with the
White states of South Africa, Rhodesia, Moçambique and Angola
discounted—the total was 169.

At the beginning of 1977 a survey for this book made another
count. It used a slightly elastic yardstick to define a newspaper,
being less concerned with who produced it than what it looked like
viewed by a professional newspaperman sympathetic to the circumstances under which it was produced. This revealed that the
1964 United Nations' total of 220 had slipped to 156—almost
40 per cent down. In those twelve years the population of the
Continent had risen from 250 million to 350 million—perhaps
more.

Arab Africa accounted for thirty-five dailies and White Africa
(Rhodesia and South Africa) another twenty-four, bringing Black
Africa's total to just ninety-nine. And if the two islands of
Mauritius and Malagasy are discounted, the total for Black Africa
proper—thirty-six different states—is a frightening sixty-seven.

And like it or not, if the governments of Africa had not taken over the control of many of these, the total would be substantially lower. The soaring cost of newsprint, which has hit the press in the most affluent countries of the world, would have decimated the newspapers of Africa.

THE MASS MEDIA OF AFRICA, 1975/6

	Dailies	Non-dailies	Population	Radio Sets	T.V. Sets
Algeria	4	8	15,300,000	700,000	150,000
Angola	3	15	5,500,000	110,000	—
Benin	1	2	2,800,000	97,000	—
Botswana	1	2	700,000	12,000	—
Burundi	—	3	3,700,000	100,000	—
Cameroon	2	4	5,900,000	222,000	—
Central African Empire	1	—	1,650,000	60,000	—
Chad	—	4	3,900,000	60,000	—
Congo (Brazzaville)	3	12	1,000,000	65,000	2,500
Djibouti	—	2	230,000	7,000	2,500
Ethiopia	3	2	25,500,000	500,000	25,000
Gabon	—	1	570,000	65,000	1,300
Gambia	—	11	510,000	50,000	—
Ghana	3	35	8,900,000	750,000	16,000
Guinea	—	1	4,025,000	85,000	—
Ivory Coast	2	2	4,480,000	86,000	40,000
Kenya	3	12	13,000,000	775,000	23,000
Lesotho	—	2	955,000	10,000	—
Liberia	1	4	1,600,000	400,000	6,000
Libya	7	10	2,100,000	85,000	1,000
Malagasy Republic	13	19	6,800,000	600,000	6,000
Malawi	1	3	4,700,000	110,000	—
Mali	2	2	5,280,000	60,000	—
Mauritania	1	2	1,220,000	150,000	—
Mauritius	12	14	900,000	108,000	29,000
Morocco	6	52	15,900,000	1,500,000	225,000
Moçambique	4	6	7,400,000	110,000	1,000
Namibia	3	2	580,000	47,000	—
Niger	1	1	4,225,000	100,000	Schools only
Nigeria	11	65	70,000,000	1,280,000	76,000
Rhodesia	2	10	5,750,000	215,000	115,000
Rwanda	—	1	3,900,000	50,000	—
Senegal	1	4	4,030,000	268,000	1,600

(Continued)

	Dailies	Non-dailies	Population	Radio Sets	T.V. Sets
Sierra Leone	2	13	2,650,000	50,000	5,000
Somalia	1	2	2,960,000	50,000	—
South Africa	22	130	23,000,000	2,350,000	650,000
Sudan	3	12	16,650,000	1,600,000	100,000
Swaziland	—	2	440,000	13,000	—
Tanzania*	4	22	14,100,000	150,000	—
Togo	3	4	2,050,000	40,000	—
Tunisia	4	7	5,150,000	287,000	177,000
Uganda	3	21	10,500,000	509,000	15,000
United Arab Republic	14	20	35,000,000	5,000,000	530,000
Upper Volta	—	3	5,500,000	87,000	500
Zaire	5	12	22,520,000	20,000	6,500
Zambia	2	12	4,560,000	250,000	18,500

* Zanzibar, constitutionally part of Tanzania, has 3,000 television sets

2 West Africa: A Black Press for Black Men

Though he had been in the office of the *Daily Times* until past midnight seeing Black Africa's biggest daily to bed, Peter Enahoro was up at dawn on the morning of 29 July, 1966. These early hours, before the heat and humidity and the dust and the noise of Lagos began to jangle the nerves, were the best time for writing his books and he always tried to get a few hundred words down before going back to the office.

That morning he was in the first chapters of a book extolling the Nigerian Army which had seized power from the corrupt civilian regime of Abubakar Tafawa Balewa. Enahoro still remembers the paragraph he was typing when the telephone rang that was to change his life: 'Nigeria had sunk into a quagmire and there was no politician on the scene with the stature and the command of wide-spread support to redeem the nation. In this environment of shame and frustration, a group of five young and high-minded majors stepped in to rescue their country from the murderous grip of . . .'

Then the phone went.

The man on the other end had arrived that morning from London and was one of the first witnesses to the military counter-coup against Major-General Aguiyi-Ironsi as the mutineers seized Lagos Airport.

Enahoro never finished the sentence he was typing. Troops began roaring through Lagos in lorries and jeeps with wailing sirens. The city seemed to be under siege. Crackling gunfire

13

erupted in half a dozen directions.

Enahoro had only the haziest idea what was happening. In a country that had been rocked with civil war and revolution and where nerves were always on edge, it was anybody's guess what was going on.

But for Enahoro, it really didn't matter what it was this time; this was the day that broke him and sent Black Africa's best newspaperman into permanent exile. What had happened was all too familiar in Africa. Though Ironsi had been hailed as the saviour of the nation only six months before, he had hardly vested himself with the full trappings of office before a powerful group of young officers had begun plotting to oust him. One of them was Lieutenant-Colonel Yakubu Gowon. Throughout that confused and bloody day, the soldiers and the journalists of Lagos had a lot in common; both groups wondered whether they were on the new wanted list.

Some of the soldiers and journalists teamed up. Two young Lieutenant-Colonels, with a hastily acquired suitcase of tinned food, were hiding in the home of one of Peter Enahoro's senior reporters. A major found sanctuary during the day in the offices of the *Daily Times* itself. In fact no newspaperman's blood was spilt in that coup. For days, military execution squads combed the streets of Lagos looking for soldiers who had not returned to the barracks. General Ironsi had been killed during the first minutes of the coup.

At this time Enahoro was the most important person in Nigeria not wearing a soldier's uniform. His prestige was enormous among hundreds of thousands of educated Nigerians, but that prestige represented his greatest danger, for the new soldier rulers were unlikely to tolerate a free-thinker running the country's largest and most influential newspaper. During civilian rule he had regularly spoken out against the corruption and negligence which were rampant throughout the State. Even the Ironsi coup had not silenced him, though he had been obliged to temper some of his hardest criticisms.

Enahoro had become editor of the *Sunday Times* when he was just twenty-three. Four years later he was appointed editor of the *Daily Times*, and at thirty, group editor-in-chief.

The soldiers of the coup left him alone. He refused to write a word about any of the activities of the new regime. He even refused to read his own paper. He was very depressed about events in

Nigeria. For though he had supported the first takeover by the army from the corrupt civilian government, he had always said that this must only be a short, sharp police action to clear the mess up and that democracy should be restored as soon as possible. But now that another group of soldiers had seized power from their own commanders, he realised that Nigeria was in for a long, long bout of military rule.

There are two ways of looking at his decision to leave Africa. There are those who say that he was very scared. They believe that notwithstanding military rule, he would still have been able to exercise a tremendous influence over affairs in the new Nigeria given his expertise as a journalist with the most deft touch in Black Africa and his enormous prestige.

But Enahoro was sick at heart at the awful upheavals, the civil war that had ripped the new state—Africa's showpiece it was called at the time—the corruption, the blood-baths of the military coups, the counter-coups and the endless planning of yet more coups.

The Nigerian personality, effervescent, capitalistic, very similar to the early American personality, almost enjoyed this turbulent way of life. Not so Enahoro. He looked ahead. He wanted a proper foundation laid for Africa's biggest nation.

'I felt alone,' he says now in voluntary exile. He had to get away long enough to clear his mind and gather a perspective. He left the country for three months. Ten years later, he has never been back and doubts if he ever will.

'It is easy for people to understand if you say you ran away if you were frightened for your life', he says. 'But much less easy when you leave because you do not want to be sucked into a situation where you will let yourself down to yourself.'

There is a cruel irony in Peter Enahoro leaving Africa. Since after early and primitive beginnings, the press of West Africa produced a long line of free-thinking African newspapermen right up to and beyond the era of Black Independence.

After the appearance of Black Africa's first newspaper, the *Royal Gazette and Sierra Leone Advertiser* in 1801, the idea of newspapers began to spread, slowly at first, then more rapidly and eventually almost like a bush fire out of control throughout the coastal belt of West Africa. The Sierra Leone paper only lasted a year before the English printers decided there was more money to be made selling people than papers and went into the slave trade.

It was in Ghana, then the Gold Coast, that the press really took hold, and for a long time it was exclusively African owned and edited. Apart from setting up the official gazette, the British were much too concerned with the sheer business of surviving in the face of numerous tropical diseases and the treacherous climate to worry about setting up something as precarious as a newspaper industry in a territory with a minute number of literates. They had come to raise the flag and hopefully make some money, never to settle and make a home. This was the pattern of British colonialism all along the West Coast, and it never varied until the day the flag was run down as the different states gained independence a century and a half later. In Ghana throughout the nineteenth century only two White-owned newspapers were started. One of these was owned by a man called W. C. Biblett, who between March and August 1885 produced a few spasmodic issues of the *Gold Coast News* at Cape Coast before giving up the venture. A year later, Leslie Mayne brought out the first issue of the *Gold Coast Herald*. It was supposed to be a fortnightly but it only came out once.

Not much is known about Mr Biblett but he did make another effort a year after his abortive attempt on Cape Coast, and although the paper only lasted one month, it has the distinction of being the first newspaper enterprise on the entire Continent produced in partnership with an African whose name has not occupied the history books.

The Royal Gold Coast Gazette and Commercial Intelligencer began in Accra in 1822 in handwritten form, and for three years it was recognised by the authorities as a semi-official organ of the area.

Missionary records in London are the best evidence of the vigour and enterprise of Africa's first newspapermen of just over a century ago, but the detail is scanty. Often no more is known of those first early efforts than a letter from a British missionary home saying '... a sort of journal has started, begun by one or two literates who are clearly intent upon propagating their own ideas' or 'we have seen another news sheet but it gives a very strange and garbled view of things'.

A more serious attempt was made in Liberia by an American negro named Charles Force. Before leaving home in 1826, he had been presented with a small hand-operated printing press as a gift from the Massachusetts Colonisation Society of Boston.

He started the *Liberia Herald* as a four-page monthly within six weeks of arriving in Monrovia, but within six months he was dead from blackwater fever and his paper ceased. However, in 1830, it was revived by yet another early Afro-American, a former editor of the first Black weekly in the United States. The *Liberia Herald* survived under various editors for more than thirty years. Although steeped in religious evangelical zeal, it made an earnest and thoroughly reputable attempt at decent journalism. It was a great attacker of the slave trade and presented the African as deserving no less respect than the European.

Charles Bannerman, the first African editor in the Gold Coast, was doing the same sort of thing in his *Accra Herald* (later renamed *The West African Herald*) launched in 1858.

Bannerman had been promised a press by well-wishers in London, but it seems to have been lost in the Liverpool docks. He therefore spent sixteen hours a day writing copies in his own hand, and then circulating the copies himself among anybody who could read. By 1859 he had more than three hundred subscribers, and the two-thirds of these who were Black comprised virtually the entire African intelligentsia of the Gold Coast.

The first serious confrontation of a newspaper and the governing authority occurred between the weekly *New Era* and the Governor of Sierra Leone. *New Era* had been started by William Drape, a West Indian, in May 1855. Drape was an educated man and had returned to the home of his ancestors to get away from the bad conditions of the West Indies. But he found things in Africa were even worse than what he had left behind, and he began calling for political and social reform. This displeased the Governor, a crusty Englishman, Lieutenant-Colonel Stephen Hill, who accused *New Era* of 'improper and provocative action'. Hill's predecessor had come to an arrangement with Drape that the *New Era* should publish all the official notices of the government (the authorities had tried nailing them to trees in the township but they either faded in the sun or were washed away by the rain). The contract was worth £30 a year to the little weekly—more than enough to pay for a year's supply of paper and ink. Hill cancelled this arrangement, and is thus remembered as the first advertiser in the African press to try to bring pressure on an editor. Far from succumbing, Drape hit back in his columns with greater venom. Hill retaliated by drawing upon some antiquated British press laws to which he added his own touches. Not only did these specify fines for a whole range of offences but, more sinisterly, they required newspapers to provide the names of sureties. Hill told the Colonial Office in London that he required such measures to check *New Era*, whose editor, he said 'is an adventurer from the West Indies without position or substance'.

When news of Hill's law reached London, British liberals protested. The liberal organ, the *Daily News*, took up the case, and the Colonial Office sent a message to Hill saying the ordinance should be executed with fairness and that the Chief Justice should decide whether the sureties should be accepted. Hill would not give in. He protested that Drape was 'the tool of a few characterless Europeans consisting of dismissed public officers, supporters of slave dealers and smugglers', and that the aim of *New Era* was to 'excite to discontent the native population'.

There was something of an uproar in London when Hill's reply was received. It was palpably transparent that though *New Era* was certainly anti-establishment, it was the very opposite of the supporters of slavery. From an official point of view it was more serious still that Hill was disobeying orders. The Colonial Secretary was asked in the House of Commons: 'Shall the Governor be recalled?'

Now the Colonial Secretary got really tough. He ordered Hill to repeal the press law and told him: 'Remember in future that a distinct direction from Her Majesty's Government must be obeyed.'

Communications along the West African coast were almost non-existent in those days—they are not very good now—but news of the *Era* case spread rapidly and the principles it laid down were to be those broadly accepted in all of Britain's West African colonies for the next half century.

Nigeria's first newspaper had been started by missionaries in 1859. It began as a vernacular in the Yoruba language, *Iwe Thorin*, but soon became Africa's first bi-lingual newspaper when English was added. It sold for thirty cowrie shells—even today used as currency in some parts of Africa.

A West Indian immigrant, Robert Campbell, founded the *Anglo-African* in Lagos in 1863. This was perhaps the most improbable newspaper venture of the nineteenth century in Africa, and it is astonishing that it survived for three years, for its columns were full of the sort of material which would have been much more appropriate in Britain. It ran a serial which began—and this in fetid, humid, tropical Lagos—'Hills and dales were deeply sleeping beneath a well-frozen covering of snow.'

But suddenly, and for no reason that records of that time reveal, the press of Lagos—and indeed, the entire territory of what later became known as Nigeria—were without newspapers for more than a dozen years. In those days Lagos was a colony unto itself, administered from Freetown in Sierra Leone where its Governor-in-Chief was based. Later, in 1874, Lagos Colony came under the Governor of the Gold Coast. It may be that this remoteness from the administrative centre of life was one of the reasons why the press of Lagos disappeared. But it was beginning to thrive elsewhere.

By 1900, around seventy newspapers in various shapes or forms had appeared, strewn along the little trading-posts and mission-ary settlements of English-speaking West Africa. An astronomical thirty-five of these had sprung up like mushrooms and withered almost as quickly in little Sierra Leone; another twenty had appeared and mostly disappeared in the Gold Coast and ten more in Nigeria. Africa's smallest state, The Gambia, had seen one. Virtually all of these were African papers in the sense that they were owned by Africans, or Black immigrants from North America and the West Indies or by missionaries catering, of course, for Africans. The Africaness of the press of West Africa was never to change and has never done so, unlike almost all the other parts of Africa from the Sahara to the Cape. Even when foreign press concerns like Britain's *Daily Mirror* Group and later Canada's Roy Thomson began to move into West Africa, the newspapers continued to be for Africans.

There was a debit side and a credit side to this. On the debit side was the generations of lost technical expertise which the Europeans would have brought to the African press. On the credit side was the fact that it gave the African an anti-colonial weapon which was to serve him well as the fires of nationalism kindled, caught and then inflamed West Africa in the 1950s and 1960s.

Kwame Nkrumah used to claim, in all seriousness, that God's greatest gift to West Africa had been the mosquito since it had kept the White man out in the sort of numbers in which they had settled in East, Central, and Southern Africa. In West

Africa the White man had come to trade, convert and administer. Newspapers hardly fitted into this pattern except in the missionary cause.

A clear pattern emerges as one turns over the yellowing pages of the files that survive of the newspapers of those early years in West Africa. Year by year they were testing the political temperature, seeing how far they could go, what they could get away with before the heavy hand of authority descended. And they got away with a remarkable amount. This was partly due to the benevolence of the British administrators along the Coast and probably, to their almightly Oxbridge arrogance. Those administrators believed that with Victoria on the throne, Britannia ruling the waves, and Britain the unchallenged power of the entire world, a few rabble-rousing sheets cranked out on broken-down hand presses was hardly something to threaten an order which seemed then might last for ever.

'We are not clambering for immediate independence', said an editorial of 9 March 1881 in the *Lagos Times and Gold Coast Advertiser*, 'but it should always be borne in mind that the present order of things will not last for ever. A time will come when the colonies on the West Coast will be left to regulate their own internal and external affairs'.

It was to be three-quarters of a century before the prophecy was fulfilled; first by the Gold Coast in March 1957, followed by Nigeria in October 1960, Sierra Leone in April 1961, and The Gambia in February 1965.

It was not only political change that the West African press was beginning to advocate. To the chagrin of the missionaries, a number of early African editors were expressing their dissatisfaction with the Church, which was seen to be very much a White importation.

An editorial headed 'The West African Church' in the *Lagos Times* of 3 January 1891 set out what it wanted from the missionaries: 'We mean a native Christian church to be composed of natives, supported by natives and governed by natives.'

Gradually as the bolder African editors ventured ankle, calf and knee-deep in the political waters of the times, the authorities began to take a more serious look at the press.

Lord Lugard, probably the greatest figure in Britain's colonial history and the architect of the policy of indirect rule, was very wary of newspapers. As Governor of Nigeria in 1917, he framed a law which gave him authority to appoint a censor of the Press whenever an emergency arose or he thought was about to arise. Lugard wrote into this legislation the power to seize the printing presses, confiscation of any newspapers printed and the imposition of a bond of £250 on publishers. Though London was upset when it learned of this action several weeks later when the mail ship from West Africa arrived and ordered him not to enforce such laws, Lugard ignored these instructions. When the Colonial Office in London pressed him, he claimed that their original messages had been lost.

His view of African journalists was that they were 'mission-educated young men who live in villages interfering with native councils and acting as correspondents for a mendacious native press.'

Increasingly anybody who had anything to say turned to the newspapers to express their views. It was not merely the British administration or other White imports that came under attack. The rivalries of local chieftaincies and political arguments were aired and it was this period that saw what was to become a feature of the press in many parts of West Africa, particularly Nigeria—tribalism in print.

Lagos claims the distinction of producing the first successful daily in West Africa, the Lagos *Daily News*, founded by Herbert Macaulay as late as 1925, although the Gold Coast *Daily Express* had struggled bravely for fifteen weeks in Accra thirty years earlier.

But more important than being West Africa's first daily newspaper, the Lagos *Daily News* was also the first political party paper, trumpeting the calls of Macaulay's National Democratic Party.

The franchise had been given to the residents of Lagos in 1922, so that a daily paper owned by a prominent politician was an immensely powerful weapon in a society where literacy was beginning and where the written word was accepted as gospel, mainly because almost everyone who could read had learnt to do so in mission schools where an important part of the reading matter was the obligatory page or two of the Bible at every morning assembly.

The European traders of Lagos were very nervous at the appearance of Macaulay's party paper, as, indeed, were many of the more conservative Africans of Lagos. The White businessmen, through the Lagos Chamber of Commerce, put up the money to start a paper in competition with the *Daily News*. They called it the *Daily Times* and it was to become the most important and easily the biggest newspaper in tropical Africa. The *Daily Times* was no pussy-footing, imperialist mouthpiece, though it might easily have become such but for its first editor, Ernest Ikoli, who had served his apprenticeship as a young reporter before founding the weekly *African Messenger* in 1921.

Ernest Ikoli would have been lost to journalism and the history of African newspapers made that much poorer had it not been for a gratuitous insult from a White schoolmaster. In 1919 Ikoli was a junior mathematics master at King's College, Lagos, and set for an academic career. But when a senior European master said something to him on the football field which he interpreted as a racial remark, he resigned there and then and joined the old Lagos *Weekly Record*.

The appearance of the *Daily Times* was a landmark in African journalism. From its first issue on 1 June 1926, it towered above all the others in West Africa in professionalism. It had proper headlines, as distinct from the wordy labels which were the normal title-pieces of its contemporaries; its news had a shape about them, particularly the modern summary of the essential ingredients of a story in the first paragraph, unlike anything else in tropical Africa. It was not long before it added features like a women's page and sports news. It sounded no particular political drum, and although it was very African in its appeal it was not unduly nationalistic.

All this made it very different from the Lagos *Daily News*; if choice is an essential ingredient of some sort of freedom of the press, this was the beginning of the vigorous competitiveness of the Nigerian press. It was to prosper and survive even the military dictatorships of the post independence era.

Other papers were not long in following and, as they proliferated, so editors and reporters began to have a choice of employment.

'It meant', said Ernest Ikoli at the end of his career many years later, 'that if you fell out with the owner of the paper you were not finished'. In fact, after he left the *Daily Times*, Ikoli edited the *Daily Telegraph* founded in 1927 as a bi-lingual paper, and later the *Daily Service*.

The pattern in Accra on the Gold Coast was similar. What were to become the two great nerve centres of British West Africa had assumed separate identities, though the links between the newspapermen of both towns were close.

Right through the story of English-speaking West Africa's newspapermen, there is constant movement from one territory to the next, and from one part of one state to another. Some of the great early African newspapermen worked in all three of Britain's principal West African territories, Nigeria, the Gold Coast and Sierra Leone at various stages in their careers. Another strong thread linking the major papers of those early years in a manner that no longer exists was the exchange of news and views between the different states. When James Bright, a Sierra Leonean, founded the *Gold Coast Independent* in 1895 'to create and foster public opinion in Africa and make it racy', he published all the news he could get from all over West Africa.

Many years later, when he addressed a journalists' conference in Accra in 1963, Kwame Nkrumah recalled how the early Gold Coast papers in Accra and Cape Coast, two hundred miles away, set up their own 'underground' communications network. This was long before there was any proper road between the two centres; though Nkrumah was probably dramatising things somewhat when he said that had the newspapers been carried overland they would have been apprehended by the colonial authorities, those early editions were ferried back and forth in dug-out canoes. Whatever the reason it was certainly a lot cheaper than by van.

It is a poor advertisement for modern-day African unity that this coming and going of African newspapermen and African newspapers from one country to the other ceased with the coming of independence.

It was Accra that provided West Africa with the first daily paper carrying regular international news through Reuters. This was the *West African Times* founded by Dr J. B. Danquah in 1931, though Accra's first daily was the *Gold Coast Spectator* founded in 1927. The *Spectator* had Africa's first foreign correspondent, Chatwood Hall, who from Moscow sent regular articles extolling the virtues of Communism. Another contributor to the *Spectator* was the West Indian George Padmore, who became a close friend of Nkrumah and played an important part in Ghana's struggle for independence.

Kwame Nkrumah had founded his *Evening News* in Accra in 1948. It was the mouthpiece around which the Convention Peoples' Party was built and all CPP members were expected to read it and did so. The paper was to serve Nkrumah well, and the *Evening News* was to spawn half-a-dozen papers owned by the CPP.

Its masthead carried the slogan 'The Party is Supreme' and a silhouette of Nkrumah. It was the *Evening News* that was used to create a mystique around Nkrumah which elevated him almost to the level of a god. His paper used to print open letters addressed to 'His Messianic dedication or *Osagyefo* (Redeemer), Dr Kwame Nkrumah'.

The only paper on the Gold Coast to oppose Nkrumah was the *Ashanti Pioneer*, which had been founded in 1939 in Kumasi. The *Pioneer* opposed Nkrumah throughout his rise to power and his eventual Presidency of independent Ghana. It managed to survive independence, but was constantly harassed by censorship until it was finally taken over by the government on 19 October 1962. Its news editor spent four and a half years in detention and its editor seven months. The Government said this was 'For destructive criticism of the government'. This action was the most vicious move against any newspaper in West Africa since newspapers had begun there nearly 200 years earlier.

The *Pioneer* was to reappear after Nkrumah's fall but it lived more on past reputation than merit, though from time to time it would raise its voice sufficiently stridently to merit attention from all the governments that followed Nkrumah. In 1972 it was closed down yet again by the government of Colonel Ignatius Acheampong. Anyone found with an old copy faced a prison sentence of five years or a fine of 10,000 cedis, about £3,000. As Acheampong's government mellowed in office, it lifted the ban on the *Pioneer* and it rose again out of its own ashes. But it had learned the lesson that survival meant servility.

With a few notable exceptions, the Gold Coast produced no journalists to match the calibre of those in Nigeria; certainly no newspapers to approach them. Editors were raw amateurs, often lawyers, doctors, clergymen and businessmen. Though this was also true of the newspapers of Nigeria, there was an element of journalistic professionalism. Unlike the Gold Coast, Nigeria's editor/owners, although often trained in other fields, soon evolved into full-time, thorough-going newspapermen.

Beneath the editors of both Nigeria and Ghana were a rag-bag of what Professor K. A. B. Jones-Quartey, a former Ghanaian journalist turned academic, calls 'the sorry crowd of under-educated, under-paid, untrained and unadjusted old men and young boys'.

After Nigeria's President Nnamdi Azikiwe had opened the training centre set up by the International Press Institute in Lagos in 1964, some of the students approached IPI's first Africa Director, Tom Hopkinson, who had also spoken at the ceremony.

One of them told him: 'You are just trying to make us feel good about being journalists as though we had an important career before us. Don't you realise that all of us here are the throw-outs and outcasts from other jobs?' The student pointed to one of his friends. 'He was chucked out from being a civil servant, and I was sacked as a schoolmaster. That's the only reason most of us are on this course.'

Hopkinson was unruffled. 'Well then', he told them, 'you are in the great tradition of journalism because that is how journalism started everywhere—the drop-outs from other professions'.

A major landmark in the development of the press of Africa was the appearance on the morning of 22 November 1937 of the *West African Pilot*, a new daily launched in Lagos by Nnamdi Azikiwe. Azikiwe was to become not only the Continent's greatest newspaperman, but also one of its most dynamic nationalists. He had found his way to the United States in 1925 to seek a better education, and followed the classic poor-boy route working as dish-washer, shoeshine boy, coal miner and even picking up a few odd dollars as a fairground boxer. It was not only a singular lesson on the plight of the American Negro in what 'Zik' had believed was the land of the free but, more important, he saw the beginnings of the militant Negro movement during his stay in America, and this gave Zik a lot of ideas for the liberation of his own people.

Although Azikiwe was studying political science and anthropology, he turned to journalism and took a diploma course. For a while he worked as a reporter, all the time planning his return to Africa and the use to which he would put his new-found knowledge.

In fact it was to the Gold Coast that he returned, and for three years—from 1934 to 1937—he edited the *African Morning Post*.

He worked with another major figure in West African affairs, I. T. A. Wallace-Johnson, who was a mixture of trade union organiser and journalist. A Sierra Leonean, Wallace-Johnson was a Marxist who had studied in Paris and edited the *Negro Worker* there before going to Lagos to edit the *Daily Telegraph*.

Between them, Azikiwe and Wallace-Johnson produced a dynamic though somewhat off-beat paper. It proclaimed in its masthead 'Independence in All Things and Neutral in Nothing Affecting the Destiny of Africa'.

Africa was a long way from Europe in those days, but the *Morning Post* kept a beady eye and a caustic tongue on the preparations for war that were beginning to loom. An editorial headed 'Stop this Madness' as early as 1937 declared: 'The world in general is mad but Europe is especially so. Is it the beginning of the end of the White race or is it a temporary fit which will soon subside?'

Wallace-Johnson's Marxism was evident in every issue. 'Has the African a God?', was the title of a stinging piece which landed both him and Azikiwe in court on a charge of criminal libel. They were acquitted on appeal.

All this was really a period of apprenticeship for Azikiwe as he polished the journalistic skills he had brought back from America. It was his *West African Pilot* in Lagos which for a decade set a pace which was to outstrip any other newspaper in Black Africa.

By this time the Nigerian *Daily Times* had already settled down into a thoroughly good newspaper, but it could hardly hold a candle to Zik's *Pilot*. Though the political message was to be the central core of Zik's journalism—a tradition which was to be followed by every other newspaper in West Africa—he laced that message with human interest, tabloid style techniques which within three years had brought the circulation to an astonishing 12,000 copies a day, a figure unmatched by any other newspaper in tropical Africa. This figure was to more than double in the nineteen-forties, and with a readership of between ten and twenty to each newspaper, its influence was phenomenal.

Pride in the African was the constant theme. Every new lawyer, every new doctor, every new graduate was a triumph. And the political message was direct; why were people of this status still second-class citizens in their own country?

Zik brought more than the biggest and brightest newspaper of that age to Black Africa. He created the first newspaper chain in West Africa. This was the Associated Newspapers of Nigeria, known as the Zik Group. *The Pilot* was number one in the group, but was followed by the *Eastern Nigerian Guardian* at Port Harcourt, Eastern Nigeria's first daily, founded in 1940, the *Nigerian Spokesman* at Onitsha in 1943, and the *Southern Nigerian Defender* at Warri the same year. Zik bought out a successful Lagos weekly called *The Comet* in 1945 and turned it into a daily. Four years later *The Comet* was transferred to Kano, giving Nigeria's northernmost centre on the edge of the Sahara its first daily. In the same year Zik's only failure was started at Jos, *The Northern Advocate*.

Thus Zik had papers all over Africa's most important country, and each one of them was ramming home the message that the day of the White man was coming to an end.

If the British colonial administration had been relatively benevolent towards the press before the creation of the Zik Group, it now got very tough. *The Pilot* was under constant attack at various times: its reporters were barred from the Legislative Council of Nigeria: both *The Pilot* and *The Comet* were banned for six weeks in 1945, and when they re-appeared the colonial government sought to cripple them by withdrawing all official advertising, always one of the greatest revenue earners of the press in Africa. But Zik would not be beaten. When *The Pilot* was banned in Lagos, he brought the *Southern Nigerian Defender* from Warri to operate in the capital in its place. A Colonial Office memo from State House, Lagos, of this period lapses from the usual bureaucratic language of such missives and declares: 'They [Zik's papers] are like a plague. They are afflicting the whole country.'

To edit the *Defender* at the end of 1944, Zik appointed a plump, twenty-one-year-old good-looking young man named Anthony Enahoro, who had served his apprenticeship on the *Pilot*. Anthony Enahoro, brother of Peter Enahoro, was to become one of the most colourful and controversial figures on the Continent, a giant of a personality whose career was to embrace prison cells, editorial chairs and cabinet ministries. The first leading article he ever wrote as an editor in the *Defender* was entitled *Da Mihi Locum Standi*, though how many Warri readers could translate Latin is questionable. But his Latin call 'Give me a Place to Stand and I Will Move the World' was not entirely presumptuous.

He was only a year at Warri, and as soon as the *Comet* was ready to be turned into a daily, Zik moved him to Lagos to take over as editor. Anthony Enahoro has written of that appointment; 'I assumed my editorship with a pardonable feeling of achievement and immediately came into the public eye as West Africa's reputedly youngest newspaper editor. For all I knew or cared, I may have been the Empire's or the world's youngest editor of a daily newspaper.' It is doubtful if any African journalist suffered quite as much as he did at the hands of the law; three times he was in prison for sedition and criminal libel. In 1963 he was arrested in Britain and repatriated to Nigeria under the Fugitive Offenders Act. There he was found guilty of treasonable felony and conspiracy to overthrow the Nigerian Government. He was sentenced to ten years' imprisonment, but was released when the government of Tafawa Balewa was overthrown.

When the government refused to renew the Zik Group's licence for operating a wireless station to receive foreign news from Reuters, he put the following notice on the front page of *The Pilot* and *The Comet* on 5 February 1946 under the heading 'Zik's Press and the Government'.

The Government has refused to allow Zik's Press Limited to operate a wireless station for the purpose of receiving news messages. When the Zik Press forwarded a cheque for £50 as renewal fee for the licence the government returned the cheque without giving any reason. The managing director of Zik's Press requested the chief secretary to the government to explain the government attitude on the matter but no reply was forthcoming. This means that Zik's Press cannot receive news from Reuters which is the only independent unofficial agency disseminating court news without bias here.

Zik added to that announcement an 'editor's note':

It is very significant that government should take such action without explaining its motive. Did Zik's Press commit any infringement of the Wireless Telegraphy Ordinance? If not, the refusal can be interpreted by the aggrieved party to be inconsistent with the liberty of the Press.

There was now open confrontation between Zik and the Colonial authorities, not only in Lagos but all over the country. In *The Pilot* and *The Comet* of 18 February 1946, Zik published a long list of acts of alleged victimisation against his papers by the government. He launched an appeal for money from readers and the response was immediate and enormous. Donations came not only from the readers of his papers, but from all manner of organisations throughout West Africa and even from sympathetic groups in Europe and the United States.

The newspapers were badly hit by the War along with the press everywhere else. Newsprint was rationed on a quota basis and this gave the Lagos authorities a critical curb on Zik. But he battled on and never temporised.

The age of the editor-owner was coming to an end. Zik's group was joined in the mid-forties by a government-sponsored clutch of newspapers in several tribal languages and the *Nigerian Citizen* in English. The *Daily Service* in Lagos became the mouthpiece of the Action Group party in opposition to Zik's National Council of Nigeria and the Cameroon (the NCNC). The *Daily Service* joined hands with the *Nigeria Tribune* in Ibadan to form the Amalgamated Press of Nigeria, and later bought control of a string of small provincial dailies. Nigeria had thus three developed newspaper chains, two serving political parties and one virtually government-run.

Nnamdi Azikiwe was the great Nigerian of his time and the great newspaperman of the Independence age, a larger than life figure whose imprint is still visible on both the political life of the country and the newspaper industry he helped create. But history is already noting that he lacked the one ingredient seemingly essential for lasting greatness in Africa: imprisonment.

When the Colonial authorities shut down his two Lagos newspapers for allegedly misrepresenting the facts about a strike, he dramatically announced in 'his last testament' that he was prepared to give 'my most prized possession—my life—for the redemption of Africa'. He accused the government of plotting to kill him and then went into hiding.

The older generation of Nigerian politicians believed that this was all Zik ballyhoo. Anthony Enahoro has written of Zik's action: 'The common people believed and were completely satisfied that the White man had planned to assassinate him.' But, added Enahoro, 'those who knew Zik interpreted his disappearance to Onitsha as a huge joke, a cowardly act or a wise and judicious step according to our several opinions of the man'.

With hindsight, it seems that Zik could have become more of

a hero and demonstrated his case to greater effect if he had stood his ground, defied the ban on his papers, and driven the British to jail him. The missing element in his otherwise brilliant career as a politician which was to lead him to the President's office of independent Nigeria was that the British never jailed him. Thus he did not have behind him the martyrdom of other British African leaders like Kwame Nkrumah, or—across the other side of the Continent—Jomo Kenyatta of Kenya, Kenneth Kaunda of Zambia and Hastings Banda of Malawi.

3 The Coming of the Europeans

The most potent foreign influence on the Press in Africa was the coming of the *Daily Mirror* Group after the Second World War.

Though there is today a generation of Africans who know nothing of the nationalist fervour of the forties and fifties, there is also an older generation of educated Africans who lived through those days. It is difficult to find any one among them who has anything but respect for the way that the Mirror Group conducted itself in West Africa. All the credit for this must go to a rather strange, aloof Anglo-Irishman, Cecil King, who seemed an improbable choice as the person to take West Africa into the modern post-war newspaper age but whose record, and the record of almost all the fairly small group of Europeans he brought with him from Britain in 1947, is acknowledged as unblemished by the most fervent anti-colonists still alive in West Africa.

Cecil King says in his *Strictly Personal* that the idea for the *Mirror*'s African adventure began with a visit shortly after the war from somebody in the British Colonial Office. He suggested it might not be a bad thing for the *Mirror* to have a look at West Africa with a view to doing business there. This seems improbable. With the fires of African nationalism beginning to fan all along the West Coast and with men like Zik in Nigeria and Nkrumah in the Gold Coast setting a pace which was leaving British officials breathless, the idea that an organisation which produced a razzmatazz tabloid like the *Daily Mirror* (which had given the British Government so much trouble during the War that it was almost banned) should enter West Africa seems totally out of character with what Whitehall would have wanted. King says the official from Whitehall saw the chairman of the *Mirror* Group, Guy Bartholomew.

There is an alternative version from David Williams, the British editor of the magazine *West Africa*, which seems more likely. Williams says that the *Mirror* had made a lot of money during the war and was wondering what to do with it. This was before the days of diversification, when newspaper empires began to include in their superstructure everything from television stations to pie factories. Thus, when the *Mirror* looked around for expansion, their reasoning was simple; they must produce newspapers, they must be in English and they should have good growth prospects.

None of these conditions seemed likely prospects for post-war Britain, so the *Mirror* looked to the Empire on which there was no reason at that time to think the sun would ever set.

King was put in charge of the project and was to work very closely with David Williams for many years. Twenty-nine years later, when the *Mirror* Group finally left West Africa, they had established something which even the military dictatorships of that part of the West Coast may never totally eradicate.

The *Mirror* Group's philosophy in Africa from the start was exactly the same as its philosophy in producing British newspapers: Will the reader be interested in this?

King toyed with the idea of starting an entirely new venture, but came round to the view that it was better to re-vamp an existing newspaper than start a new one. He settled on the *Daily Times* in Lagos which had two off-shoot magazines, *West Africa* and the *West African Review*. Between them, the three publications were making £2,000 a year and King bought the triple package for £46,000 towards the end of 1947.

His recipe for the new *Daily Times* was direct and simple; it must not take sides in the political gang war; it must cater for Africans and be edited by an African (if this sounds unoriginal, then one only has to look at many other parts of British Africa to realise how novel it was), and finally it should print more local news. In fact he turned the *Daily Times* into an African-style London *Daily Mirror* tabloid—but minus the sex. This was in no way a reflection on his somewhat conservative, even prudent nature which had always seemed out of character with the flavour of the *Daily Mirror*, but rather, as he put it in *Strictly Personal*, because as far as sex was concerned Africans were 'firm believers in do-it-yourself'.

The new *Daily Times* under King assembled the first rotary printing press in Nigeria and set up the most modern photo-engraving and type-setting and type-casting plant on the West Coast.

King imposed careful rules about crime reporting. With the highly volatile Nigerian temperament, he felt it was not wise to give undue prominence to crime; but with the frequent secret society killings which were a feature of Nigeria, it was often difficult to play it down.

A news service covering pretty well the whole of Nigeria was organised on a scale never attempted before or since. Some of the best Nigerian journalists in the country joined the paper and success was immediate.

King knew, of course, that it was one thing to produce a popular best seller; it also had to be marketed efficiently. This side of newspaper production all over Black Africa has always been its greatest weakness. Many an otherwise good little news-paper has failed because its editors and managers have given scant regard to actually getting it to the reader.

King went about his distribution methodically. As the tropics have a twelve-hour day and a twelve-hour night, people begin to move about the urban centres at 6 o'clock in the morning. Thus, King decided the *Daily Times* should arrive at its main selling points no later than that. Nothing like the British newspaper trains that carried his London newspapers existed, of course, so King adopted Africa's most widely used form of public transport—the bus. West Africa's buses are a joy to behold. Their only resemblance to the buses of Europe, North America or anywhere else is that they have circular wheels. For the rest, anything goes and they are festooned with exhortations, mottoes and biblical quotations in large, gaudy lettering.

One of the *Daily Times* buses is remembered to this day by old White West-Coasters as bearing the yellow and red legend 'The Lord is King'—and there was many a tight-lipped British civil servant of the day who felt that the signwriter had got the message round the wrong way.

King's buses carried not only his newspapers but also passengers and freight—even a goat or two. In fact when the conductors could be persuaded to stop stealing most of the passenger and freight fares, they even paid their way, which meant that the papers got a free ride.

So efficient was the bus service in a country still renowned for the inefficiency of its transport service that many a sharp-witted entrepreneur copied the red and yellow coachwork of King's buses, and even invented fictitious newspaper titles which were painted on the sides to con the passengers into believing they were *Daily Times* buses.

King says in his *Strictly Personal* that a recurrent difficulty in the production of the *Daily Times* was his White editorial staff. Forty per cent of the White men working on the paper went to pieces, sometimes in a matter of days. It was not merely drink and women, which have figured fairly prominently as the recreations of newspapermen in most societies, but in one instance a *Daily Mirror* sub-editor who had been sent out as editorial director of the *Daily Times* got mixed up with some local *ju-ju* men. He was sent home to the cooler climes of Fleet Street. Those other Whites who survived the climate, the frustrations, and the hundred and one pressures, King called 'pure gold'. Some were to go on later to the top-most positions in British journalism. One such was Percy Roberts, a *Daily Mirror* sub-editor of whom Peter Enahoro says fondly: 'He bullied me into a newspaperman. Everything I became afterwards I owe to him.' Roberts was to go on to become Chairman of the Mirror Group in London.

King soon ran into problems with the colonial administration when they realised the policy of the new *Daily Times* was self government for Nigeria. Although this was of course the official policy of colonialism, nobody was trying to implement it.

It was not long before the *Mirror* Group began to extend up the Coast, first to Ghana with the *Daily Graphic*, and then to Sierra Leone with the *Daily Mail*. The *Daily Graphic* was launched in 1950 and there was great suspicion not only among the colonial authorities but also among many Africans. When the *Graphic* appeared in Accra, a young political firebrand not long back from university in the United States was editing the highly volatile *Evening News*, one of no less than thirteen local newspapers which eventually fell to King's competition. He was Kwame Nkrumah, leader of the Convention People's Party (then called the Nationalist Party).

Though burning with revolutionary zeal, the *Evening News* was technically very poor and editorially boring except to the more extreme followers of the Convention People's Party. All its correspondents were CPP activists who angled everything they wrote around the Party Line.

Nkrumah's paper was no match for the professionalism of King's racy *Graphic*, and with independence now on the horizon, CPP leaders set up the *Guinea Press* with backing from generally unenthusiastic local businessmen who were told in unmistakeable language just what they might expect in a free Ghana if they did not cooperate in the venture.

This new injection of capital improved the *Evening News* technically, but it was still little more than a tub-thumping political pamphlet. For some years, as Nkrumah's star rose as the brightest African nationalist on the Continent, the *News* also published editions in several African languages of Ghana, Hausa (spoken in northern Nigeria) and French.

In 1956 the *Guinea Press* brought out its second daily, the morning *Ghanaian Times*, established with public funds. It was much more like a real newspaper than the *Evening News*, but was still very much the CPP mouthpiece and only served to emphasise the overall superior quality of the *Graphic* which outsold both the CPP party papers five or six to one.

Long after independence, in 1962, Nkrumah's Bureau of African Affairs launched the most serious attempt ever in Black Africa to produce a Marxist journal on African affairs. Although strident in tone *The Spark*, a weekly, had well researched articles on major topics from all over the Continent. Writing in the hundredth issue in November 1964, Nkrumah said that the idea for *The Spark* had been his own. 'I invited two of my associates in the Bureau of African Affairs to work out the details of a newspaper that would specialise in ideological work and thought and provide the intellectual revolution which could dispel the doubts and confusions concerning the ideology of the African Revolutions . . . I named the new journal *The Spark*'.

Before it appeared, a number of powerful Gold Coast chiefs declared their intention of boycotting King's *Daily Graphic*. They believed it was a Colonial Office front brought out to stave off independence. But King's Irish charm worked well and they relented. Then the Convention People's Party declared a boycott. This brought the sale of the first issue down from 10,000 to

2,000 and with the grip that Nkrumah had over affairs in Accra, this could have been disastrous had the boycott continued.

But it was to be White man's magic which broke it.

One Saturday shortly after its launch, the *Graphic*'s racing tipster—the local manager of the National Cash Register Company—picked five winners and two seconds out of seven races at the Accra track.

No political party on earth could withstand that sort of thing. Nkrumah's boycott was broken and the circulation took off like a rocket. King found his Ghanaian operation much easier to handle than the *Daily Times* in Nigeria. Lagos is a huge hotch-potch of a capital in a huge hotch-potch of a country. Accra was tidy, and by comparison tiny, like the country itself. In his *Strictly Personal* King strikes a tribal note when he attributes a lot of the success of the *Graphic* to the fact that the Ewes are a major tribe around Accra 'who appear to be the most intelligent and the most adaptable of all the tribes'. In fact, he had to take care to see that the entire staff were not Ewe.

Success in Ghana was even more marked than in Lagos. All the country had ever had were political sheets. Suddenly there was a newspaper with no political abuse, printing stories about people the ordinary reader could identify with, with a sports page that told you not what had already happened but prophesied with far greater accuracy than any *ju-ju* man what would happen at the racetrack and football pitch on Saturday.

King pushed on up the coast to Sierra Leone and bought out the *Daily Mail* in 1952. Because it was the birthplace of African journalism with a long British connection and an excellent University College, King thought it would be relatively easy to recruit and train a good local staff. In fact the theory proved wrong, and after many frustrations Nigerian and Ghanaian staff were moved in. With literacy low and bad roads making distribution difficult and deep political intrigue, the Sierra Leone venture was never a success and finally became a failure.

Cecil King decided to call it a day in Sierra Leone in 1965. David Williams went to see what sort of a deal could be made with Sir Albert Margai, the President. His Sierra Leone People's Party controlled two competitors to the *Mail*, and creamed off the important government advertising. When Williams said the *Mail* was not able to carry on, Margai replied that he knew the paper had been making plenty of money. He clearly believed this and Williams, rather dangerously, asked whether the President was suggesting that the *Mail* was defrauding the income tax authorities as the paper's returns clearly showed the financial state of the company. Williams finally said that if the Government did not wish to buy the *Mail*, then the *Mirror* would merely close it down. Margai bought it for, in Williams' words, 'a song'.

Though King's *Graphic* was always the circulation leader against Nkrumah's *Evening News* and Ghanaian *Times*, it had supported the CPP in the campaign towards independence. But it had also given a fair showing to Nkrumah's opponents, and as the nationalistic atmosphere of independent Ghana intensified, operations became more and more difficult. There was never a show-down, but King realised that the writing was on the wall. He sent David Williams to see Nkrumah about getting out. Williams told the President that it was an anomaly that a revolutionary state like Ghana should have a leading newspaper owned by a capitalistic company from the old imperial power. Williams pointed out that under the law in Ghana, it was not possible for a public company to be floated and the *Graphic*'s shares sold to Ghanaians.

Would the Government buy it, asked Williams? Nkrumah said no. Then Williams suggested what he called 'a sort of half-way house' arrangement. The *Graphic* would be placed under a trust, modelled (somewhat loosely) on the London *Observer* one. Nkrumah agreed to this, and terms were arranged. King had always ploughed the profits made by the *Graphic* back into the paper, and Nkrumah knew that Ghana was getting not only a very good paper but also a very good bargain. King became a trustee of the new company which was set up in 1963, and payments to the *Mirror* group were spread over three years. The sum involved was well under £500,000, lock, stock and barrel.

The stage was thus set for the beginning of government control of the press of Ghana, and though Nkrumah was to fall, as was his successor, and governments to alternate between civilian rule and military dictatorship, the pattern was to remain the same with only occasional flickerings of freedom from papers like the old *Pioneer*.

Eddie Agyemang, a leading Ghanaian journalist who went on to become editor-in-chief of the *Times*, told an international seminar on Reporting Africa held in Sweden in 1970 what it was like for newspapermen under Nkrumah: 'Friends of the politicians became automatically the friends of all the writers', he said. 'In the same way the adversaries of the politicians became the adversaries of the journalists. Ghanaian newspapers were specifically ordered to castigate such African countries as Nigeria, Ivory Coast, Senegal and Togo, whose policies did not please the President. Also nothing done anywhere in the Western world was deserving of praise in any of the state-owned papers. Lavish praises were to be showered on Eastern European countries for the minutest thing that they did.'

THOMSON'S COSTLY SAFARI

It was almost certainly the Mirror group's success in West Africa that tempted another British Group, Roy Thomson's, to the tropics.

Russell Braddon's biography of Thomson, *Roy Thomson of Fleet Street*, says that the inspiration for the Thomson African safari began when his number one adviser, James Coltart, impressed upon him the duty of a publisher like himself to spread to less enlightened countries the gospel of the freedom of the press, literacy and democracy.

But Roy Thomson was hardly the sort of man to be greatly moved by talk of duty and ideals. He had never pursued any course of action unless he could see profit in it. Braddon believes that Coltart's missionary fervour coincided with Roy Thomson's style for well publicised philanthropy. Thomson went into Nigeria on the invitation of Chief Obafemi Awolowo, leader of the Action Group in the Western Region of Nigeria. Awolowo partly owned the *Daily Express* (formerly the *Daily Service* of old) but it was badly run and unprofitable.

When Cecil King learned that Thomson was going into West Africa, he commented sardonically: 'I wish him success'. He was not to have it.

Awolowo wanted Thomson to put his whole operation on to a professional and profit-making basis. Thomson took 50 per cent of the shares of the group, the Amalgamated Press of Nigeria, in 1960. White management was put in, but the editorial staff remained all Black. James Coltart told Awolowo that the paper would not be the voice of the Action Group, and in fact this was specified in the contract signed in the Nigerian High Commission in London. It is difficult to believe that a long-time political wheeler-dealer like Awolowo could not have had his tongue in his cheek when he accepted this clause.

Now in retirement Coltart merely says: 'This gave us a bit of trouble.' He refers to 'the odd intrusion' of a party political nature in the paper. Others have a more vivid memory.

Nigeria was in the run-up period to independence and the elections for the Federal House of Representatives were only months away when Thomson moved in. He had left it too late. The Nigerian cauldron was bubbling fiercely, fuelled by the three great tribal groups of Hausas in the North, Yorubas in the West and Ibos in the East. The political knives were being sharpened ready for use, and one of the keenest of the grinders was Awolowo. The *Mirror* group had been around long enough to stand a better chance of survival in this atmosphere, but Thomson was soon in trouble. Nigeria's first Prime Minister, Abubakar Tafawa Balewa, became unhappy with the line the *Daily Express* was taking. He began complaining, not merely to Thomson's head office in London, but direct by telephone to the British Government in Whitehall. Winston Churchill's son-in-law, Duncan Sandys, was then Commonwealth Secretary and Tafawa Balewa would ring him up direct to complain about the *Express*.

Coltart recalls that Sandys, in turn, 'came blistering on to us'. It is one of the ironies with which Africa is riddled that a generation later Sandys, long out of politics, was to appear as a director of another English group, Lonrho, who moved into newspapers in Africa. Sandys' receipt of his director's fees from the parent company via the Cayman Islands was part of a financial operation that was to move Prime Minister Edward Heath to refer to the Lonrho operations as 'the unacceptable face of capitalism'.

Coltart flew out to Lagos to see Tafawa Balewa, and remembers him as the most responsible African politician he ever dealt with. He puts Tom Mboya of Kenya as the best brain, Black or White, he ever came up against in Africa.

Coltart had told Balewa that if he did not like the way the Thomson papers were being run the partnership with Awolowo would be dissolved. Tafawa Balewa quoted one example of the sort of thing that had upset him in the *Daily Express*. This was

a reprint of a British newspaper editorial which was critical of
Nigeria and especially of Tafawa Balewa. The London office of
the *Express* had lifted this, and it was reprinted in Lagos. Tafawa
Balewa told Coltart that it was one thing to criticise the government, but if the finger was pointed directly at the leader of it—
he himself—then anybody who read it would feel that he had
made a mess of things. 'You have to realise', he told Coltart,
'that this country is two or three hundred years behind Britain.
When Africans read something in the newspaper they take it as
gospel',—a sentiment expressed time and time again by responsible African leaders over all the Continent and the greatest
rationalisation for curbing the press they have.

There were a number of brushes like this, and more and more
Roy Thomson felt that the West African game wasn't worth the
candle it was supposed to be lighting in the name of Western
civilisation. He and Coltart felt they ought to get out, but Britain's
High Commissioner in Nigeria, Anthony Head, urged them to
remain.

Although the *Daily Express* and the *Sunday Express* were highly
professionally produced, they had an unmistakeable flavour of
Europe about them. It was not merely their wide coverage of
events in Europe and America, but the whole emphasis often
seemed slanted towards the White man. The death of Sir Winston
Churchill filled three pages.

Finally Tafawa Balewa decided to set up his own newspaper.
He felt he was not getting the support he merited in any of the
other Lagos papers.

Coltart went to see him, and told him that whatever his views
on the existing press in Nigeria, if he was planning to set up a
Government paper, he would, to use Coltart's own phrase to the
Prime Minister of Africa's biggest state, 'lose your shirt'. And
the ankle-length, richly-embroidered shirt-type robes which are
the Nigerian national dress are expensive items indeed. Coltart
quoted the case of Britain's *Daily Herald* and *Daily Worker*, the
Labour Party and Communist Party-backed British newspapers
which had both failed.

But Tafawa Balewa was very determined. He planned a great
new paper for the people, the *Morning Post* and its Sunday sister
the *Sunday Post*. Money was no object. It bought not only the
best equipment but the best editorial staff it could find. But it
was never a success. It rapidly lost £300,000, but being govern-

ment-owned that was of little consequence.

The competition from the *Morning Post* and even from the ever-thriving *Daily Times* which was going from strength to strength, affected Thomson's *Daily Express* less than a still prominent Nigerian journalist-politician who has breast-beat his way through several continents on the theme of press freedom. He would approach Lagos businessmen, generally foreign businessmen running large companies in Nigeria, and casually say 'I see you are supporting the Action Group'. The startled foreigner would retort with something like 'Good God! what makes you think that?' and the reply would come back: 'But I thought I saw an advertisement for your company in their newspaper.'

Slowly the squeeze was put on the *Express*. It found that work permits for foreign executives were not being renewed. The paper had just gone into profit, but now it began slipping deeper and deeper into the red as one advertiser after another cancelled his contract.

Coltart flew out to Lagos to close the operation down. But Tafawa Balewa pleaded with him not to. He admitted freely that his own *Morning Post* and *Sunday Post* had failed, and said that if the *Express* were to close, it would leave the field very largely to the *Daily Times* which, he said, was 'so neutral they are useless'—a magnificent commentary on what Africa's political leaders think of newspapers they cannot control.

So Coltart agreed to carry on for the time being. But a little later Tafawa Balewa sent an emissary to London with a proposition that Thomson's *Daily Express* should merge with the ailing government *Post* newspapers. Coltart, whose evangelical zeal had been sorely tested in Africa, was wary. But he told the emissary: 'Let's see the deal.'

The proposed deal was that the *Express* should virtually take over the ailing *Morning Post* and *Sunday Post*, and with its more modern plant and equipment produce a joint operation under tight, professional Thomson management. It was to be called the *Post Express*. The contract was for Thomson to run it for a minimum of ten years.

It is curious now to think that so canny a Scot as James Coltart, who many say was the financial mastermind behind Roy Thomson's huge media empire, could have believed that you could plan ten years ahead in post-independent Africa.

But the contract for the merger went through. The first step

was the closure by Thomson of the *Express*. It should re-appear
shortly afterwards in its new guise with the *Post*. But before the
new venture got off the ground in January 1966, Tafawa Balewa
was found dead in a ditch. The army had come to power.

Thomson decided to cut his losses and get out. Coltart sold
off the plant and closed the books on their West African venture.
It had been a costly safari.

In late 1976, sitting in his sixteenth-floor office at London's
Press Centre, Coltart was asked whether it had been worth
Thomson's while to go into Africa. He answered almost before
the question was finished.

'No.'

As the nineteen-seventies came in, the only foreign newspaper
influence in English-speaking West Africa was the London
Mirror Group's *Daily Times* and its Sunday sister, the *Sunday
Times*, in Lagos. They had not merely survived the several
changes of government from civilian to military rule and the war
between rebellious Biafra and the Federal Government, but had
continued to prosper. The *Daily Times* was selling 200,000 copies
a day and the *Sunday Times* 350,000. Cecil King had long since
returned to Britain, and though there were still *Mirror* executives
in ultimate control, the editorial and managerial staff was African.

The *Times* had become a public company in 1967, and just
over a quarter of the ordinary stock was owned by Nigerians.
In 1972 the Nigerian Enterprise Promotion Decree was introduced in Parliament. This meant that control of all foreign
companies had to be vested in the country itself. The deadline
for local ownership was 31 March 1974, and a few weeks before
this the *Mirror* sold its remaining one million shares.

It was just twenty-seven years since Cecil King, now deposed
as chairman of the *Mirror* Group and living in exiled retirement
in Ireland, had set out for the tropics.

4 The Going of the Europeans

The withdrawal of the *Mirror* Group and the Thomson Organisation from West Africa left the newspapers of Nigeria and Ghana in the hands of African journalists and African managers. But even before the last Britishers had left, control of the press had been taken over by the politicians, civilian or military.

Because of the widely differing philosophies of the principal West African nationalists who gained independence for their countries from Britain—the benevolent capitalism of Nigeria and the fanatical neo-Marxism of Kwame Nkrumah's Ghana—the two states had become virtual enemies. They were certainly highly distrustful and disdainful of each other. These suspicions were to survive and even strengthen with independence as governments came and went in a series of coups, counter coups, and just one election (the short-lived Kofi Busia Government of Ghana in 1969).

And yet the evolution of the press in both countries in the post-independence years is strikingly similar. Both in Nigeria and in Ghana newspapermen were to be subjected to a frightening switch-back roller-coaster of highs and lows. Many were thrown off. Some—like Nigeria's Peter Enahoro—got sick and jumped clear. As the second half of the nineteen-seventies came in and military regimes for both states seemed a strong probability for the foreseeable future, the switch-back flattened out, with the high and the lows now no more than the odd jolt and jar. Newspapermen still aboard could never be sure that the track ahead was not blocked or mined, but by now they had been able to organise a makeshift braking system which, though greatly slowing their progress, made for a much safer ride.

It proved more difficult for the soldiers of Nigeria to get a saddle and bridle on to the press than for those in Ghana. There are three reasons: the Nigerian press is a much bigger animal; it has a huge paddock and most important of all, it is better bred.

With one exception, Ghana's newspapers are all in the capital, Accra, a fifteen-minute drive from the military headquarters of Colonel Ignatius Acheampong. Three-quarters of both dailies, the *Graphic* and the *Times*, are sold in Accra. Nigeria's eleven dailies are spread all over the country, and although there are military governors in every state, the centre of power in Lagos is often hundreds of miles away. Even editors of government-owned papers feel less inhibited. As an editor in Kano, over five hundred miles from Lagos, on the edge of the Sahara, put it: 'Absence makes the heart grow stronger—and the pen, too.'

But it is the quality of Nigeria's newspapermen which makes them buck and kick every time a soldier tries to mount, a quality born of the high-spirited nature of all Nigerians, but brought to a professional pitch in the country's journalists by the long tutelage and example of the Mirror Group's *Daily Times*.

With bayonets at the ribs and rifle-butts between the eyes—often literally—the soldiers of Nigeria were finally to subdue the newspapermen and women, but there was still enough snorting and champing at the bit to hope that given half a chance they would one day break out of the garrison stable and run free again.

Kwame Nkrumah was far away in Peking on a self-appointed Vietnam peace mission when a group of army and police officers seized power on the morning of 24 February, 1966. The coup had been planned by J. W. K. Hartley, Commissioner of Police, two army brigade commanders, Major-General E. K. Kotoka and Brigadier A. K. Ocran, and a dashing thirty-year-old Sandhurst-trained officer, Colonel A. A. Afrifa.

When they met in secrecy to finalise plans for the coup twenty-four hours before the seizure deadline, Major-General Kotoka ticked off the moves to be taken in the vital first hour: the two major priorities were Flagstaff House, the strongly-guarded residence in Accra of Nkrumah where his Soviet-trained bodyguard was stationed, and the transmitting station of the

Ghana Broadcasting Corporation.

General Kotoka consulted his list and said: 'Both of these at five a.m. The cabinet can wait until six.'

Colonel Afrifa asked: 'What about the newspapers?'

Kotoka replied: 'They won't cause any trouble. Just send half a dozen men round during the morning.'

The other coup-leaders nodded in agreement.

So subservient had the Ghanaian press become that the rulers-to-be took it for granted that it could be put into reverse without so much as grinding its gears. All subsequent governments of Ghana have gone on taking the Ghana press for granted. By the time Colonel Acheampong was ready to seize power on 13 January 1972, the newspapers of Ghana were so conditioned that they did not even figure in the plans of the plotters. Several hours after the coup had taken place, anxious newspapermen were ringing the Ministry of Information to ask: 'Is anybody coming round to see us?'

An official answered them: 'What for?'

On the morning of the coup that ousted Nkrumah, a detachment of troops made the rounds of the newspaper offices picking up Eric Heyman, editor of the *Evening News*, Thomas Baffoe, *Ghanaian Times* and Kofi Batsa, *Spark*. All were senior members of the Convention People's Party and enjoyed substantial benefits like free housing and government cars. They were only detained briefly, but all were dismissed.

The papers continued to appear with the same staff and the reporters and sub-editors who had long grown used to filling page after page with praise of the Osagyefo performed an immediate *volte face*. A sub on the *Evening News* remembers that there had been a story about Nkrumah held over from the day before the coup, and it was marked to appear in the issue due out a few hours after the military seized power. A young captain was in the news room, nominally in charge but happy to sit quietly drinking tea as the newspapermen went about their work. The sub handling the old Nkrumah story tossed it aside and said 'We won't be needing this now'. The captain took the proof, which had a headline including the almost mandatory 'Osagyefo' and said 'Just take out Osagyefo'. The sub explained that the headline would then be one line short and thus out of balance. The captain did not at first understand. The sub explained and said there would have to be another word used in the headline in place of Osagyefo and also in the text wherever it appeared. So that it would cause a minimum of resetting, explained the sub, the new word would have to be no longer than the old one, that is, eight letters or less. The captain thought a moment and then totted up on his fingers.

'Tyrant will fit', he said. The amended story duly appeared— and tyrant became the favourite term of reference for Ghana's deposed president, until eventually all references to him were banned.

The military junta soon closed *Spark* and also two new government papers just started by Nkrumah, the *Daily Gazette* and *Sunday Punch*. The President of the National Liberation Council, Lieutenant-General Joseph Ankra, announced to the foreign diplomatic missions in Accra that the military 'is determined to open a new page in the journalistic ethics of Ghana'.

The elation throughout the country at the overthrow of Nkrumah was almost euphoric among newspapermen. Censorship of outgoing press stories was lifted and Nkrumah's black list of foreign journalists—most of them British (who had been banned from entering the country)—was cancelled. The *Ashanti Pioneer* was resurrected and Kwame Kesse-Adu, its old editor, released from Fort Ussher. Among the many hundreds released from preventive detention without trial were a number of journalists, including a German freelancer, Lutz Herold, who had been sentenced to forty years' imprisonment.

Colonel Akwesi Afrifa sent a special message of goodwill to the *Pioneer* on its re-appearance (it had dropped Ashanti). He said: 'Those of us who carried out the coup did so in the firm belief it would create the needed atmosphere for freedom of expression, the bedrock of all democratic institutions. We fought so that our newspapers should be free to begin this process of democratisation. Liberty is here with us. But I have a feeling of disappointment and sometimes dismay when I see the quality of journalism that still lingers. I am aware that the press is owned by government. But that is no excuse for mediocrity and sycophantic adulation.'

A group of academics at the University of Ghana took the military's call for 'freedom of expression' in the press at its face value, and in July 1966 seventeen lecturers produced the first issue of the bi-weekly *Legon Observer* (Legon is the suburb of Accra in which the University is sited). It immediately established itself as the most literate and provocative publication on the

West Coast, with a circulation of 10,000, several hundred of which went abroad.

For more than a year, the press under the National Liberation Council felt its way towards something approaching free expression, but the new editors of the government-owned *Daily Graphic, Ghanaian Times* and *Evening News*, although untainted by the bootlicking policies of their predecessors, were still, in the last resort, civil servants and the editorials they wrote and the coverage in the news columns reflected this relationship with authority. But things were undoubtedly getting better and the *Pioneer*, published at Kumasi but also circulating in Accra, and the *Legon Observer* were revelling in the new atmosphere.

It was one of those honeymoon-like periods common in new African states in transition, and it was not to last for long.

During the Nkrumah regime a state-owned pharmaceutical company had been set up by the Hungarians. As part of the dismemberment programme of several such enterprises, the military government negotiated terms with an American drug firm, Abbott Laboratories, to take over and run the state company. Not only were the *Pioneer* and the *Legon Observer* critical of the terms negotiated by the government, but also the state-owned *Graphic, Evening News* and *Times*. The editors of the government papers knew they were on delicate ground, but as they pondered how far to go in their criticism, Brigadier Afrifa, who was emerging as the strong man of the regime and who was shortly to take over as head of state, made a speech saying that journalists would not be victimised for speaking their minds as long as they worked within the law.

The government editors then took the cue from the *Pioneer* and the *Legon Observer*, and came out with editorials condemning the deal with the American drug firm. A few days later, on 14 December 1967, they received identical letters from the Principal Secretary of the Ministry of Information summarily dismissing them. The fourth man sacked was Oscar Tsedze, John Dumoga's assistant on the *Graphic*.

The entire press world of Ghana was rocked on its heels. The military's civilian Commissioner of Information, Kwabena Osei Bonsu, resigned in protest, saying the firing of the four men '. . . jeopardises the freedom of the Press to which the NLC had irrevocably committed itself'.

Three weeks after the military sacked the editors of its own newspapers, it brought to court twenty-nine people associated with the *Legon Observer* (including six printers) and charged them with contempt of court. Although the *Observer* had been even more critical of the Abbott contract than the newspapers, the charge it faced concerned an article criticising delays in hearing court cases. The military did not wish to have a trial which would allow the academics to lay out in public all the arguments against the drug contract they had negotiated, but they were determined to administer a rap on the knuckles of the academics. Twenty-two lecturers and the editor were fined small sums. The printers were found not guilty. The *Pioneer* was untouched, and it followed up its criticisms of the drug contract by demanding that the NLC explain why it had sacked its own editors.

The military was badly shaken by the whole Abbott affair which had undermined a great deal of the growing faith in the new regime which the high command had been nurturing since they came to power. They reacted by increasing their grip on the press even tighter.

One of the country's newspapermen who felt the military squeeze hardest was Chris Asher, owner, editor, reporter, advertisement manager, circulation director, accountant and proof reader of *The Palaver*. Asher is one of the rapidly declining breed of editor-owners anywhere and certainly the most colourful in Africa. *The Palaver* (Trouble) is a razzmatazz weekly packed in fairly even proportions with expose, campaigns and off-beat human interest stories which often strain the credulity of its readers to the limit.

Asher has travelled widely, and spent some time in the United States where he acquired a taste for a life-style as flamboyant as his newspaper. He dresses impeccably, runs two large American cars, and his business card is crammed with titles like managing director of United Press International, executive chairman of Trans World Associates, managing director of various public relations and advertising companies and editor-in-chief of *The Palaver*.

He first went to prison in 1967 for allegedly 'jubilating over an attempted coup'.

Before he was taken away by a detachment of troops, he sat down at his desk and typed out a message to the military high command saying 'Political imprisonment of a journalist cannot be his end; it cannot even be the beginning of his end, but the end of the beginning of a more uncompromising journalist who will always publish the truth and be damned'.

He was kept behind bars for ten months and says he found the experience 'very useful spiritually'. Every morning he preached in hot-gospelling style to the other prisoners, and ever after he was to begin the day in similar vein, with an 8 o'clock morning prayer and hymn (always the same, 'Come Down O Love Divine') for his not very enthusiastic reporters and sub-editors.

Before he launched *Palaver*, Asher made two earlier attempts to get into publishing. His first paper was the *Western Tribune* but its maiden issue carried two stories, 'Workers Laid Off in Western Region' and 'The Tragedy of Tribalism', which the military considered incitement.

It took the high command four months to decide how best to deal with this. The law officers found it difficult to frame satisfactory charges, and finally his passport was impounded and he was placed in protective custody. In prison he was closely questioned about his connections in the United States. The government-owned publishing house which printed the paper refused to accept any more issues when Asher was released. For more than a year he worked as a free-lance, stringing for a number of Afro-American newspapers in the United States and all the time saving to start a successor to the *Tribune*. *The Herald* appeared in April 1969 and it was soon in trouble. At this time the military was preparing to hand back power to a civilian government and the head of state, Lieutenant-General Afrifa, called on the electorate to support Dr Kofi Busia's Progress Party in the elections. Chris Asher felt it was no service to the country for the final act of the military to give the seal of approval to any one party, and the *Herald* came out with a stinging editorial saying that it was unfortunate that the Head of State could descend to the level of 'jungle politics' and become the champion of 'political khakistocracy' which, said the *Herald*, would be the worst form of government.

When Asher went to deliver the copy for the next issue of the *Herald* the printers said they could no longer publish the paper as there was a shortage of newsprint. Asher went back to work, this time into public relations, saved again and brought out *The*

Palaver in October 1970. The soldiers were back—for the time being—in their barracks and Kofi Busia's Progress Party was in power. *Palaver* prospered in the freer environment, but trouble of a different kind was around every corner. Rising production costs and a bigger staff to produce the increasing number of pages soon brought the operation money problems. *Palaver* moved offices three times because of rent rises, and Asher had to borrow money at 100 per cent interest to keep his paper going.

When the soldiers moved out of their barracks an hour before dawn—'coup time'—once more on the morning of 13 January 1972 to travel the familiar route to Flagstaff House and the Ghana Broadcasting Corporation, *Palaver* welcomed them. It was, of course, standard journalistic practice for newspapers in every state where the military seizes power to do so, but for months Chris Asher had been aware of the growing corruption in the government of Kofi Busia. One of his morning prayers included the exhortation 'O Lord, keep their hands out of the till this day'. Now he could publish the corruption stories he had been collecting for months, and week after week *Palaver* regaled its readers with the details. Some of *Palaver*'s revelations were obtained through what he admits were 'unorthodox methods'. Almost certainly the new generation of soldier rulers under Colonel Ignatius Acheampong were supplying him with chapter and verse. In the next year *Palaver* was served with seventeen libel writs, a minimum claim for 10,000 cedis (just over £3,000 at the then rate of exchange) and a maximum of 100,000 cedis. Not one came to court. 'We had documents to defend ourselves', says Asher.

His relations with the military were excellent, and in April 1973 he was summoned to Flagstaff House by Colonel Acheampong and commended for his good work in the cause of the revolution.

For several years after the military seized power in Nigeria the country's newspapermen were sustained by the repeated promise of the soldiers that once corruption had been cleaned up and the country was back on an even keel they would return to the barracks and hand over to a civilian government. There was also a certain amount of common cause between the military and the press. Though they did not like the principle of authoritarian rule, many newspapermen had watched with dismay the mess made by the politicians who had taken over from the colonialists. 'Africa's Showpiece State'—the title given to a *Time*-magazine cover story on Prime Minister Tafawa Balewa—had become a pretty sordid advertisement for Black rule. The war with the rebellious Biafra probably only postponed a military take-over; it certainly strengthened the case of those officers who believed that only a firm grip, backed by the gun, would pull Africa's biggest and most complex state together.

Even when General Aguiyi-Ironsi, the military leader who was leading the clean-up, was killed with many of his top command at the end of July 1966, most of Nigeria's newspapermen, though badly shaken, clung to the belief that this was only a temporary aberration which would not affect the declared goal of a return to democracy.

Though the new military regime under General Yakubu Gowon brought in emergency decrees which gave it almost unlimited arbitrary powers, the press retained a large measure of freedom. When he addressed the University of Ife in August 1974, Lateef Jakande, publisher of the *Nigerian Tribune* and just retired as chairman of the International Press Institute, said that the Army's emergency decree of 1966 was 'sufficient to turn the Nigerian press into a captive press'.

But, he said: 'That this has not actually happened is due to the tradition of press freedom which dates from the colonial era, the courage and professional spirit of Nigerian editors and publishers and the good sense of some of those in authority.'

Although the powers were there, no attempt was made to introduce Press censorship.

Not that life was easy for newspapermen by a very long way. At the top of the military high command there was general agreement to give newspapers a fair amount of rope, but lower down the ladder there were many officers and ordinary soldiers who saw in the newspapermen of the country the embodiment of how things had been under civilian rule—much too lax. Soldiers in the streets of the towns were able to assert their authority over the common man by stopping his car, demanding proof of identity and generally bullying anyone they took a dislike to. Anyone who answered back was likely to get, at best a boot up the backside, or a few days cooling his heels in the local jail.

Newspapermen were much more difficult to bring into line. They stood their ground when challenged and answered back—

both by word of mouth, and later, in the columns of their papers. There began to develop a sort of cat and mouse game between reporters and soldiers, and it was not always the soldiers who were the ones waiting to pounce. Typical of the sort of minor brushes which existed was an incident when a cameraman on the *Daily Times* was picked up by security forces for allegedly failing to stand to attention while the national anthem was being played. When he was brought to court, he was cleared. On another occasion, at an airport press conference on the arrival of President Leopold Senghor of Senegal for a state visit, a reporter who had submitted his written question, as required, was tapped on the shoulder with the crisp order 'Get out of the conference room'.

Gradually the soldiers adopted tougher tactics. Military governors had been appointed over all the country's twelve regions, and in many cases they began to exercise authority like little war lords. Chief Theo Ola, news editor of the *Daily Times*, was at his desk in Lagos when he was picked up and taken under a detention order to a prison at Ibadan, one hundred miles away. He was later released, almost certainly on the orders of the high command.

Every time an incident like this occurred, the Nigerian press raised its voice. In February 1964 the editorial staff of the *New Nigerian* in Kaduna, upset by constant harassment by the military, asked their managing director, Adamu Ciroma, to do something about it. He came out with an editorial which said: 'In the last twelve months life for *New Nigerian* reporters and correspondents has been difficult. If the present trend continues there will come a time when it will be impossible. The result, if these actions continue, would be that the vital service of collecting and disseminating information to much of this country—where the *New Nigerian* is the only daily newspaper distributed—will be paralysed. And the public should know who is responsible.'

Gradually the press, which had welcomed the military, came to realise that the promise of democracy for Nigeria and freedom for itself was a mirage. By 1973 General Gowon, though still declaring the intention of the military to return to their barracks by 1976, had shifted his ground. He said that only an administration which included the military could guarantee political stability, and he suggested a 'diarchy' civilian-military government to succeed the soldiers. Pressmen reported that speech at

Lagos University with tight lips.

By 1974 bitterness between the press and the military was at a peak. *The Christian Science Monitor* news service reported: 'A new crisis of confidence has developed between the Nigerian police and the Press.'

The soldiers who had come to power in 1966 to eliminate corruption were now as crooked as the civilians they had ousted—more crooked, for Nigeria's oil wealth was beginning to flow, bringing in wealth undreamed of by any other Black State.

What had happened in Nigeria was the ultimate example of what had happened in almost every other state in Africa—and in other continents, too—where the military had seized power. Civilian regimes were ousted by officers incensed at corruption, and not only incensed, but bewildered by the whole crooked system. After all, nobody had ever tried to bribe *them*. Thus, the military came to power with much breast-beating about cleaning out the old stables, and for a year or two corruption and bribery were taboo. If democracy was the price to be paid, most people thought it was worth it. But a couple of years was enough to initiate the soldiers into the habits of the erstwhile civilian politicians. Slowly the captains, the majors and the colonels, who had never had more than their military pay, found themselves in positions of power and realised that their patronage was worth a fortune.

The circle was thus joined—until it started all over again, but this time with soldiers taking over from brother soldiers.

Many of Africa's military regimes govern states so poor that the fortunes to be made by corruption are relatively modest, but in the case of Nigeria wealth was vast. One newspaper alleged that soldiers who had joined the army virtual paupers had in a few years become millionaires. With much of the oil revenue going on major public works projects, thousands of millions of dollars were spent importing building materials like cement. Such international deals eased the way for illicit fortunes to be acquired outside of the country—the 'just in case money'—as it is known in Africa.

Another newspaper spoke of 'vast wealth hidden abroad, especially in Swiss banks'. The military high command reacted to these attacks by warning the press to behave or face the consequences.

Alhadji Kam Salem, Inspector General of Police, told a press conference: 'The press has recently mounted a campaign against the Federal Government, putting pressure on it to institute an inquiry into the conduct of certain government functionaries and levelling accusations against individuals. The Federal Government will no longer tolerate press indiscipline and calculated attempts to undermine its authority. It may be forced to take drastic and unpleasant measures to curb the excess of the press.'

The *Nigerian Tribune* challenged the government to substantiate its charge that the press had attempted to blackmail the authorities by publishing misleading stories; what the press was doing, said the *Tribune*, was mounting a campaign against corruption in line with the declared policy of the government.

Recalling that the rooting out of corruption had been the principal reason why the military had seized power, the *Tribune* said: 'It will be damaging to the reputation and good name of the Federal Military Government if, instead of encouraging the press to expose this evil, it imposes restrictions on the freedom of the press and the personal liberty of journalists.'

The military was divided in its attitude to the press exposes, just as it was divided over corruption. There were many officers as appalled at what was happening under military rule as they had been at the name Nigeria had earned as the most corrupt state in Africa when it had been governed by civilians. Brigadier Oluwole Rotimi, Governor of the Western State, issued a statement saying it was important to give journalists adequate freedom. 'I have never made any attempt to gag the press', he said, 'and I will allow them to enjoy their freedom. This is how it should be'.

Although the corruption issue was the major cause of friction between the press and the military, there were many cases where pressmen, and presswomen, fell foul of senior officers who resented the slightest examples of what they considered indiscipline or the questioning of military dictate. The most serious case, and one which united the entire press of Nigeria against the government in a way unprecedented since independence, was the treatment of Mineri Amakiri, a reporter on the *Nigerian Observer*, Port Harcourt.

On 30 July 1973, Amakiri, who was his paper's chief correspondent in Rivers State, reported that teachers throughout the State were threatening to resign *en masse* if their working conditions were not examined. In comparison to many stories carried by the Nigerian press, this was pretty innocuous, but it appeared on the thirty-first birthday of the military governor of the State, Alfred Diete-Spiff, who interpreted it as an attempt to embarrass him.

Amakiri was summarily arrested, given twenty-four strokes across his back with a cane, had his beard and his hair shaved off, locked up for twenty-seven hours and thrown out into the street.

Every newspaperman in the country, every journalists' association, the Newspaper Proprietors' Association, the Guild of Editors, the Association of Radio and Television Journalists (all Government employees), demanded action.

'Amakiri: Press Fury on the Rise', said a *Daily Express* headline.

'We Call for Freedom, Justice', said a story in the *Daily Times*.

'The Port Harcourt Scandal', said the leading article in the *Nigerian Observer*, which describing the incident as 'jungle-style manhandling' commented: 'It amounts no less to a primitive attempt to muzzle the truth and compromise an elemental right— the freedom of the press.'

The military high command was shaken and divided. Amakiri filed suit against the police officer who had carried out the assault and the acting Chief Justice of Rivers State—who was directly under the Military Governor—awarded damages of £100 for each one of the twenty-four strokes laid upon the newspaperman's back, plus another £1,300 for having had his head shaved, £1,300 for 'illegal and unconstitutional detention' and costs of £375.

It is the only case on record of a journalist in Africa successfully suing an official of a military junta.

If the Amakiri case was a high point in the friction between the press and authority in Nigeria it solved nothing; it may even have made the military and the police more determined than ever to bring pressmen to heel. On 18 July 1974, writing in the *Daily Sketch*, Titus Ogunwale said: 'Police invitations to editors are so frequent that no one can blame an editor who lists "possible chat with police" as an item on the schedule to be considered at the daily editorial conference.'

Soon after the Amakiri affair, three journalists on the *Daily Express*, Fola Ashiru (chief sub-editor), Miss Toyin Johnson (features editor) and Goody Emegokwue (feature writer) were charged with sedition. When they came to court, the director of prosecutions withdrew the case and they were discharged. No doubt mindful of the outcry and the substantial damages in the Amakiri case the governors of the country's States were now a little more circumspect in their handling of errant journalists. When Femi Ogunleye, *Daily Times,* and John Anishere, *Daily Sketch,* who worked in the Kano offices of their newspapers, fell foul of the Kano State Military Governor, Auda Bako, he simply deported them out of the State. The *Daily Sketch* commented: 'The mind boggles at the prospect of what would happen to a Nigerian journalist who has been declared *persona non-grata* in all the states of the Federation' and a columnist in the same paper said that but for the deterrent effect of the High Court decision in the Amakiri case, the two journalists barred from Kano State 'would have suffered worse personal indignity than Minere Amakiri'.

Relations between the press and the military were now at a low point. Each accused the other of corruption.

On 9 April 1975, thirty journalists from different Lagos newspapers marched in protest on the office of Edwin Clark, the Federal Information Commissioner, and handed over a letter calling on General Yakubu Gowon, the Head of State, to make a policy statement on the press. A few days earlier the Army Chief of Staff, Major General David Ejoor, had told an interviewer that the military government held 'the strong view that Nigerian journalists are corrupt, not only in terms of money but also politically'. Still the old champions of the Nigerian press held to their belief that freedom would survive. As the newspapermen of Lagos were marching on the offices of the Federal Information Commission, Alhadji Babatunde Jose was in London. More than any other practising Nigerian journalist, Alhadji Jose symbolised the generations of struggle the Nigerian press had undergone. Long before Cecil King arrived from Fleet Street to bring West African journalism into the twentieth century, he was at the *Daily Times,* not in the editorial department, but hand-compositing the type before the first linotypes were installed.

By sheer determination, he fought his way right to the top, as admired by successive imports of British *Mirror* executives as he was by Nigerian newspapermen all over the country. On 10 April 1975—the day after the Lagos march—he addressed the Royal African Society in London on press Freedom in Africa. 'What does the future hold?' he asked, after reviewing the hazards of the fifties, the sixties and the coming of the military regime.

He had this answer: 'I want to hazard the opinion that we have been through the worst. With continued courage, improved professional skill and mass political awareness, tomorrow, I am confident, will be a better day.'

Alhadji Jose had less than eighteen months remaining as chairman, managing and editorial director of the *Daily Times* group before the military moved in.

Oluwole Rotimi, the Governor of Western State, who less than a year before had spoken out on behalf of press freedom, had now come round to the soldiers' conventional view that the military was supreme. He ordered the removal of the manager of the government-owned *Daily Sketch* because of a story which, he alleged, incited the public against the military. The Head of State himself, General Gowon, a soft-spoken and generally courteous man, returned from a state visit abroad in August 1974 and dismissed waiting pressmen with 'Get out of my sight'.

He was not to be troubled by Nigerian journalists for very much longer. On 29 July 1975—the ninth anniversary of the coup that brought him to power—Gowon was attending a meeting of the heads of state of the Organisation of African Unity in Kampala, Uganda. The week before his departure from Lagos, Nigeria had been rife with rumours of a fresh military take-over. Gowon had asked one of his closest associates, Brigadier Murtala Ramat Mohammed, if there was any truth in the rumours. He was assured there was none—but Gowon thought it appropriate to send his wife and children on a visit to Britain.

Gowon learned of the seizure of power by Murtala while at his desk in the O.A.U. conference in Kampala. He joined his family in Britain.

The Murtala coup was a totally bloodless one, almost gentlemanly. There was not even a house arrest. Some thirty senior officers were quietly retired, all on full pension. The governors of Nigeria's twelve states were changed. The press waited to see what was in store for them. Murtala made the standard declarations about the role of the press in society and 'invited' newspapermen to co-operate. It sounded ominous and it was.

By the end of the month, on 31 August 1975, the Federal Government took a 60 per cent shareholding in the *Daily Times*, the *Sunday Times*, and eight other magazines and newspapers produced by the country's biggest publishing house. The *New*

Nigerian group, run since 1962 by successive governments in the Northern Region, went the same way. The acquisitions brought the entire newspaper industry virtually under central government control since the *Sketch, Standard, Herald* and *Observer* were state-owned. Six radio and television stations run by state governments were also taken over by the Federal Government.

The official statement from Lagos on the take-overs said that they would allow the press 'to expand their activities and enhance channels of communication with the public'.

Nigeria was left with three independent newspapers, the *Nigerian Tribune,* the *West African Pilot* and the *Daily Express,* all with small circulations. When the country achieved independence in 1960, three times that number of newspapers were freely expressing their views on major national issues.

The Continent's biggest state still has the best journalists in Independent Africa. But they are no longer independent.

5 French-speaking Africa: A Different Shade of White

French-speaking Africa is as different from English-speaking Africa as France is from Britain. Independence has had practically no effect in bridging this gulf.

Michel de Breteuil, whose father Charles was the founder of modern newspapers in French-speaking Africa, sums up the difference in the two colonial approaches: 'British colonialism was concerned with capitalism: French colonialism was concerned with culture.'

Britain managed her African possessions rather like Charles Dickens's Mr Micawber, always waiting to see what turned up. If it was trouble, they sent a ship or a plane with a battalion of troops to put it down—that is, until the trouble came from Rhodesia's rebellious Whites.

The British dismembered their African empire constitutionally in the same way as they had acquired it—haphazardly. Protectorates, colonies, mandated territories were juggled by a succession of Colonial Secretaries in London who had seldom visited any of them and had only the haziest idea where most of them were. They all had their independence negotiated separately.

The British view was to hand over their possessions to the local peoples 'when they are ready'.

The French did not for a moment operate their African empire in this way. They just took one step forward at a time for the whole lot.

As late as the years after the Second World War, independence for France's African colonies was not even a contentious issue in Paris: it was not considered. It was only when Guy Mollet formed his Socialist Government in 1955 that a new deal was forged for French Africa.

During the sixty years from 1857–1918, France had acquired in Africa an area eight times the size of France itself. You could start a journey at the mouth of the River Congo and travel 2,000 miles to the Mediterranean without leaving French territory. Dakar, the capital of Senegal, was the centre of French West Africa in a way not comparable to anything in British Africa. French Equatorial Africa had its headquarters at Brazzaville in the Congo.

Fourteen independent states were to emerge from France's African Empire. But between them they could hardly muster a Press worth the name.

As far as an African-owned press went, there was little of the enterprise shown by the Africans in the British West African states, most of which bordered on the French colonies.

The earliest African paper of any significance in French West Africa was a weekly, *L'A.O.F.* which appeared in 1907 in Senegal as the organ of the local branch of the French Socialist Party. It is very much in character with the way the French operated in Africa that such a paper should have been linked to a political party in France. There was never anything remotely equivalent in British Africa.

An early editor of *L'A.O.F.*, Lamine Gueye, was one of the first African members of the French Parliament.

In such an improbable territory as Dahomey (renamed Benin in 1976), today still one of the least developed countries on the Continent, there was a burst of newspaper activity in the twenties, including *La Voix du Dahomey*, *Le Cri Nègre* and *Le Phare du Dahomey*.

Although fairly primitive publications, they hammered away at the theme of nationalism. How they managed to survive for any length of time is difficult to understand. The explanation lies probably in a mixture of benevolence on the part of the local French governor, and the belief by the authorities that self-government by Africans was such an absurd idea that it did no harm to let the natives play with the thought.

During the thirties, the first African elections to the French

Parliament were held, and though these were limited to Senegal, they produced a spate of political broadsheets financed by the political aspirants. Most of them closed down immediately after the elections, but they had at least whetted the appetite of the small number of literates for newspapers and four of them, *L'Ouest Africain, Le Journal de Dakar, La Sirène Sénégalaise* and *Rumeur Africaine* all flourished for several years.

The first anti-colonial paper in the Ivory Coast appeared in 1935 and was financed by a number of small African business-men. This was the *Eclaireur de la Côte d'Ivoire*. In spite of strict government censorship, *L'Eclaireur* campaigned for social recon-struction, the reform of the chieftain system and consistently put forward the cause of urban unemployment and the peasant farmers.

Although it cannot be considered as part of the indigenous press, *Afrique Nouvelle*, the Dakar based bi-weekly produced by the Catholic White Fathers, became the most widely-read publi-cation in Francophone Africa. It was founded in 1947, and though produced by the Catholic Church, it never pushed religion and was always consistent in its support of African nationalism.

In its early years it was edited by Father J. de Benoist who had been trained as a journalist, so that it provided a profession-alism far superior to any other religious sponsored publication in West Africa. In the sixties it was taken over by an all-African team in Dakar with correspondents in most of the French-speaking states of West Africa.

The totality of African-owned newspapers in French Africa was minimal, however, compared to the African press in British Africa. It is doubtful whether it had the slightest effect on the attainment of independence by the French colonies.

In modern terms, Africa only entered the newspaper age by chance when young Charles de Breteuil realised the potential in producing a newspaper for the large French community in Dakar, capital of Senegal. De Breteuil was no newspaperman himself. He had not been trained for any particular profession in France after the First World War. He used to drink with journalists from the Paris evening paper *France-Soir* and was friendly with Paul Reynaud who was later to become French Prime Minister but before the Second World War was Minister for Colonies.

It was his friendship with Paul Reynaud that probably inspired young Charles de Breteuil to have a look at France's African Empire. He set out with very little money in his pocket, first to Morocco, then Tunisia and finally into tropical Africa. He did a variety of jobs, even some diamond mining for a British company in Sierra Leone.

In all the French colonies he found an ex-patriate community whose only contact with home, apart from letters, were newspapers which arrived infrequently and sometimes months late by ship. He realised there was a ready market for local newspapers publishing fresher news about France than was brought by the Parisian imports.

He began his publishing venture cautiously and though it grew to considerable proportions he, and later his son, Michel, always kept the operation uncomplicated. In no country where he established newspapers was there a commitment greater than a couple of small rooms rented as offices, a desk or two, a couple of typewriters and a filing cabinet. And a highly effective operation it was. There was no problem of expensive expatriate technicians to man printing presses. De Breteuil had all his papers printed by local printers.

There were many Frenchmen like Charles de Breteuil in French colonial Africa, men running small businesses, cafés, bars, shops.

In British Africa large corporations were the employers of the majority of Europeans. You rarely saw a British shopkeeper in Britain's African Empire. The British may have been a nation of shopkeepers in Britain, but the French were the nation of colonial café proprietors, electricians, plumbers and a whole range of other *petit-bourgeois* entrepreneurs.

Because of this de Breteuil was able to get his papers printed from little backyard print-shops, often using machines old by half-a-century or more, but kept going by the skill of their French owners.

In Abidjan, capital of the Ivory Coast, for example, less than twenty per cent of Frenchmen there before independence were employed by big French companies. The rest worked for themselves in small family concerns.

Charles de Breteuil's newspaper chain began by following the same route that he had taken when he had set out on his travels; first in Arab Africa, with papers in Tangier and Casablanca.

His first paper in tropical Africa was *Paris-Dakar* in Senegal, which began as a weekly in 1933 and became a daily two years later. The name reveals all. It was a French newspaper, produced by a Frenchman, to be read by Frenchmen.

In 1938 de Breteuil launched *France-Afrique* (which became *Abidjan-Matin* in 1954) in the Ivory Coast. In 1954 he started *La Presse de Guinée*, but this was suppressed in 1958 after Guinea had voted to stay out of the French Community which General de Gaulle had grandly offered to France's African Empire. Guinea paid a dreadful price for daring to say 'non' to its French masters, a price unmatched by any metropolitan power over a former subject people. Immediately the vote to remain independent was known, the four hundred French aid officials in Guinea were withdrawn. They ransacked the files to make sure that an administrative mess was left for the new and totally inexperienced government as it took over. The departing French officials wrecked the electricity generating plant in the capital, Conakry, and left the telephone system in ruins. Even electric light bulbs in government offices were smashed. Guinea's currency was refused convertibility against the French franc. This meant economic and industrial chaos, since all the machinery in the country was of French origin and the spare parts had to be obtained from France.

It is little wonder that in their bitterness, which has never subsided, the Guinea Government lashed out at anything French-owned that was left, and de Breteuil's newspaper was an obvious target. But because of the neatness of the operation, all de Breteuil's two expatriates had to do was clear their drawers, pack their bags and fly out.

De Breteuil had also started papers in Brazzaville and Madagascar but the War finished these.

It is remarkable that anything survived of his newspaper chain in Africa because de Breteuil himself joined the French Army and was out of the Continent for most of the War. To a large extent his papers in Senegal and the Ivory Coast were able to continue because local French Army officers posted to the colonies used to go down to the printing works for a few hours two or three evenings a week and supervise their production.

At the end of the 1950s the de Breteuil Group comprised: *Dakar-Matin* in Senegal, *Abidjan-Matin* in the Ivory Coast and *La Presse du Cameroun* in Cameroon.

When France's African colonies achieved independence between 1960 and 1962, these were the only daily papers in the entire region. De Breteuil had one other publication, *Bingo*, which was the only thing he produced designed for Africans. It was a picture monthly aimed at the growing numbers of new literates coming out of secondary schools. He could hardly have realised when he started *Bingo* that it was to become the prop of the publishing empire his son was to inherit and expand in post-independence French Africa.

But even with independence, de Breteuil was making no more than a gesture towards producing newspapers relevant to their immediate societies. The underlying philosophy that all cultural thought came and went back to Paris was reflected in every issue of his newspapers in every country.

With independence, de Breteuil recognised that his newspaper empire was going to suffer the same traumas as the French Empire itself. He also believed that with French law specifying that foreigners could not own daily papers in France (though this did not apply to the French colonies) it would be morally wrong for him to continue in Africa.

This is another example of the disparity between the British and French philosophies in colonial Africa. For as independence came to British Africa, there was never the slightest thought by the owners of the European press there that there was any moral obligation upon them to leave. Indeed, a generation after *uhuru*, both of Kenya's big newspaper groups are foreign-owned.

De Breteuil looked around for a new way of operating, and the solution that he worked out, almost certainly with the co-operation of the French Foreign Ministry, has ensured a much greater French influence in the old French African Empire than Britain has been able to command in its former colonies; a simple, subtle arrangement that looks as though it may do something few other imperial importations anywhere in Africa look like doing—survive.

Because de Breteuil's operation was so compact, with virtually no capital or equipment, the problem posed by independence was of a purely technical nature. French printers who had been printing his newspapers were uncertain of their future. They were unwilling to invest in new machines, particularly as de Breteuil himself, always their best customer, was unsure of the future.

As the new states established themselves, they finally got around to looking at the printing industry in the various countries. The old machines which had been kept going by French printers were clearly inadequate for what the new governments had in mind.

The French Government was quick to see the opportunity that was offered. They realised not merely that he who pays the piper calls the tune, but that he who pays for the printing press is likely to have a very great influence over what those pressmen print.

This was something that never occurred to the British in Africa, where British publishing houses were well established with modern equipment. The fact that that equipment was in many cases soon to be taken over, or at the very least brought to heel by the new Black governments, did not occur to Whitehall.

One is bound to say that even if it had, so different was the attitude of the new governments of British Africa towards London that the link, even the stranglehold, that the French had over their old colonies could not have been maintained by Britain over its former territories by all the printing presses in creation.

'The French did more important work in education than the British' says Michel de Breteuil, 'and they made an especially strong effort to promote their language'. British critics of French colonialism question whether perfect fluency in French is as big a contribution to a young state seeking its way in the world as an independent nation as some Frenchmen suggest.

'When you see the way the French-educated Africans speak French and the way the English-educated Africans speak English, you see all the difference in the two colonial approaches', says de Breteuil.

'Many Africans speak a perfect French—more than a perfect French, a distinguished French. The level of English in English-speaking Africa is very low.'

That is only true at the topmost level of society. While a tiny veneer of political and civil service Africans in the French-speaking states speak this 'distinguished' French, the great mass of the populations speak none at all. In the former British possessions, even at the top, the level of spoken English is generally poor and heavily accented. But right down to peasant level most Africans speak some English.

But whichever the better system, it is undeniable that the 'Frenchness' of the political and administrative centres of the new

Francophone states created a relationship with Paris unknown between any Anglophone states and London.

After the Second World War an organisation called *La Société Nationale des Entreprises de Presse* (SNEP) was set up in France as a state enterprise to dispose of the assets of newspapers that had collaborated with the Nazis. SNEP had a number of subsidiaries concerned with providing technical advice, the training of printers and journalists and finance for new equipment. One of SNEP's subsidiaries is *La Société Nouvelle d'Editions Industrielles* (SNEI), one of France's biggest publishing groups which produces the Paris evening *France-Soir* and the magazine *Réalités*. As independence came, the resources of all these organisations were now turned towards the French-speaking states of Africa.

In the Ivory Coast a partnership was formed between de Breteuil and SNEI which allowed *Abidjan-Matin* to continue on the new press until the day, literally the day, the new independent Government of Houphouet-Boigny was ready to start its own paper.

On 7 December 1964 *Abidjan-Matin* came out with an announcement that a new newspaper would be appearing the next morning, *Fraternité-Matin* 'which we recommend to our readers'. When this publication appeared the next day, it was virtually the same as its predecessor.

SNEP provided both technical and editorial aid and de Breteuil's two or three expatriates left. Two separate companies were formed, one to run the editorial and the other the printing works, following the pattern that Charles de Breteuil himself had set, though now there was no reason why the operation should not be one. The contract with SNEP was to run for fifteen years from 1965, and by the end of 1976 there was only one Frenchman involved in the operation, the head printer.

President Houphouet became Board chairman and no expense was spared to produce a prestigious-looking newspaper. The contents were something else.

A Goss off-set press was bought from Chicago and phototypesetting was installed. The policy of the paper was a simple one and followed virtually the same successful path as de Breteuil: no criticism of the head of state or the government, but a certain amount of latitude allowed of a general nature when discussing other official issues.

In Senegal the new Government printing press provided by

France was not ready until May 1970. A new company was formed consisting of the Government, which held 65 per cent of the shares, and SNEP and de Breteuil sharing the rest. The old *Dakar-Matin* became *Le Soleil du Sénégal*. The Minister of Information, who for a year had been trained by de Breteuil on *Dakar-Matin,* took over as editor. The French Government sent a team of technicians and editorial advisers. This is an indefinite arrangement, unlike the fifteen-year-old agreement in the Ivory Coast. In 1974 SNEP provided a new off-set printing plant. The operation is, in every sense, a Government venture which is not expected to be viable.

The de Breteuil group now concentrates on its string of magazines published in Paris but circulating throughout Francophone Africa. *Bingo* is the linchpin. Michel runs things in exactly the same way that his father did in Africa, with just a few rented offices and printing done wherever the price is right.

Michel is a shrewd, imaginative innovator and his magazines range from general interest to agriculture, taking in children and pop music. They are printed anywhere the price is right. He will switch his printing from North Africa, to Paris, to Belgium, always looking for the cheapest quote. And because of the strong identity with France that the former French colonies have, the magazines are distributed throughout the old French African empire. All are exclusively in French.

No British publishing house has been able to match this sort of operation. Britain's former colonies feel little or no kinship with each other, and from a highly practical point of view exchange control makes it always difficult and generally impossible to remit money from English-speaking Africa back to London.

Michel de Breteuil has no such problems. He thinks that as the sun sets on the British publishing houses in Black Africa, there are many more dawns for the French. He puts this down not to the strong identification Francophone Africa has with France, but to the size of the British ventures by comparison with his own. He believes that just as the *Daily Mirror* group and the Thomson organisation reached a point where the frustrations of the tropics were just not worth the managerial trouble in London and the small financial returns, so the other big groups like the Aga Khan and Lonrho in Kenya will finally come to the same conclusion.

But for de Breteuil's tight little organisation, Africa is all they know, and they know it backwards.

'The British super-markets are closing down', he says, 'but the small French shopkeeper has a long way to go'.

The Cameroon is in many ways the most intriguing country in Black Africa. It came to independence in 1960 after seventy-five years of German, French and British rule. French and British troops occupied the territory during World War I and in 1919 the League of Nations carved it up and shared out various parts to the two great European colonial powers, Britain and France. The greater part went to France, and it is clear that almost a generation after independence the predominant foreign influence is going to be French. Diplomatically it rates low at the British Foreign Office.

The net result of these two very different cultures super-imposed on a fledgling state trying to establish its own identity has created stresses which Cameroon could well do without.

France is busy in a whole range of fields, not least the newspaper business. It took no less than ten years of planning for the new African Government of the Cameroon to decide finally on the sort of daily newspaper it wanted.

From 1964 the de Breteuil group had been publishing a modest daily, *La Presse du Cameroun*, in Douala, the fetid little port tucked right in the crutch of the great West African bulge.

The new Government wanted a paper in the capital, Yaounde, so the pattern de Breteuil had set in the Ivory Coast was followed. The last issue of *La Presse du Cameroun* appeared on 30 June 1974, announcing its own demise, and the *Cameroun Tribune* followed on the streets of the capital the next morning. The Government's holding in this venture is some 70 per cent, with the de Breteuil Group sharing the balance with the Société Nouvelle d'Editions Industrielles (SNEI).

The Cameroon Government, although leaning far more to-wards Paris than London, has always been anxious to demonstrate its independence, and there was concern in the cabinet of President Ahmadou Ahidjo that the official Government news-paper should not be seen to be French controlled.

They asked a Scotsman working for the Thomson Foundation in Britain, Norman Cattanach, to help them get the paper going, but he had only recently recovered breath from a nightmarish five months running papers in another part of the Continent and declined the offer.

Although both French and English are supposed to be the official languages of the Cameroons, because Yaounde, the capital, is in the former French region, it is the French language which has, if not a stranglehold, then certainly a very firm grip among the decision makers of the country. But as they are anxious to demonstrate to the English-speaking regions that the country is not manipulated from Paris, there is a good deal of latitude allowed to English-speaking publications and to some extent this has rubbed off in the French-language press. The *Cameroun Tribune* is published in French but has an English edition on Wednesdays.

The most important English language newspaper is the *Cameroon Times*, printed in Victoria. This comes out three times a week, and on the blank days *Cameroon Outlook* takes over with the *Weekender* on Sunday.

Outlook and *Weekender* are owned by a free-thinking former school-teacher, Tatu Tatu Obeson, who makes no secret of his fears that the English language will eventually become second to French, a fear widely held in West Cameroon. During General de Gaulle's Presidency, the formidable cadre of French aid advisers in Yaounde were pushing hard to stamp French upon the government and civil service. The French advisers did not disguise their dislike of 'the English' in Victoria. Though the top level of African ministers and civil servants in Yaounde were to a large extent much better educated—often at the Sorbonne—than Africans in West Cameroon, the Westerners had a broader educational base. While in Yaounde the air-conditioned offices of government were occupied by 'Black Frenchmen' who shared the bottles of Vichy water on their desks with their French advisers and spoke literally and metaphorically the same language, there were a lot more West Cameroonians in the bars of downtown Victoria who knew how many beans made five—or, as the saying still goes—'How many beans make *cinque*.'

Though the end of the de Gaulle era weakened French influence in the capital, there is still a division between the two parts of the country and the newspapers of West Cameroon are more guilty than the newspapers of Yaounde for perpetuating this. But it makes for lively journalism. Tatu Tatu Obeson writes a cheeky gossip column, and in February 1973 when President Ahidjo paid a state visit to Victoria, Obeson publicly tackled him about the future of English. Ahidjo's aides were appalled. The President is said to have 'tried to laugh, but not quite succeeded'. The President answered that there were two official languages, French and English. But the hard-line Anglophones of West Cameroon remember that he replied in French.

There is official censorship of the press, but it works in rather a hit and miss way and is, on the whole, benevolently applied. Tatu Tatu Obeson is obliged to print five copies of his newspapers and deliver them to the Victoria censor two hours before publication. If the censor does not like something, then it is changed, or—as seems to happen most of the time—the offending item is blacked out.

Occasionally Obeson is directed by the Victoria censor to report to the authorities in Yaounde, but as often as not when he gets there he finds the offending article has not even been noticed, or if it has, not upset anyone. Obeson is an example of a dozen or so newspapermen—no more—scattered throughout tropical Africa, who by maintaining some degree of freedom have set a pattern which the authorities have now come to accept. It requires both professionalism and courage to achieve this, and it cannot even be attempted in many states. But whether anything resembling freedom of the press survives in Africa will largely depend on this handful of editors.

Sometimes this independence rubs off on other publications. In the Cameroon the Yaounde papers will often ask *Outlook* for a translation of something mildly audacious it has printed, which is often just as easily available in the first instance to the papers in the capital.

A Yaounde newspaperman was quite frank about it. 'We use *Outlook* as a sort of temperature gauge', he said. 'If nothing happens when it oversteps the line, then we will follow.'

A case in point occurred when *Outlook* carried a report about a senior government minister who had been taken to court in a civil action in Victoria and ordered to pay a substantial sum in damages.

The attitude of the Yaounde papers to *Outlook* was 'How can you publish something like that?' And when Obeson raised a superior Anglophone eyebrow and answered 'Because it happened and it is news' the reply came back: 'Can you let us have a translation?'

The very delicacy of the Francophone/Anglophone relationship in the Cameroon nourishes this sort of thing. The French-speaking establishment in the capital does not want to be seen wielding the big stick over the English sector in Victoria.

6 East Africa

They used to call West Africa's humid coastal colonies The White Man's Grave, and there was some truth in the description. But across the other side of the Continent, East Africa was the White Man's seventh heaven.

If it was the mosquito that kept Europeans out of West Africa as settlers, it was the cool clear air of Africa's east and central plateau that attracted them as a place to put down roots.

The development of the press there was very different to that of West Africa. For though there were certainly papers started by Africans, they were never in the same class as those produced by the nationalists of the West Coast. It is probably true to say that one of the principal reasons Britain's major West African colonies achieved independence before their East and Central African lay in the lack of a virile nationalist African press.

Indeed, in the case of Kenya, the most important of Britain's East and Central African colonies, the fact that independence came relatively late in the day was due in part to the resistance to African nationalism by the White-owned press, representing not the Whitehall attitude but the settlers' viewpoint: 'What we have we hold.' Up until the morning of independence on 13 December, 1963, Kenya's biggest daily newspaper, the *East African Standard*, carried on its masthead the British coat-of-arms.

Though both Jomo Kenyatta and Julius Nyerere of Tanzania

71

had dabbled in journalism in their early days it was not on the scale of Azikiwe and Nkrumah in Nigeria and Ghana.

Thus the story of the Press in East and Central Africa is essentially part of the story of White settlement. This is even more true of the press in Portuguese Africa, both in Moçambique and Angola, and of Rhodesia and South Africa.

The beginnings of what was to become for a long time the most powerful press group in East Africa was the founding of the weekly *African Standard* in Mombasa in 1902. Although it had been started by an Asian, A. M. Jeevanjee, who had made a fortune supplying the builders of the railway from the coast inland, he soon sold out to two Englishmen. In 1910 the renamed *East African Standard* moved three hundred miles up country to Nairobi. It became a daily on 24 May—Empire Day—1910 and its only competition, the weekly *Leader of British East Africa*, which had been founded two years earlier limped on until 1923 before ceasing publication.

In 1930 the colonial government in Tanganyika invited the *Standard* to set up a newspaper in Dar-es-Salaam, and thus the *Tanganyika Standard* was born.

Britain's third East African colony, Uganda, was to wait until 1953 before the same group established the daily *Uganda Argus*. Up to then its only newspaper was a weekly, the *Uganda Herald*. The record of the Standard group of newspapers in East Africa is not an honourable one. It is to the enormous credit of the first generation of African nationalists who came to power in East Africa in the early nineteen-sixties that they did not close down the three leading dailies of Kenya, Uganda and Tanzania. Not only were they to survive, but for a remarkably long time after independence they continued to wield great influence—in the case of Kenya very great influence. This was due to the shrewdness of Kenneth Bolton, the British editor, whose dexterity developed the *East African Standard* in Nairobi from being the mouthpiece of the White settlers of the territory to being the newspaper of the new Black establishment. The principal reason he was able to bestride these two vastly different and opposing philosophies is generally believed to be his close friendship with Kenya's Attorney-General, Charles Njonjo, easily the most British orientated African of all Britain's former African empire.

The late Tom Mboya, who before he was to die from an assassin's bullet in 1969 was among the two or three likely successors to President Kenyatta, described the colonial history of the Kenyan press as 'a pretty tawdry advertisement for so-called British fair play'.

If the *East African Standard* was smug to the point of arrogance in its near total disregard of the African, it was almost liberal compared to the *Kenya Comment*, a weekly that as Rosalynde Ainslie says 'for sheer bigotry deserves to be recorded as what White-owned newspapers were capable of inflicting on their readers'.

The *Kenya Comment* was the mouthpiece of the extreme right-wing settler clique led by Sir Ferdinand Cavendish-Bentinck, who resigned as Speaker of the Colonial Legislative Council in 1960 as a protest at the undertaking by the British Government of eventual independence for Kenya. When Kenya's Minister of Finance, Mr Ernest Vasey, declared in 1958 while visiting Britain that an African majority in the government was inevitable, the editorial in the *Comment* villified him as being 'bent on pushing a cause which will end us up in the arms of Russia'.

Another publication, not nearly so extreme because it barely took any notice of Africans, was the *Kenya Weekly News* which survived for a good many years after independence though in a very different form from what it had been in colonial times.

The non-European press of East Africa owes more to Asians than Africans, and while it is true that the great majority of Asians in East Africa were supporters of the colonial *status quo*, happy to be used by the British as traders, and the middle men between the White elite and the Africans, there was also a significant number of Asians who aligned themselves with African nationalists. The African nationalists of the day were happy to use them, and one of the most despicable chapters of independent Africa is seen in the way these Asians were discarded by the very men they helped to bring to power.

Three of the major Asian-owned publications were the *Kenya Daily Mail* of Mombasa and the *National Guardian* and the *Daily Chronicle* in Nairobi. There was also a clutch of Asian-owned weeklies. The *Chronicle* was edited until the declaration of the state of emergency over Mau-Mau in 1952 by Pio Pinto.

Pinto had nailed his colours to the Black Independence mast very early on and the British were determined to get him. He went into detention with all the African nationalist leaders when the emergency was declared. He was to die of an assassin's bullet in

February 1965, the victim of the vicious politicking that began almost with the birth of independence in Kenya in December 1963.

The mushrooming of the African press was an important factor in fostering political action in the urban centres of Kenya after the Second World War. Publications appeared in several of the tribal languages and also in English. Most of these were printed in Nairobi, though Mombasa had the *Coast African Express* and on the shores of Lake Victoria, in Kisumu, there was the *Nyanza Times*.

All were nationalist and highly militant, expressing bitterness at colonial discrimination and the poverty and insecurity of the African tribes against the affluence of the settlers.

The Kikuyu papers around Nairobi were the most successful and the most influential was *Mumenyereri* ('He who looks after'). This was a weekly edited by the Kenya Africa Union's assistant general secretary, Henry Muoria, and with a sale of 10,000 was probably read by six times that number.

As the tension grew which was to ignite finally in the Mau-Mau uprising, it became more and more uncompromising in its nationalism. The colonial government had banned political meetings but *Mumenyereri* was regularly referring to 'tea parties' in the shanty towns around Nairobi, which were, in fact, occasions for the secret and blood-thirsty oathing ceremonies.

Jomo Kenyatta had dabbled in journalism in the middle twenties and edited *Muigwithania*, but it was much more of a straight political sheet than anything produced by the nationalists of that era across the Continent in West Africa. Forty or fifty mainly African language publications appeared and disappeared in Kenya during the twenties, thirties, forties and fifties. When the Mau-Mau emergency was declared in 1952, all African publications in the vernacular were instructed to publish in Swahili to make the censor's job in Nairobi easier.

As nearly half of these publications were catering for people who could not read a word of Swahili this was a particularly inane demand, though probably intended as a not very subtle way of suppressing them without actually closing them down. Few survived the emergency.

Tanganyika had always been ruled by the British with a much looser rein than Kenya. Originally a German colony, it had been given to Britain to run by the League of Nations and then, when the United Nations was formed, became a Trust Territory. Unlike Kenya it had virtually no settlers, and thus what repression there was came from the much more benevolent hand of Whitehall's colonial civil servants. There were one or two mission publications in the twenties, but the first important African press was the duplicated *Sauti ja Tanu*, in a mixture of English and Swahili propagating the Tanganyika African National Union. Julius Nyerere, the Tanu party leader, always wanted a daily paper. However, apart from a brief period when the *National Times* appeared under his editorship, he was to wait until long after independence before he could take over the White Tanganyika *Standard*. The eighteen months that followed that takeover provide one of the most bizarre stories of Africa's changing press.

The fact that by common consent there is more freedom of the press in Kenya today than in any other state in Black Africa is because the Aga Khan established newspapers in East Africa as the curtain was going up on independence.

The man selected by the then young Aga Khan to spearhead his newspaper operation was Michael Curtis, former editor of London's *News Chronicle*, who was still not forty when he went to Africa. The Aga Khan had, and still has, a large community of Ismailis in East Africa, but from the start he told Curtis that he did not want newspapers which merely represented the Ismaili interest.

In the same way as Cecil King in West Africa, Curtis believed it was easier to take over an existing newspaper than to start from scratch with an entirely new venture. He selected a modest Swahili weekly called *Taifa Kenya* which had been started by one of those rare things in East Africa, a liberal European, Charles Hayes. Roy Thomson's group became marginally connected with the Aga Khan's papers, and it is likely that James Coltart felt that there were some rich pickings in East Africa. Coltart became a director of the Aga Khan's group, but the only investment Roy Thomson had in it was in the form of a debenture. Certainly the Thomson organisation never exercised any real influence.

The English language *Daily Nation* and its *Sunday Nation* began in Nairobi in 1960, and the little paper Curtis had acquired as his launching-pad, *Taifa Kenya*, became the Swahili daily *Taifa Leo*. They survive today as vigorous, thoroughly professional publications which have produced a generation of African newspapermen who though they know well the line beyond which they must not tread are proud and jealous of the freedom they have achieved and get very angry when any politician starts pushing them around. They wait now, as does the whole of Kenya, to see what fate has in store for them in the post-Kenyatta era.

From the very beginning, Michael Curtis embarked on a programme to turn the whole organisation into an African venture. This was more difficult than what Cecil King had found in West Africa where there was a long tradition of African newspapermen. The number of Black journalists in East Africa worth the name when the Aga Khan group set up could be counted on the fingers of one hand. For a long time White journalists had to be recruited from Britain for the key posts of the *Daily Nation*, but Curtis was always pushing for promising Africans to be promoted, even at a pace likely to entail a lowering of professional standards. Only the considerable financial reserves of the Aga Khan could have kept what became known as the *Nation* Group afloat as it battled to make inroads into the *East African Standard*, which long after independence even was still *the* newspaper.

But slowly the message of the *Nation* got through. Its tabloid presentation was much more attractive than the staid broadsheet format of the *Standard*, and though it had many professional weaknesses as Curtis pushed Africans into positions they were barely qualified to hold, it began to assume a character much more in sympathy and keeping with the new young state of Kenya as it moved from being the most exclusive White conclave in the tropics to a Black nation.

When Michael Curtis addressed the annual assembly of the International Press Institute two years before Kenya became independent, he told them that he was under no illusion that the toughest pressures on the press would come when Kenya and the rest of East Africa were free of colonial rule and when the relatively inexperienced politicians would expect the newspapers to support them in all circumstances.

This was exactly what happened after independence, but because of the skill and often the courage of the three Africans who, in turn, edited the *Daily Nation*, those political pressures, though intense at times, have been resisted in a way unknown in any other part of Black Africa.

The *Nation* group's first African editor-in-chief was Hilary Ng'weno, a graduate of Harvard. He had a very fierce baptism of fire in the editorial chair as his appointment coincided with the Congo rising, the murder of Patrice Lumumba and the landing of Belgian paratroopers. The Western press was almost exclusively preoccupied with the fate of Belgian and American missionaries in the Congo, but Ng'weno saw to it that readers of the *Nation* also heard the other side of the story; the thousands of Africans who died in the civil war or at the hands of the European mercenaries.

Curtis commissioned surveys to find out just what Africans wanted to read and, surprisingly perhaps, they revealed that they wanted to know more about the world outside their own country, particularly the other states of Africa.

The *Nation*'s second editor-in-chief was Boaz Omori, who from uncertain beginnings, grew into the job and gave the *Nation* its real African flavour. The third man to become editor-in-chief of the *Nation* Group, and certainly the most controversial newspaperman in Black Africa, was George Githii. Githii, a colourful blend of philosopher, academic and newspaperman, was above all a free-thinker.

He began as a reporter on the *Nation*, but was particularly close to Jomo Kenyatta, having been his private secretary and then personal assistant. When Boaz Omori was persuaded by the Government to move to the *Voice of Kenya* broadcasting station as its editor-in-chief, George Githii took his place on the *Nation*. But the academic in George Githii was strong and he went to Oxford for four years. A frustrated Boaz Omori, who had found life virtually impossible as the servant of the political bureaucracy controlling the *Voice of Kenya*, returned to the *Nation*.

George Githii thought he had left journalism for good, and probably because of this he spoke with remarkable freedom at a conference in Sweden in 1962 organised by the Scandinavian Institute of African Studies.

Although he paid tribute to the way the Aga Khan had run his newspaper chain, Githii coined the phrase 'the survival criterion' for African journalists which, he said, often imposed rigid and almost immutable limitations on an African editor's freedom; the choice between publishing the truth on the one hand and surviving on the other.

White journalists who worked for Githii during that period, now long back in Britain, give instance after instance of the stand he took against the White management of the paper in Nairobi who were not unnaturally concerned with the survival of the group. It was this management that once demanded of Githii the withdrawal of an editorial critical of General de Gaulle because the Aga Khan lived in Paris. In another case, when the *Nation* commented on Moise Tshombe's flight from the Congo to Ibiza, Githii clashed with the management because Tshombe was supposed to have embarked on the flight in Sardinia where the Aga Khan had extensive business interests. The probability is that these White managers were being over-cautious, but for the most part George Githii was able to assert himself as he so felt.

But, he says, he has always found President Kenyatta 'very, very tolerant'. On one occasion he published an editorial attacking preventive detention which greatly angered a number of influential members of the Cabinet. He believes that one of his White reporters was deported in retaliation. But he continued to attack the detention orders. Eventually he felt it was time to see Kenyatta about the impasse. Kenyatta told him: 'Those were your views. Now remember to print *ours*.' Githii lost his campaign against preventive detention, not because of any action by the government but because of lack of public support.

Gradually the *Nation* won acceptance as a Kenyan newspaper even though it was owned by a foreigner. After ten years of losses, it broke even and then began making money. The company had branched out into commercial printing and packaging, and in 1976 it was paying a 20 per cent dividend to shareholders.

There are still Europeans in the newsroom of the *Nation*, but they are the last generation of Whites. The reporting staff has long since been exclusively African, with one or two Asians who are Kenyan nationals. The greatest problem in its Africanisation drive has been on the sub-editor's desk.

All over Black Africa, the greatest editorial weakness of the press has been among sub-editors. Late nights, no by-lines, no glamour, has created a resistance to sub-editing by African reporters, although it is significant that those who have been lured to the sub's desk have gained quicker promotion than from the reporter's room. The libel bills settled because of sloppy sub-editing on Africa's newspapers is astronomical, and the *Nation* itself is very near the top of the list in lost libels. It had to provide a special item in the budget for them. But slowly the sub's desk is being Africanised, though the last White post in the newsroom will clearly be that of chief-sub-editor.

As the *Nation*'s star rose, so did the *Standard*'s sink. There is often a certain bitchiness about the sniping of the *Standard* at what it calls the Paris-controlled *Nation*. Certainly Michael Curtis, now in Paris, freely admitted to palpitations when George Githii not only flexed his editorial muscles, but often exercised them in a most vigorous way. On several occasions Michael Curtis has left for Nairobi by jet in a fury from Paris to pick up what he thought would be the pieces of the *Nation* after some particularly violent piece of editorialising by Githii.

As one Kenyan cabinet minister put it in late 1976, talking about George Githii: 'He sails so close to the wind that most of the time all you can see is the bloody keel.'

A lot of stormy water was taken aboard on 4 September 1974, and there were many in Kenya who thought that George Githii might well have fallen overboard, or even the *Nation* itself, sunk.

During Kenya's general election campaign, an article appeared entitled 'Language of Elections: Trash, Politics and Nonsense'. It was signed by George Githii as editor-in-chief. This was a hard-hitting attack on Njoroge Mungai, the Minister for Foreign Affairs and one of the half dozen most important men in the country. Mungai was one of four candidates fighting a parliamentary seat on the borders of Nairobi. Githii supported Dr Johnstone Muthiora, who, in fact, won the seat. Githii's article created a major political row and was interpreted as being intended to denigrate Mungai's performance as a Minister.

Michael Curtis took the night' plane from Paris to Nairobi, had a personal interview with Mungai, other cabinet ministers, the *Nation* board of directors and George Githii himself.

On 27 September the *Nation* appeared with an editorial entitled 'A Balance of Views'. This read very much like a considerable climb-down. It said that the earlier article 'was not intended to denigrate Dr Mungai's performance as Kenya's Foreign Minister, and if that is how it has been interpreted it is a cause for regret and a reason to put the record straight'.

The competing *Standard* seized upon all this, and the next morning came out with a story headlined: 'Aga Khan disassociates Nation Group from commentary.' The *Standard* story began: 'The head office of the Nation Group of newspapers in Paris has taken an extraordinary step of publicly refuting a commentary by the editor-in-chief of the Group, Mr George Githii.'

Michael Curtis was furious at this suggestion that the *Nation* was controlled from Paris and published a statement in the *Nation*, in turn refuting the *Standard*.

In itself this whole incident may not appear to an outsider to be very important. Newspapers and politicians, even influential ones, are always falling out. But it is rare for a newspaper in tropical Africa to be able to so much as voice a whisper against one of the major establishment figures of the state.

Again, the whole incident reflects to the credit of everyone in Kenya; George Githii said what he felt he must say—and he must have known the danger he was courting. The fact that he survived is testimony to the amount of press freedom in Kenya.

Another Kenyan Cabinet Minister, Julius Kiano, was moved as Minister of Commerce after a *Nation* campaign on inefficiency and negligence within his Ministry.

By his singlemindedness—his critics call it bloodymindedness— Githii won for himself his very dangerous position as the most powerful man in Kenya outside the inner political circle. He clearly had friends in high places, but equally clearly he had enemies. Everything the *Nation* did was put under scrutiny as no other newspaper in Black Africa has been since the leading organs in Nigeria were taken over by the military government.

Just after dawn on 11 October 1976, a police car went to Githii's home in the suburbs of Nairobi. An inspector told Githii that the Commissioner of Police, Bernard Hinga, wanted to see him. Githii asked whether he was under arrest. When told that he was not, Githii refused to leave. Ninety minutes later the police car returned. This time the inspector was firmer. Githii demanded to know whether he was under arrest. Only when told that he was did he agree to go to see the Police Commissioner— but he drove there in his own car. According to the *Weekly Review*, the news magazine owned and edited by the Nation Group's first editor-in-chief, Hilary Ng'weno, Hinga warned Githii to stop serialising the book 'Operation Thunder', the story of the Israeli commando raid on Entebbe Airport.

The *Weekly Review* said: 'It was Hinga's view that the *Sunday*

Nation should not publish any further instalments. "Don't play about as we can ban the *Nation*," Hinga reportedly told Githii before letting him go.'

That would have been enough for almost every editor in Black Africa. But, said the *Weekly Review*, the same morning as the incident, Githii instructed his lawyers to seek compensation from the Government or to sue them for wrongful confinement.

In October 1973 the *Nation* Group, which with its associated companies in the printing and packaging field employed over 800 people, became a public company. The Aga Khan made available 1.2 million shares, and this offer was more than twice over-subscribed among some 3,200 different individuals and institutions. The Aga Khan's holding is now some 60 per cent. He is on record as saying that he wishes to make the group a locally controlled company as soon as possible, and will undoubtedly do so as soon as a reasonable offer comes along which does not compromise the Group's independence.

There was an attempt in 1973 to launch Kenya's first evening paper. This was the *Evening News*, owned by Narain Singh who had been the last editor of the *Sunday Post* before it closed after years of trying to compete with the much more professional *Sunday Nation*. The *Evening News* was printed by the *Standard* but purely as a commercial proposition. During the election campaign of 1974, the *Evening News* suddenly ceased publication and there has never been a satisfactory explanation as to just why. But it may be significant that the closure came shortly after the *News* had published a story supporting the same man who was opposing Mungai (as the *Nation* had).

Another attempt to create a press outside of Kenya's big two groups occurred when a number of local journalists, among them several who had been sacked by George Githii from the *Nation*, launched the *Weekly Star*. But it was under-capitalised, and finally folded leaving a 50,000 shillings print bill unpaid.

Crystal ball gazing in any African country is a very negative pastime. Black faces seem to blur much more than White. New men tend to appear very suddenly. But one guess for the future of Kenya is that the *Nation* Group will become part of the Lonrho empire. Lonrho's chief in Kenya is Udi Gecaga. A long-time member of the *Nation* Group's board is Udi Gecaga's father, Mareka Gecaga.

A fairly safe prophecy about the press in Kenya is that its

future is likely to be very largely determined by what happens when the dust has settled at the end of the Kenyatta era. An organisation called GEMA, which is an association originally formed to provide welfare services for three of Kenya's most important tribes, the Kikuyu, the Embu and the Meru (Kikuyu is sometimes spelt with a G) may come into the press picture. Through GEMA's business company, Gema Holdings Ltd, an approach has already been made to the *Standard*. This came to nothing, it is believed, because of the failure to agree over the price of the cuttings library of the *Standard* which forms East Africa's best contemporary record, going back to the turn of the century.

Lonrho did not want to separate the newspaper from the cuttings library. The *Standard* operation was not an *à la carte* operation: GEMA was told they must take the whole menu or nothing.

But prominent politicians within GEMA are still clearly attracted to the idea of getting hold of a newspaper.

This is partly for the political influence they would then have at their finger-tips but probably just as much for the financial gain they think would accrue. In such a highly capitalistic state as Kenya, there has always been the belief that in spite of the evidence   of   the   balance-sheet   newspapers   must   be money-spinners.

The leaders of Kenya's other tribes, particularly the powerful Luo and the Kamba, are far from happy at GEMA's newspaper overtures. For them, it is very much a case of better the white devil they know, which can always be lambasted whenever the mood prevails, than one more powerful weapon in the hands of Kenya's 'Royal Family', the Kikuyu.

While the *Nation*, from its very beginning, was making a brave attempt to Africanise, the old establishment of the *East African Standard* under Kenneth Bolton continued along its great White way. Though it had been obliged to take a dramatic new turn in editorial policy now that an African government was in power, under Bolton it was still in a very real sense a White paper, owned by Whites, largely staffed by them and dedicated to the White way of life.

The early years after independence in Kenya were a curious period, with an atmosphere unlike any other of Britain's African territories. Those Europeans who remained—and many of them did— were naturally enough apprehensive at what life under Jomo Kenyatta, who the British authorities had described at the outbreak of the emergency as 'a leader to darkness and death', would be like.

For a long time, and then only gradually, the African position at all levels other than the new political establishment, remained virtually the same as it had done throughout the whole of the colonial period.

In every other respect, except in politics, the White man was still the 'Bwana'. It was to be a decade, even a generation, before this was to fade away finally and even in the second half of the seventies, there was still plenty of evidence of the old servant and master relationship between Blacks and Whites in Kenya.

The position of the White journalists in Kenya after independence was still entrenched, but they became among the first group to feel the new pressures from the Black establishment. For the rest of the White business establishment, an African government merely meant an adjustment in terms of openings for Africans in positions barred to them during colonialism. There was a lot of window-dressing as Africans were pushed into positions for which they often had few qualifications and less training. The phrase was born: 'Every Black man has his White man.'

It was a much more vulnerable situation for White newspapermen. Kenneth Bolton, through his close relationship with Charles Ngonjo, Kenya's ultra-British style Attorney-General who was closer to Kenyatta than any other member of the Cabinet, walked with supreme confidence along this highwire and to that extent must be given credit for not falling.

But what happened to two successive assistant editors illustrates the position of the White newspaper executive in 'settler' Africa.

After Tom Mboya's assassination in July 1969, tribal rivalries were sharpened and ugly memories of Mau-Mau returned as oath-taking campaigns developed among the Kikuyu tribe, the Royal Family' of Kenya's tribes, led, of course, by Kenyatta himself. The aim of the oath-taking was to bind the solidarity of the Kikuyu tribe but it caused great alarm, not only among Europeans and Africans of other tribes, but also among some Kikuyus.

Eric Marsden, a thoroughly professional British newspaperman who had led something of a frustrated life as assistant editor under Bolton, was in charge of the *East African Standard* during Bolton's absence on overseas leave when the oath-taking ceremonies came to a head. At first he played the stories very quietly and never on the front page. They could hardly be ignored, for prominent personalities were daily making statements about them. Things came to a head after an African lay priest had been chopped to death in a manner identical to the killings which had occurred during Mau-Mau for refusing to take the Kikuyu oath. It was impossible to keep this story off the front page, though it is doubtful whether what subsequently happened would have been different had the story been used elsewhere in the newspaper.

On 26 September 1969 the *Standard* carried a front page story of an assistant minister who at a press conference had come out very strongly against the oathing ceremonies and the damage they were doing. Marsden himself went through the story with great care three times, removing the names of prominent personalities and places identified with some of the highest in the land. He also removed all the more chilling descriptions of the oath-taking ceremonies. That night he and two other White journalists, one from the *Standard* and one from the *Nation*, were picked up by the police at 9 o'clock, given an hour to pack and driven to the airport to catch the London plane at 11 pm.

In fact, after strong representations by the British government and almost certainly because of Kenneth Bolton's influence, Marsden was allowed to return three weeks later. But he knew that his days were now numbered in Kenya, and after a series of nerve-racking experiences ranging from threatening phone calls in the middle of the night to a corpse being thrown into his front garden, he decided it was time to take his wife and children out of the country.

Frank Young, a seasoned British journalist who had worked in South Africa, Rhodesia and then Zambia became deputy editor to Bolton.

He had sought the job in Kenya after organising and running the Zambia News Agency with considerable success at the invitation of the government. He had preached the 'Get the news moving' message to his African staff in Zambia so effectively that while he was sitting in the press gallery in Parliament one day in 1970, he was handed a message from his own agency's teleprinter announcing his replacement by an African.

When Young flew up to Nairobi to decide whether he should take the job as the *Standard's* deputy editor, he had an immediate taste of the prevalent attitude of mind of many Whites in Kenya at that time. He was sitting in his hotel when one of the *Standard's* White journalists came to see him and began to talk about the 'thick' Africans on the paper. Young was astounded. This was exactly the sort of language that had made him move from South Africa to Rhodesia and from Rhodesia into Black Independent Africa. Kenya at this time had been independent for seven years. Nevertheless, he decided to stay in Nairobi. He was designated chief training officer, the only way work permits could be obtained for White journalists. In fact he set about Africanising the reporting staff, and within six months had completed the job. As the competing *Daily Nation* had found, it was relatively easy to produce an African reporter; something else to turn an African reporter into a sub-editor.

Young organised an in-service training scheme, and fourteen Africans were designated to attend. One refused outright, and most of the others did so with varying degrees of surliness. Whenever there is a chance to get additional education outside of Africa, there is always a queue of applicants, whether it be to Moscow in the winter or Britain in the summer. But in-service training has never been popular among African journalists. It is probably because they resent being shown 'how to do it' in their own environment—literally at their own desks. And often, it must be said, the White 'training officer' is of dubious quality. Young recalls the first night a new White sub-editor from Britain took his place at the sub's table on the *Standard*. On being handed a piece of news agency copy to sub-edit, he turned despairingly to the African alongside him and asked 'Can you help me with this?'

Kenneth Bolton had been in bad health for some time, though he was still working. He rang Young late one Sunday night in 1973 saying he would not be in the next morning as he was going into hospital for investigation. The next morning Bolton's wife phoned Young; Bolton had died in the night. It was a traumatic moment, and the beginning of different days for the *Standard*.

Lonrho, a multi-national property company with innumerable

investments all over Africa, had bought control of the Standard group in May 1967 at a cost of more than £1 million. This included the money-making commercial printing and packaging interests run by the *Standard* as the financial prop of the newspaper, in a similar way to the *Nation*. A week after Bolton's death, the pressures began to mount. Young was lying down on a Saturday afternoon at home after an exhausting week when the phone began to ring. He left it unanswered, and it rang on and off for over an hour. When he finally picked it up, he was told he had to be in State House, Mombasa, three hundred miles away at the coast, by 7 o'clock next morning.

When White editors in Black Africa receive those sort of messages, they can produce a prickly feeling at the back of the neck. Young telephoned State House and delicately enquired what was happening. 'You will be here', was the only answer he got. He left at once, and was somewhat relieved when he found that George Githii from the *Nation* and Narain Singh, editor of the *Sunday Post*, had also been summoned to Mombasa.

The three men sat together in a room waiting for Kenyatta to call them in. When at last he did so he told them: 'I have Uganda's President Amin here, and I am very angry with him because he has banned your newspapers. And when I say your newspapers, I mean Kenyan newspapers, and although they are privately owned, they are still Kenyan newspapers and if they are Kenyan newspapers they are my newspapers.'

The grizzled old African nationalist paused, eyes glinting, and all the President's men nodded. 'So', he went on, 'that means that if he has banned my newspapers, he has banned me—and I don't like it'.

He then asked the three editors what they felt about the situation and why it had happened. It was rather a tall order, asking anyone why President Amin does anything. What the three editors did not know as they sat before Kenyatta in Mombasa was that Amin himself was in State House. The Ugandan President had arrived in Mombasa, not merely uninvited, but unwanted. He had flown there from Entebbe to supervise the unloading of a cargo of Russian arms which had arrived at the Kenyan port addressed to him. Amin himself wanted to see them safely ashore—ashore on the docks of a country he was always threatening to invade.

Kenyatta called Amin in, but Young recalls that the ensuing

discussion was not very rational. Amin said he had banned the Kenyan papers 'because they are always reporting bad things about us'. But he reinstated them all, though later he was to ban them again.

Young told Amin that he had given up reporting anything from Uganda other than official announcements from the Uganda Command Post, Amin's Army Headquarters, which issued them at the behest of the President himself. Young did not add that this provided the *Standard* with all the light entertainment any paper could wish for.

With Bolton gone, the editorial chair of the *Standard* became very much a hot seat. Vice-President Arap Moi began to make regular phone calls to Young complaining about things in the *Standard*. Young found that the servility which was needed in some African quarters was not the best line with the Vice-President, and so he replied to Moi with as much vigour as Moi used to him. Things often ended up virtually a shouting match between the two. This again is an illustration of how a professional newspaperman with courage and the facts on his side can often get away with much more than the editor who will kowtow.

Young believed that the Kenyan hierarchy felt that with the death of Bolton it had lost its grip on the *Standard*. At one time the Kenya Government had plans to start their own paper, and as the Prime Minister of Nigeria, Tafawa Balewa, had asked James Coltart of the Thomson Group for advice, so did the Kenyans ask Bolton for his views on the venture. Bolton had replied in exactly the same way as Coltart; that they must expect to spend a fortune and then lose another one. It is an ironic reflection upon those times in Kenya that the Government was prepared to accept this advice from a man who for years had edited a newspaper which not merely represented White settler interests but opposed African nationalism until it was obvious that the Black man was going to win.

Frank Young believes that the Kenyan Government's decision not to start their own paper was mainly due to their feeling that through Bolton they had the *Standard* anyway, and it would be not only a costly but unnecessary exercise to start one of their own.

But Young insists that though the *Standard* could be said to be the servant of the new African government, it was never this in an improper way. He believes that in a developing country—where there is often only one and rarely more than two newspapers—the press generally speaking has a duty to support the government.

Bolton was far from happy when Lonrho bought control of the *Standard* group. He was determined there would be no interference from anybody with editorial policy—anybody, that is, outside the higher echelons of the Kenyatta Cabinet. Lonrho was quite satisfied with this arrangement. For them newspapers were only a means to an end, the end being the much more profitable businesses of packaging, breweries, transport, mining and other ventures in different parts of the Continent.

But there was one occasion when the editorial direction of the paper was questioned by its new owners, the major upheaval of directors of the Lonrho parent company, in London which led the Prime Minister, Edward Heath to mint the 'unacceptable face of capitalism' phrase which was to become common coinage in Britain. The Lonrho affair and its political reverberations were a major story in Britain and carried by all the news agencies.

Frank Young was at home on the night Heath spoke in the British House of Commons. The local Lonrho chairman, Udi Gecaga, President Kenyatta's son-in-law, telephoned him and enquired: 'I take it that you are not going to use this story.' Young said he was certainly going to use it. He pointed out to his chairman that there was really no choice. Lonrho was a name well-known in Africa, and the *Standard* could not afford to omit the story. In any event, he pointed out, it was odds on that the rival *Nation* was going to carry the story. But, pressed by Gecaga, Young agreed to telephone Bolton who was on leave, though still in town. When Young explained the position to Bolton, the response was immediate: 'You're in the chair. You edit the paper'.

Young phoned Gecaga back and told him what he was going to do. Gecaga replied: 'I may be forced to use my prerogative.'

Young told him: 'As far as I know, Mr. Gecaga, you do not have any prerogative as far as editorial policy is concerned, but even if you have that is my decision and that is what we are going to do'.

The *Standard* ran the story in full. It was served to them by telex from their London office upon whom no pressure whatever had been brought by Lonrho headquarters.

It is doubtful whether an African editor could have resisted such pressure from his chairman, who was also the son-in-law of the President.

Bolton was back in his office the next morning. He asked Young what Gecaga had said, and when Young told him, Bolton picked up the phone and asked for an immediate call to Lonrho's London headquarters. He wanted to speak to 'Tiny' Rowlands, the remarkable and somewhat mysterious figure who had built Lonrho into the huge multi-national corporation it is today.

Rowlands was not in the office, but Bolton spoke to Gerald Percy, then his number two. He told Percy: 'I will not have any interference with editorial content'.

Percy replied: 'You are quite right. We do not interfere with editorial policies. You were right to do as you did and if you wish I will telephone Gecaga and tell him so.' A tight-lipped Bolton replied: 'You can if you wish but I am going to tell him so now.'

Bolton had served in the Tank Corps during the war, and as Frank Young put it: 'He had never really got out of his tank from Alamein onwards.'

Young tried hard to gather the reins that Bolton had so skilfully manipulated through White settler colonial rule to Black nationalism, but his approaches were not well received by Kenya's new African establishment.

Charles Njonjo, the Attorney-General, too, would begin to telephone the *Standard*, though *sotto-voce*, which was far more unnerving than the raised tones of the Vice-President.

Njonjo always prefaced his complaints the same way: 'The President is very angry . . .', he would begin.

Young knew full well that half the time Kenyatta was not angry at all but totally unaware of the offending story. But he could never say 'The President should not be angry'. It was the fable of the King's clothes come to life.

Lower down the Kenya hierarchy the complaints to the *Standard* were often nerve-tingling. A permanent secretary from one of the Ministries would ring and say 'You haven't got a picture of the President on the front page today'. Or if there was a picture of Kenyatta inside, someone would want to know why it was not on the front page.

The general election of 1974 presented many problems for the Kenya Press. Both the *Nation* and the *Standard* felt obliged to report the speeches of all candidates as fairly as possible. Young, and probably Githii too, were asked by the Government why they were reporting 'the unfavourable people'.

After the election, there was a delay of several months in announcing the Cabinet while a lot of tribal in-fighting went on.

The whole country awaited news of the Cabinent with an interest much greater than is ever found in the West. Young's African reporters had been digging hard to find out who was likely to get what in the new order. It is a credit to the way Young had Africanised the newsroom, and also to the increasing professionalism of Kenya's African journalists, that although coming from a number of different tribes the *Standard's* reporters never displayed tribalism among themselves.

The word came finally that the new Cabinet was to be announced. Young planned a special issue, and with very little time at his disposal, put together the pictures and the names of all the new cabinet ministers.

This special duly appeared and sold out. But twenty-two Cabinet names had been announced and the *Standard* came out with twenty-three pictures of new Cabinet ministers. It was a classic case of a mistake made under pressure. But the uproar was immediate and immense. Members of the Cabinet believed this was some White Lonrho plot to get a new man into the Cabinet.

This error clearly called for something more than a telephone call from either the enraged Vice-President or the urbane Attorney-General. The call when it came—and it came quickly— was anonymous and peremptory: 'You will report to the Commissioner of Police at once.' Young was on drinking terms with the Commissioner of Police, and when he explained that it was a genuine mistake made in the fervour of getting the special edition out, the Commissioner said he believed him but whether anybody else would he couldn't say.

No newspaper has ever sold so well in Kenya as that special edition. It is now a collector's item of African memorabilia.

The Police Commissioner advised Young to go to the Minister of State, Mbiyu Koinange, and explain what had happened. Eventually the matter was resolved, not merely with an apology but an apology to the President for daring to appear to usurp his function in appointing cabinet ministers.

As the level of civil servants' telephone complaints got more and more junior, Young's temper and nerves became more ragged. One day an assistant information officer in one of the ministries rang up with a complaint. Young exploded. 'I'm not having any bloody civil servant dictating to me how to run my paper', he roared, 'and you can tell your minister so'. As the information officer put the phone down, he said 'You will be hearing from the Special Branch'. As Special Branches go in Africa, Kenya's is not particularly frightening, but it is none the less not to be taken lightly.

The pressures mounted. Early in 1975 the *Standard's* chief reporter was picked up by the police following a headline about a story which, by some stretch of the imagination, could be interpreted as denigratory to a decision about educational policy. When the reporter told the police that reporters did not write headlines on stories, they returned to the newsroom and picked up the chief sub-editor.

George Githii's number two man on the *Nation*, Joe Roderiques, a Kenyan Asian, was also picked up once and detained for thirty hours for printing a story that the President was to make a special announcement. He had taken this from the official Government Gazette.

The greatest newspaper drama of postwar Kenya occurred in March 1975 when a prominent Member of Parliament, James Kariuki, disappeared. Kariuki, a Kikuyu and a former junior minister, had become something of a champion of the under-dog. It is probable that he felt this was a way to power. His disappearance was a sensation. Rumours abounded, and the firmest of these, which proved true, was that he had last been seen leaving Nairobi's Hilton Hotel in the company of a security policeman.

Although the Kikuyu tribe was still very much the Royal Family of Kenya after a dozen years of independence, the tribe was splitting into various factions, rather like the old Florentine families of medieval Italy, and for precisely the same reason— money and power. It seemed increasingly likely, and still does today, that Kariuki was murdered as part of this Kikuyu in-fighting.

Then the *Nation* broke the news. Kariuki was alive and in Zambia. Under a by-line shared by George Githii and one of his senior journalists, Michael Kabuga, there appeared a detailed account of Kariuki in Zambia, saying he was now on his way back to Kenya. It was a considerable scoop—except that it was fiction from first to last. For on the very morning that it appeared, the *Standard* broke the news of Kariuki's murder. Their chief reporter, Fred Nyagah, had been digging deep for days and was finally present at the Nairobi mortuary when Kariuki's relatives came to identify the body. It was a sensational story, and more than anything else since Kenya had become independent it threatened the survival of Kenyatta's Government.

For the *Nation* it was a disaster. The immediate interpretation by the entire country was that the *Nation* story that Kariuki was in Zambia had been deliberately planted by Kariuki's murderers to allay fears of his death. Every journalist on the *Nation* felt humiliated. Indeed—and this says a great deal for the degree of professionalism of African journalists in Kenya as a whole—this feeling of shame was shared by journalists on the rival and triumphant *Standard*. As George Odiko, general secretary of the Kenya Union of Journalists, and a *Nation* reporter, said: 'There was a feeling among all journalists that the *Nation* story had destroyed our credibility. We felt we had been used.'

Odiko went to both George Githii and Michael Kabuga, seeking an explanation. Kabuga said that as he and Githii had come into the newsroom fairly late on the night in question, the telephone had rung, Githii had answered it. Kabuga had moved away to another part of the newsroom but when he returned Githii, still on the phone, began handing him a hastily written outline of the Kariuki in Zambia story. Kabuga typed it out, and Githii replaced the lead story on the front page of the *Nation* so that the Kariuki 'scoop' could be accommodated.

When Odiko tackled Githii in the name of the Union, the editor-in-chief said that he had written the story in good faith, but that he could not reveal the name of the contact who had given him the false information.

This was the first occasion that on a major story—the most sensational story of postwar Kenya—the *Nation*, which had pioneered Africanisation of the press in Kenya, had ever been beaten by the old colonial *Standard*. It cost the *Nation* dearly in circulation. The *Standard's* circulation figure soared, and it was to be a long time before the *Nation* was able to climb back to its pre-eminent position. There was never a satisfactory explanation, either of the murder of James Kariuki, or of how George Githii came to write the story that he was still alive.

But achievement though the revelation of the death of Kariuki had been for the *Standard*, Frank Young felt that his days were numbered. He used an English cricketing metaphor to sum up its feelings: 'The wicket, which had always been sticky, was now crumbling almost to dust.'

And so, a British newspaperman who had left South Africa disenchanted with apartheid, who moved on from Rhodesia when the pretext of racial partnership proved utterly hollow, had reached his final disillusionment in free, Black Africa.

He left for Britain.

The end of George Githii's editorship of the *Nation* Group was very much in keeping with the traumatic, even emotional and always courageous way he had occupied his position since returning from Oxford for his second term at Nation House.

The first occasion Kenyans knew about Githii's removal was from the newscast on the *Voice of Kenya* radio on the evening of Friday, 29 April 1977. Announcing Githii's resignation, the radio said that he had objected to interference in the editorial running of the newspaper. The next morning's *Nation* carried not a word. The *Standard* had a brief front page announcement quoting the newscast. The whole political establishment and virtually everyone in the country who was literate enough to know what had happened was intrigued. The full story quickly unfolded. Six weeks earlier, the Tanzanian Government had warned leaders of the Bohra Muslim Community to 'stop imposing their will' upon members of their Community in such a manner as to threaten law and order. The Government alleged that the Bohra leaders were harrassing dissidents of their sect by forcing them out of business and preventing them working in certain professions.

The *Nation* had done an investigation of the situation among the Bohra Muslims in Kenya, and as a result George Githii had written a characteristically strong but, on the face of it, not unfair leader calling for an investigation.

It is doubtful whether Githii, when he wrote the editorial, knew that the Bohra and Ismaili Communities both belonged to the same sect as Islam. The Aga Khan is the head of the Ismailis. But whether Githii knew this or not, it is unlikely that it would have made any difference. There was consternation in the Aga Khan's Paris headquarters, and an editorial was despatched to the *Nation* with the request that it be published. The Paris editorial, almost certainly written by Michael Curtis, was moderate in tone, well argued and designed to calm matters.

In the event it had just the opposite effect. In George Githii's eyes it challenged not merely the *Nation's* views on the Bohras but also his position as editor-in-chief. He refused to publish the editorial, and the local board of the *Nation* backed him. The Aga Khan was told from Nairobi that though the majority of its shares were held by a religious leader, the *Nation* papers themselves were secular and that the dual role of the Aga Khan as spiritual head and big businessman made things difficult for the *Nation* in the delicate political and social environment of Kenya.

Before Paris could respond, George Githii resigned.

He wanted his letter of resignation to the local chairman to be carried in the *Nation*. When it did not appear, he went to the newsroom of the *Voice of Kenya* and gave the story to them.

Githii's letter of resignation to the chairman was couched in bitter terms. 'You will recollect', he wrote 'that I maintained as a matter of principle that the encroachment by the chief shareholder upon sacred editorial space in order to express sectional and communal interests amounts to direct interference with editorial integrity and press freedom. This interference has become the rule rather than the exception'.

Githii then went on to speak of the sores between himself and the Aga Khan. Among them, he claimed, was an editorial which was withdrawn because it had referred to General de Gaulle 'and the Aga Khan lives in Paris'. Githii's letter accused the Aga Khan's office of trying to persuade the *Nation* to take a pro-Arab and anti-Israel line 'which, so far, I have resisted as a matter of principle'.

Githii's resignation letter concluded by asking the chairman of the board to tell the Aga Khan that 'my conscience and my principles are not for sale'.

The whole affair was not merely unfortunate, but even tragic for the cause of press freedom in Kenya for, almost certainly, George Githii's removal from Nation House could only be seen as a diminution of press freedom in the African state which is still able to boast that it has more of it than any other north of the Limpopo.

Free-thinking editors are a rare and diminishing body everywhere in Africa, and the gap left by Githii at Nation House posed a problem for the management greater than that of merely replacing him.

Since the beginning of the Aga Khan's newspaper activities in

East Africa, the editorial bedrock at Nation House had been Joe Rodrigues. Rodrigues is an Asian, though a Kenyan citizen. He totally identifies with the country in which he was born. He had seen the *Nation* fight through the long unprofitable years prior to independence and watched successive editors, Black and White, of both the daily and Sunday editions come and go.

With Githii's removal, he was the natural choice as editor-in-chief of the Group and there was nobody at Nation House in Nairobi—certainly no African journalist who ever worked under him—who felt that he was not the man to take over. But he was only made acting-editor-in-chief, and the weeks turned into months while the management chewed its nails and faced the political realities that they thought the situation demanded. These were that the editorial chair in Nation House must be filled by an African—a Black African. It was paradoxical that the newspaper group which had championed every decent cause by which the new nation of Kenya had confounded its critics in the wake of the bloodshed of Mau Mau in which independence had been won should now hesitate before confirming Rodrigues because he was Brown instead of Black.

Hilary Ng'weno, the Nation group's first African editor-in-chief, was asked to return but he was not interested. Encouraged by the success of his *Weekly Review*, which was quite the best news magazine produced anywhere in Black Africa, Ng'weno was busy raising capital for a newspaper of his own. This duly appeared at the end of October 1977 as the *Nairobi Times*. A Sunday broadsheet complete with colour magazine, it was as near an imitation of the London *Sunday Times* as it was possible to get. The pre-launch advertising had proclaimed that it would be a 'quality' newspaper.

It lived up to its claim, an outstanding example of private enterprise, professionalism and sheer courage, both in commercial and political terms. It was the only newspaper of any substance launched by private enterprise in tropical Africa for a decade. If it had a weakness, it was that though strong on comment, features and views, it was light on hard news. The first issue did not even carry the previous day's sporting results in Kenya.

Towards the end of 1977 there was another incident in Kenya, virtually unique in the post-Independence newspaper story of tropical Africa. The Kenya Union of Journalists at Nation House called a strike of protest over the dismissal of the *Nation's* labour relations director. About 450 employees of the Group stopped work and on the sixth day of the closure of the *Nation* George Odiko, the Union's General Secretary, and six other Union leaders, were arrested and charged with inciting the strike. Strikes are illegal in Kenya unless twenty-one days notice is given to the Government.

The strike, if not the subsequent arrests of the Union officials, was very similar to that prevailing in newspaper offices in much more developed societies than Kenya. It was significant that such a thing could happen in a one-party Black state. With the possible exception of Nigeria, whose journalists have evolved a pretty gutsy attitude to officialdom now that their papers are owned by the military government, there is certainly no other African state where journalists would for a moment contemplate going on strike.

Put in the context of the Continent a generation after independence, the walk-out from Nation House, was, in its own curious way, another assertion of the independence of journalists in Kenya. In the long run that could be no bad thing.

UGANDA: THE KILLING OF THE PRESS AND THE PRESSMEN

When Britain administered East Africa, although the three territories of Kenya, Uganda and Tanganyika were separate entities, to a very great extent they were regarded by London as one. They shared many common services such as railways, the airline, postal services and the ports and harbours of both the Indian Ocean and the inland lakes of Victoria and Tanganyika.

The three African Nationalist founding fathers, Jomo Kenyatta of Kenya, Julius Nyerere of Tanganyika and Milton Obote of Uganda, had planned that their three nations should form a federation as soon as the last of them became free. But it was not to be. They went their separate ways and are now ideologically as far apart as it is possible to be; Kenya an unashamed capitalist state; Tanzania making the Continent's most honest attempt at socialism, and Uganda ruled by an army which has all but obliterated not merely formal opposition but tens of thousands of people who in some way or other got in the way of the bayonets, the bullets and the rifle-butts.

The earliest papers in Uganda emerged in and around the capital, Kampala, where the elite tribe, the Buganda, are centred. The Buganda probably had among the highest literacy rate of any tribe in the interior of Africa. The early missionaries, the Catholics, had always been particularly strong in Uganda, and played an important part in the creation of newspapers by lending their printing equipment to a whole spectrum of people who wanted to print something. Some of the earliest papers which appeared at the end of the nineteenth century had no names. In 1907 *Ebifa mu Uganda* was established, and twenty years later *Gambuze* appeared, followed the next year by *Dobozi Iya Buganda.*

But it was as late as 1953 before an African newspaper of real significance emerged. This was *Uganda Eyogera,* the voice of the Uganda National Congress, the founding movement of the Uganda Peoples' Congress which was to campaign for and eventually achieve independence for the country. The Uganda National Congress leader of those years was Joseph Kiwanuka who was in and out of jail through most of the fifties, sometimes for publishing what the British said was seditious material, but generally for political activities of one sort or another. With another Nationalist paper, *Uganda Empya, Uganda Eyogera* successfully campaigned to bring back the ruler of the Buganda people, the Kabaka, who had been exiled to Britain by a colonial administration which was floundering about all through the fifties, totally unable to deal with the mounting nationalism. When the campaign to have the Kabaka returned from Britain was successful, he sat in the 'plane that had brought him from London on the tarmac at Entebbe Airport, and insisted on the humiliated British Governor coming in to meet him first while tens of thousands of delirious Bugandans went wild outside.

The wheel of fate was to make a cruel spin for the young Kabaka, 'King Freddy', as he was known. After becoming his country's first President following independence, he was to flee from the new government of Milton Obote, and finally to die poverty-stricken and heartbroken in a seedy part of London.

Apart from a brief attempt by the Aga Khan to gain a foothold, the only foreign-owned paper in Uganda during the colonial period and for a decade after it was the *Uganda Argus,* part of the Kenya *Standard* group. Because there were virtually no White settlers in Uganda, the *Argus* was always a much more

reputable paper than the *Standard*, although with its White
editor and staff, it still projected a European viewpoint which
was totally out of character with the country. But at least it
recognised the existence of Africans and catered for them more
and more. After independence when Uganda was thrown into a
series of upheavals which led to the emergence of Idi Amin,
the White editorial staff had a nerve-racking time keeping their
heads above water. Amin threw the last two Europeans out in
1973.

Obote had been determined to get a newspaper of his own,
and soon after Uganda became independent he went knocking
on the doors of foreign embassies in Kampala seeking money to
start one. The *Uganda Press Trust* was set up, and also the *Milton
Obote Foundation*, with funds from an American organisation called
Freedom Incorporated in New York and a West German charity,
World Wide Partnership in Bonn. The end product of all this was
the English-language weekly, *The People*, which appeared in
March 1964.

The People was a bright and breezy tabloid, very different
from most newspapers set up by African politicians. Although
financed by the West, neither its editorials nor its news coverage
made any concessions to this.

When Idi Amin came to power in the military coup which
ousted Milton Obote in 1971, he listed eighteen reasons why he
had taken over. One of them was 'lack of freedom in the airing
of different views on political and social matters'. Although he
suspended most of the Uganda constitution, he left the section
on 'Freedom of expression and press' as it was. Idi Amin is only
matched on the continent of Africa for his ruthlessness by two
other men, Jean-Bedel Bokassa, whose military career as an
N.C.O. in the French army followed a similar pattern to that of
Amin's in the British army, and South Africa's Johannes Vorster.

On Amin's second day in power, he gave a press conference
to end all press conferences. All the journalists in the country
were summoned. When they arrived, they found that Amin was
to take them on a conducted tour of the whole country to
demonstrate, as he said, that unlike other coups in Africa and
Latin America his had been a bloodless one. This was very
largely true. It was only a little later that his soldiers began the
wholesale slaughter of his own people which has been unmatched
as a blood-bath by any other military regime on the Continent

outside of a Civil War.

For a while after Amin came to power, the press took him at his word and there was more outspokenness in the columns of the *Argus* than there had ever been before. Amin gave a bull to the staff of *Taifa Empya* (previously *Uganda Empya*), and another to the reporters of *Munno*, the Catholic vernacular paper 'because during the former regime they printed my statement that I feared nobody but God'.

John Ejalu, a giant of a man, was the first Ugandan editor of both the *People* and the *Argus*. A close friend and supporter of Milton Obote, he had thus been a natural choice to succeed Daniel Nelson, the English editor of the *People,* and his relationship with Obote was very much in the minds of the management of the *Argus* when in June 1970 they appointed him to take over from the paper's long-time editor, Charles Harrison, another Englishman. But seven months after moving to the *Argus*, Obote was ousted in the coup led by Amin.

One of the first things Amin did after moving into State House was to send for the English managing-director of the *Argus*, William Buse. Buse, mindful of the links between Ejalu and the deposed Obote, asked what the position of the editor now was. Amin told him that as long as Ejalu stuck to his job, and did not dabble in sensitive political matters, he could remain. At that same meeting Amin told Buse that he 'loved the British', but that he despised the Asians in the country.

Notwithstanding Amin's assurances, John Ejalu was soon in trouble. One day in March 1972 for no apparent reason a contingent of soldiers arrived at the offices of the *Argus* and picked him up. They took him to his house, and, according to Buse, roughed him up. Shots were fired, but Ejalu survived. He gave no explanation to Buse as to what had been the cause, but it seemed clear that it was his past links with Obote, who was now in neighbouring Tanzania and planning to invade Uganda and overthrow Amin. Buse believes that it is more than likely that Ejalu was picked up by the military without the knowledge of Amin. At that time—and ever since—the Ugandan Army were a law unto themselves, and right down to the lowest ranks frequently operated as thugs and gangsters.

A few days after the incident, Ejalu asked Buse whether the *Argus* would help him to take up the offer of a study tour of India. He resigned as editor of the *Argus* and left the country.

He was later appointed Director of Information Services for the East African Community based at Arusha in Tanzania.

Though this post covered all three of the East African territories, the respective heads of which were the supreme authority, Ejalu has never set foot in his native land since.

It was shortly after this that Father Clement Kiggundu, editor of the Catholic *Munno*, was found strangled and shot in his locked car which had been set alight. Five years later another editor of *Munno*, John Sawiniko, died in a police cell to which he had been taken with two of his reporters, Bob Kakembo and Jim Luzima after, it was claimed, leaflets criticizing Amin had been found in the *Munno* offices. And a few hundred yards from the spot where *Munno*'s first editor had been murdered in a forest just outside Kampala, Jimmy Parma, the country's best news photographer, was found shot.

Amin spent an undue amount of time dealing with the press in the early days of his rule. He set up a school of journalism, and when the first course was opened by the Minister of Information and Broadcasting, the students were told: 'If papers want to be meaningful they should try to dig out news and offer intelligent opinions in the great place of ideas.'

In June 1971 there was a press seminar when another minister declared: 'This Government believes in the freedom not only of the press but of everybody.'

Three months later, yet another seminar on press freedom was held and the then Attorney-General, Nkambo Mugerwa, described the press as 'a watchdog of freedom'. He said that the former regime of Obote had fallen because it had so stifled liberty of opinion that it 'ceased to be in touch with the needs and aspirations of the people'. He said the press in Uganda had been like a modern court jester 'telling the King what he wants to hear'. As a result, he said, the nation's press was dull and uninteresting.

His parting message to the seminar was 'Uganda's journalistic history is at a turning point'. It certainly was—to disaster.

The speeches of Amin and his ministers in those early days of Uganda's first military government are a classic instance of the breast-beating, cliché-ridden hyperbole with which most military dictators come to power. The turning point in Uganda's journalistic history had been reached and slowly, then more vividly, Uganda's newspapermen realised what was happening to them.

When Amin came to power his speeches, which were generally short, sharp affairs, were, of course, given considerable prominence but they could be edited. Then as Amin waded deeper into the political and administrative waters of the Presidency, he surrounded himself with all the trappings political leaders all over the world acquire—speech writers, public relations aides and general hangers-on. His speeches began to get longer. By 1972 the editors of Uganda's newspapers began receiving telephone calls from the Presidential office telling them that such and such a story—always concerning Amin and generally one of his speeches—was a 'must'. The editors accepted these directions with resignation. The slide began. Soon not only was every speech and everything that Amin said 'a must', but instructions were being issued as to just where in the newspapers the President's speeches should be printed.

When Amin expelled the Israelis from Uganda in 1972 a continual front-page story in all the papers was either of Amin or of an unnamed military spokesman warning 'saboteurs, imperialists and Zionists or their agents' and saying that if they stirred up trouble they would be eliminated. From April to June that year there were ninety-six such warnings in the *Uganda Argus* alone.

Uganda newspapermen now knew what was expected of them in so far as the projection of Idi Amin and his regime was concerned, but there was constant difficulty with all sorts of other stories. When the *People,* which survived Obote's downfall, ran an agency story about the shortcomings of the Tanzanian Government, the editor was declared by Amin to be a 'suppressive element', because, said Amin, he had criticised a neighbouring government.

The fact that Amin was almost daily threatening to launch a war against Tanzania at this time did not save the editor from being sacked.

When Amin declared 'economic war' in August 1972 and began the mass expulsion of Asians from the country, the *Argus* started running stories condemning anyone who sympathised with the Asians. As a result of the expulsion of the Asians, many factories in Uganda found their production targets impossible to meet. There was a national shortage of sugar, and when the *Argus* carried a story explaining why there was a shortage, the Government came out with a denial and said it was an 'imperialist paper not working in the interest of the country'.

It threatened to nationalise the paper and finally did so on November 30, 1972 'because it is conflicting with the Government's interests'. The name was changed to the *Voice of Uganda*. All journalists had to be registered as employees of the Ministry of Information. Early in 1973 Amin's honeymoon with *Taifa Empya* and *Munno* was over. The bulls which he had given to the editorial staffs of the papers when he came to power had long since been digested. Both papers were constantly threatened with closure for 'confusing the people'. The Government said that as *Taifa Empya* was owned by the Aga Khan it was 'serving its Asian master'.

The *Nation* group in Kenya had brought control of *Taifa Empya* in 1960, but Michael Curtis saw the hopelessness of trying to carry on under Amin and abandoned the project. Amin closed *Munno* down and a statement from the Presidential office said that 'the public had requested the Government to ban *Munno* because it is working as a confusing agent'.

The *People*, which had become a daily in January 1969, staggered on for a while, but after its employees had not been paid for many months they sued the management for breach of contract. As the ownership was virtually the Government this was not merely fool-hardy but dangerous. In fact all Amin did was to close it down.

The new editor of the *Voice of Uganda* was Horace Awori, an intelligent graduate and a passionate nationalist who was bending backwards to accommodate his conscience as a journalist with the demands of the new regime upon his newspaper. In October 1973, as Uganda celebrated its eleventh independence anniversary, a press conference was held with a number of distinguished foreign visitors present. One of them was from Tanzania which at this time, unlike Uganda, had not broken diplomatic relations with Israel. Awori asked an Israeli visitor what his country's stand was in the Arab/Israeli war. Amin interrupted. He said this was an embarrassing question because the war was between Africa and Israel and it was known, he said, that all African countries supported the Arabs. Therefore, said Amin, the question implied that Tanzania 'sided with the Zionists'. There was a deathly silence at the press conference as Amin's astounding logic ground to its conclusion. Then he concluded with what virtually amounted—in the Uganda of 1973 where life was very cheap—to a death sentence for Horace Awori.

'That question', said Amin, 'must have been asked by a White African and surely not by a Ugandan'.

Awori expected to be seized there and then by the guards looking on, but probably because of the foreign visitors present they bided their time. Awori was able to slip away and after living rough in the bush as the army mounted a major search for him, he crossed the border to the sanctity of Kenya.

This was the end of the *Argus* as a newspaper. It became literally the organ of the Ministry of Information and Amin himself took over the portfolio as Minister of Information.

It now has no reporters but merely an editorial production team which waits to receive the official hand-outs from Government. Amin operates with his own Presidential press unit, which consists of a chief information officer, two information officers, two senior news reporters and several photographers. They are concerned exclusively with his activities, and they supply the *Voice, Taifa Empya,* which limps on as a public company, and *Munno,* which since the murder of its editor and its banning has re-appeared, with Amin's speeches, the activities he wants reported and an endless stream of photographs of him.

Amin came to power on 25 January, 1971 and for the five-month period to 25 June of that year 101 pictures of him appeared in what was then the *Argus.* In the same period 87 pictures of members of his cabinet appeared and 73 other pictures of a non-political nature. A year later, over the same five-month period from January to June, this ratio had changed to: Amin 157 pictures; cabinet 55; foreign 63. The progression continued and by 1976 it was Amin 215; cabinet 26; foreign 15. It is not unusual for Amin's picture to appear a dozen times in the same issue. If he makes a speech in the morning and the same speech elsewhere in the afternoon, it will dutifully appear, word for word, twice in the *Voice of Uganda.*

It still prints a form of editorial, generally in strident, defensive tones. A typical example is from the leading article which appeared on 20 May 1976. This declared: 'We have enjoyed the pride of standing clean before the eyes of the world to disprove all shit smeared over our face.'

The *Voice of Uganda* is so pre-occupied with its primary function of projecting Idi Amin that it pays scant attention to other news. When it does so, there is often an air of confusion about the stories. On 26 May 1976, it got what was presumably a news agency report of President Giscard d'Estaing's visit to the United States in connection with the bi-centenary celebrations there. The story in the *Voice* said: 'French President Valery Giscard d'Estaing gave President Gerald Ford on Wednesday 1.2 million dollars (9.6 million shillings) spectacle tracing the life of George Washington as France's bi-centennial gift to the United States.'

The story gave no clue as to what this gift was and the curious headline above the story could have meant little to the average Ugandan reader—or anyone else. It said 'D'Estaing Offers a Dear Spectacle'.

Yet there is another side to Amin, which the world, in its awe and horror at the viciousness of his rule, rarely hears about. He can be kind, gentle and, if the fancy takes him, helpful even to newspapermen.

Barbara Kimenye, a strikingly beautiful woman, the child of a White mother and a Black father, who went to Africa when she married a Tanzanian student in the early fifties, worked as a reporter and feature writer when the Aga Khan started the short-lived *Uganda Nation* in 1962. This was a revolutionary role for a woman in the conservative society of Uganda with its almost Victorian traditions. But Barbara Kimenye was close to the Kabaka. She had worked in his office. He told her: 'If you want to write for the newspapers, then try it. If it does not work out you can always come back to the Palace.' He wanted to see women progress, and he knew that this meant that they would have to start entering the male domains. Barbara used humour as her ally, for the Buganda have none of the subservience of the tribes in 'settler' Africa. They have great humour—or did have until Amin's army knocked it out of them—and could laugh at themselves.

She began to write lively feature articles about social etiquette in the new independent Uganda.

One article of that period which she wrote pointed out that if you received an invitation 'requesting the company of' to a function, that did not mean the whole company was expected to turn up. Slowly the barriers fell, and the more progressive Buganda women began to use her to promote their own aims. In no time she was a household word all the way from the Kabaka's Palace to the down-town shanties of Kampala. She remembers with affection how she was turned into a reporter by a hard-graft English newspaperman, Manning Blackwood, who edited the *Nation*. This sort of tribute by Black journalists to the Europeans they worked with is found time and time again throughout tropical Africa. It is one of the most rewarding memories of the colonial and immediate post-colonial times.

As a feature writer, Barbara Kimenye found it difficult to adapt to the brevity of news reporting, where the essence of the story had to be condensed into the first paragraph. Manning Blackwood became so exasperated with her one day that he got a pile of her wordy copy and hit her about the head with it.

Her output—and this was customary with many journalists all over Black Africa—was enormous. It was not unusual for a single issue of the *Nation* to carry four full-length features by her, three or four news stories and a full report of Parliament. Her striking beauty was a great asset in what was predominantly very much a masculine society. Many a time the Speaker coughed discreetly into his lace-edged sleeve in an effort to bring back members' attention to the parliamentary business as Barbara leaned a little further over the rail of the press gallery to catch what was going on.

She was writing so much that she needed extra by-lines. The Kabaka gave her one; Sara Namukasa. It was not unusual for her to arrive back at the office at eleven o'clock at night to find that the advertisement manager had managed to sell advertising space to justify another couple of pages and editorial filling was needed. She and the only other reporter—they shared a motor-scooter to cover their beats—would pull out their typewriters and provide the necessary copy.

But the *Nation* was never able to make the breakthrough to viability that was necessary, and after eighteen months Michael Curtis closed it, though retaining the office as the Uganda depot for the Nairobi *Nation* in Kenya which began editionalising for the neighbouring territory. Barbara continued in her new role as Uganda correspondent.

Obote wanted Barbara Kimenye for his *People*. She did not want to leave the Aga Khan, but Obote said that if she refused to join *The People* he would make things unpleasant for *The Nation*. She joined *The People*. There she found herself working even harder than ever. By now she was a fully-seasoned journalist and professionally far superior to the editor. To her duties as news reporter, feature writer and parliamentary corre-spondent was added staff photographer and proof-reader. But the rift between the Kabaka and Obote, which was to lead to the Kabaka fleeing to England, was beginning to widen.

Violence, although not on the scale that in turn was to be used when Obote was overthrown by Amin, was beginning; vicious murders, heads chopped off, entrails torn out. Barbara Kimenye reported the official enquiry into one particularly brutal bout of murdering. Her copy was sent for by the government and censored to a travesty of what she had written.

During this period she got to know Amin fairly well and remembers him as a kindly if not very literate or bright man. At a particularly crowded official conference, she was being jostled and pushed by a surge of men. A burly figure with a colonel's tabs cut through the throng like a knife through butter. A slow voice announced in schoolmasterly tones: 'It is not nice for a lady to be pushed like this.'

In January 1964, during the days of the Obote Government when a number of soldiers attempted a coup, she reported their court-martial but was lost at some of the military jargon used. Amin sat with her long after the court-martial had risen, explaining what all the military terms meant.

Idi Amin has always been a great military man in the tradition of the British Army that created him. A decade later another story emerged to underline a little known side to his nature. The *Voice of Uganda* had standing instructions to publish on the front page of every issue a picture of Amin at least two and a half columns wide and four columns deep. The pictures were supplied by the Ministry of Information which was run by Amin himself. One afternoon, a message was received in the newsroom of the *Voice* saying that a new photograph would be sent along that evening for publication the next day. But when with press time almost upon them no picture had appeared, a frantic sub-editor rushed to the library and pulled out an old picture of the President.

Amin had recently promoted himself to field-marshal but the picture that appeared the next morning showed him with colonel's epaulettes.

Just after dawn Amin personally telephoned the *Voice* and said that he wanted everybody who worked in the news department to be ready when he appeared. There was genuine terror when the message was hurriedly relayed to the staff. At this time people were disappearing or being found murdered every day, and there were many among the editorial staff who thought that their last hour had come. Amin duly arrived, driving his own jeep but escorted by a bodyguard of soldiers with bayonets fixed to their rifles. Amin entered the newsroom and the soldiers took up their positions. But then the President began a long, laborious but very friendly talk about military ranks, and moving almost affectionately amongst the awe-struck staff of the *Voice*, produced from his pocket a picture of Britain's Field-Marshal Viscount Montgomery. Wagging his finger at it, he explained that he, too, was wearing the same uniform as Montgomery and that 'it is silly if you put a picture of me in the paper wearing a colonel's uniform'.

A charitable view of what has happened in Uganda under Idi Amin is that sharper minds in the Army Command have been as responsible as Amin himself for the blood-letting. The Press long ago gave up any pretence of proper journalism. The last two White journalists on the *Voice of Uganda* were dismissed early in 1973. The editor of *Taifa* was sacked because the newspaper attributed measures announced in a budget speech to the Minister of Finance rather than to the Government as a whole.

The last whimper of the *Voice of Uganda* went in the middle of 1974 when Amin sacked its sports editor, Sammy Katerega, who was alleged to have written 'unconstructive criticism of the national football team'.

The news contents of the radio and television programmes are travesties. When Amin makes a speech, it will automatically be the first item on the news, which is supposed to last for twenty minutes. But if Amin has spoken for two hours, then the news broadcast may go on for as long as this, Then the same speech will be repeated later that night and again on the early morning news before finally appearing on the front page of the *Voice*.

While the *Uganda Argus* was White-owned and White edited in the new Independent Uganda, it was so cautious that it avoided any serious trouble with the Government. The outstanding case of persecution of the press during the first years of independence was against the magazine *Transition*, which was the most successful literary magazine produced anywhere on the Continent and with an international reputation. It was edited by a Ugandan Asian, Rajat Neogy, who had been born in the country. *Transition* was not a Ugandan publication in the sense that it dealt with Ugandan affairs. It addressed itself to a much larger audience. But the thirty-seventh issue of the monthly magazine in October 1968 contained a letter from a former Minister in the Parliament of the Kabaka's Kingdom of Buganda, Abu Mayanja.

In the letter Mayanja took issue with an official who worked in the office of President Obote, who in an earlier issue of *Transition* had argued that the judiciary should take ideological considerations into account when deciding cases. Mayanja went on to accuse the Government of prolonging the use of outmoded colonial laws and of dragging its feet over the Africanisation of the Ugandan High Court.

Both Rajat Neogy and Mayanja were charged with sedition. While they awaited trial in prison for several months, the Government began a campaign to discredit Neogy and *Transition*, saying it was backed by the C.I.A.-financed Congress for Cultural Freedom.

Neogy was stunned when he learned that C.I.A. money was behind the Congress for Cultural Freedom which was the principal support of *Transition*. When he was asked by the *Sunday Nation* in Nairobi what his reaction had been when he learned the truth about his magazine's sponsorship, he replied: 'Shock, later turning into a massive two-month depression. The depression came out of a feeling of being smeared by something one neither knew about nor was prepared for. There was also a great and helpless resentment at seeing one's work of more than five years tarred over by this C.I.A. brush.'

Neogy said there had never been the slightest influence on editorial policy exerted by the Congress for Cultural Freedom. 'What the C.I.A. was doing was exploiting integrity', he told the *Sunday Nation*. 'Taking an honest man or an honest organisation and exploiting the very fundamentals of its success, its proven honesty and integrity.'

During their time in prison awaiting trial, both Neogy and Mayanja suffered considerable privations and Neogy, particularly, was broken in mind and body. They were both acquitted by the Ugandan Chief Magistrate who ruled that the basic freedoms granted in the Ugandan Constitution would be morally impaired if Mayanja's letter were interpreted as sedition. Even though they had been found not guilty, they continued to be held in detention. Eventually Neogy was released and *Transition* reappeared, published from Ghana. But Neogy's health had gone and the magazine fell away to a shell of its former self. Finally it disappeared.

The journalists of Uganda are no longer under pressure for they no longer practice journalism. 'As long as we do exactly what we are told, which means just putting all the hand-outs straight into the paper and in the right position on the page, then we are safe', was the frank observation of one of them.

TANZANIA: THE CYCLONE IN A SARI

If an identi-kit picture had to be made of the most improbable choice of an editor for a newly-nationalised African nationalist newspaper in Africa it might be something like this; a South African, an Asian and a woman.

And yet this was exactly the person whom Julius Nyerere selected to edit the *Tanganyika Standard*. The *Standard* and its Sunday sister, the *Sunday News*, had been part of the Nairobi-based Lonrho Group which ran Kenya's *East African Standard* and the *Uganda Argus*.

Julius Nyerere had long wanted a press which reflected what he considered should be the proper message of Tanganyika. In 1959, two years before independence, his Tanganyika African National Union (TANU) had set up a company called the National Times Press to promote just such a venture. The plan was to publish an English daily, a Swahili daily, and a weekly catering for the Asian community. But poor equipment, insufficient capitalisation and a general lack of experience in publishing never allowed the venture to really get under way. In 1961 TANU established a weekly in Swahili, *Uhuru*. There was another independent weekly, *Mwafrika*.

Tanganyika became independent on 9 December 1961. The ruling Tanganyika African National Union created *The Nationalist* in April 1964, and an experienced Ghanaian, James Markham, who had worked with Nkrumah in the days of the old Accra *Evening News*, was appointed managing editor. The shortage of African journalists was so acute that many of the staff were Whites from the *Tanganyika Standard*. But the *Nationalist*, after a promising start, never really made the impact that TANU wanted and the old *Tanganyika Standard* remained the principal daily.

When TANU came to power they began a major programme of nationalisation. But Nyerere was constantly embarrassed by the incongruity that the country's largest papers, the *Standard* and the *Sunday News,* which were supposed to be the main instruments for projecting the socialist aims of Tanzania, were owned by foreigners. He was constantly reminded of this in the fairly free-speaking atmosphere of Dar-es-Salaam. On one occasion, in February 1967, when he was making a major speech about nationalisation a voice from the crowd shouted: 'The Standard! The Standard!'

Nyerere replied sarcastically: 'Can you edit it?'

But two years later, the pressures on Nyerere to take over the *Standard* and the *Sunday News* were too strong to resist. They were nationalised.

It was this most sensitive of all TANU's take-overs that Frene Ginwala was recruited by Nyerere to edit. Frene Ginwala is a South African-born Asian, a Marxist, a dedicated African nationalist with a first-rate mind and considerable single-mindedness. Born of wealthy parents, she studied law, was called to the Bar in London and then gravitated towards journalism. But politics was always her driving force.

In South Africa law has always played a major role on the ultra-liberal and left political scene. After graduating at the University of London, she intended to go back to South Africa, practise law and continue to fight for independence. But it did not work out like that. In London she free-lanced and travelled widely, working, for among others the BBC. She travelled widely in Asia, writing and broadcasting. The end of 1959 saw her back in South Africa, and she became involved with the African National Congress, then led by Nobel Peace Prize winner, Chief Albert Luthuli. This was a period in South African Black nationalist history when it looked as though great events might be beginning. The ANC executive decided to send a senior man out of the country to begin the organisation's first ambassadorial exercise. Frene Ginwala was asked to help to get Oliver Tambo, the A.N.C's Deputy President General, out of the country.

The nearest independent African country in those days was Ethiopia, half a continent and many British colonies away. Frene Ginwala engineered Tambo's escape from South Africa. The day after the Sharpeville massacre, in March 1960, she herself left South Africa via Portuguese-ruled Moçambique. Sharpeville was traumatic for Blacks and Whites in South Africa. Nobody knew what was going to happen. Frene Ginwala was one of the few people in the ANC with a passport, and as her father had been born in Moçambique, she had joint South African and Moçambique citizenship. She made her way to Salisbury in Rhodesia and organised a small aeroplane to fly to Bechuanaland (now Botswana) to pick up Oliver Tambo. When the 'plane delivered him to Tanzania, still administered by the British, her connection with the escape became clear and her name, then only lightly pencilled on the wanted list of the South African Special Branch, was inked in heavily.

World opinion was not yet mounted against South Africa as was to be the case as Black Africa became powerful in the United Nations, and in those days the British Government had firm links with the South African security forces. Thus Frene Ginwala found she was a prohibited immigrant virtually everywhere in Africa. But with Tanganyika on the threshold of independence, the British did not want an incident with Julius Nyerere and it was agreed with TANU that she and Oliver Tambo would be allowed to stay in Dar-es-Salaam.

She joined a publishing group called the *National Times* which was owned by the Tanganyika African National Union and travelled around East Africa trying to raise money to launch a daily paper. With Britain still administering Uganda and Kenya, she found she was banned in both territories. She was unable to raise the sort of finance needed for a daily newspaper but finally a monthly magazine called *Spearhead* appeared with her as editor. It was technically poor but editorially gutsy, providing a platform for nationalism all over East Africa. It was very much a one-man— or in this case, one-woman—show and in the great tradition of the political journalism of the early years of West Africa. At this time she was also on the editorial board of *Révolution Africaine*, the Algerian-based paper. With Frene Ginwala's intimate knowledge of the African nationalist scene, she was a valued stringer for the *Guardian* and the Sunday *Observer* in Britain.

But as was pretty well the standard pattern in the early post-independence period of any new African state, she became involved in an internal TANU problem and in June 1963 was declared a prohibited immigrant. Back in Britain, she busied

herself with her old ANC work and began a thesis at Oxford.
Then out of the blue, in October 1969, she got a letter from
Dar-es-Salaam saying Julius Nyerere wanted to see her and that
she should come to Tanganyika as soon as possible.

Consumed with curiosity, she flew to Tanzania where Nyerere
told her he was nationalising the *Standard*. He asked her if she
would take over as managing editor. Nyerere also wanted her to
start a training programme within the *Standard* for Tanzanian
journalists.

She was more than intelligent enough to know the difference
between turning out little monthly magazines beating the political
drum, and editing a big national daily which would have not
merely technical and staffing problems but almost certainly highly
delicate political problems too. 'I was scared stiff', she says. 'I
thought I was going to be a sitting duck.' She made all these
points to Nyerere, and said that she felt she might not be cut
out by nature to be editor of a government paper. All her life
she had been in opposition and she wondered how she could
switch to the other side—the 'establishment' side of the fence.
Nyerere replied that this was exactly what he wanted. He did
not want the *Standard* to be a government mouthpiece. But
Frene felt it was one thing for the President to tell her this
privately; it needed to be said publicly. Nyerere agreed. And so
what became known as the Charter was issued. This is what the
Charter said:

> The new *Standard* will give general support to the policies of
> the Tanzanian Government but will be free to join in the
> debate for and against particular proposals put forward for
> consideration of the people, whether by Government, by
> TANU or by other bodies. Further, it will be free to initiate
> discussions on any subject relevant to the development of a
> socialist and democratic society in Tanzania. It will be guided
> by the principle that free debate is an essential element of
> true socialism and it will strive to encourage and maintain a
> high standard of socialist discussion.

To dispel any fears of censorship or control on news, President
Nyerere said:

> The new *Standard* will aim at supplying its readers with all

domestic and world news as quickly as possible. It will be run on the principle that a newspaper only keeps the trust of its readers and only deserves their trust if it reports the truth to the best of its ability and without distortion, whether the truth be pleasant or unpleasant.

Having got her brief for the new *Standard*, Frene Ginwala felt she should have a crash course on a daily paper and so it was arranged that she should go to the *Times of Zambia*, which although owned by Lonrho, had its editor appointed by Nyerere's close friend, President Kenneth Kaunda. She was only there a week before flying back to Oxford to put her unfinished thesis away. It was not to turn yellow with age.

Lonrho had owned the *Standard* when it was nationalised, and the White editor, Bernard Grimshaw, was only given forty-eight hours notice before Frene moved into his chair. All the senior posts on the paper were held by Whites. Of a total editorial staff of about thirty, a third were European and doing three-quarters of the work.

Although Tanzania had been independent for eight years, the Africanisation programme had merely been a window-dressing exercise of taking on a lot of Black faces with very little or no experience. On 4 February 1970, Frene Ginwala moved in to the editor's office of the *Standard* to produce the next day's paper.

She had spent several nights before having nightmares that if Lonrho, in a pique over the nationalisation, should pull out all their expatriate staff, she would be in trouble. In fact the Europeans on the paper, both editorial and management, took the whole thing well. Grimshaw got the staff together and introduced her to them. The Europeans were on contract and they stayed until these ran out.

Frene Ginwala brought with her to Tanzania a number of socialist newspapermen from Britain. Chief of these was Richard Gott, a well-known writer from the *Guardian* who specialised in Third World affairs. He had just completed a book called 'Guerilla Movements in Latin America' and a series of articles for the *Guardian* on 'Cuba Revisited'. He was to take charge of foreign news. Another was Tony Hall, a first-class South African journalist who had worked in Kenya on the *Nation*. He was to be in charge of the training programme. The newsroom became part newspaper office and part classroom. Her other White recruitments took the European expatriate strength back to pre-nationalisation level.

Black and White editorial staff stood apprehensively about the newsroom as Frene Ginwala addressed them for the first time. The Whites were frankly sceptical and the Blacks bemused. Everyone had known for a long time that the paper was going to change hands, to be either bought out or nationalised. They assumed it was to be Africanised. Then suddenly, at virtually no notice, this most remarkable of managing editors swept in in her silk sari and sandals with her troupe of White left-wingers. One of the Whites who was present on that occasion summed up everyone's feelings when he said, long afterwards, 'An Eskimo in furs would have been as much in character as Frene Ginwala was that morning'.

She told them what she wanted: 'There is no such thing as objectiveness', she began. She elaborated by explaining what she meant. Hadji Konde, editor of the *Sunday News*, remembers that moment well. He says he will do so to his dying day. 'It was as though the new vicar had started his sermon by telling the congregation that the New Testament was a load of rubbish', he says. The African journalists on the *Standard*, though far from happy that for so many years after their nation had become independent they had been obliged to continue working for a newspaper which was owned by not merely a European group but one of the biggest capitalistic organisations in Africa, had all been reared in the British tradition of journalism. Most of them had attended training courses at centres such as those run by the International Press Institute or the Thomson Foundation, and they were to a great extent imbued with the idea of objectivity, arguable though the meaning of that might be.

Frene Ginwala told them that stories were written by human beings, and human beings selected the stories. Thus personal values were inevitably reflected in what stories were selected for publication. She said this was certainly so in the case of the British press, with what she referred to as its 'much vaunted' objectivity. Sub-editors blue-pencilled out other people's attitudes. There were people in positions who did not see certain things as important; they saw other things. The urge to be objective, she said, was in a sense an unreal thing. She told the editorial staff that what was needed in Tanzania was a committed paper, not a neutral one, because objectivity implied neutrality

'We are not going to make any bones about it. We are not going to pretend to be objective', she said. On the other hand, the new *Standard* would be fair. They would not obliterate all other ideas and refuse space to anything they did not agree with. She summarised her philosophy by saying that she was talking about a fair press, not an objective press.

Gott looked around for more socialist sources of foreign features. Material from *Prensa Latina,* the Cuban-based agency, *Granma,* the Cuban newspaper, the *American Liberation News Agency* and the *Africa Research Group* began to make the feature pages of both the *Standard* and the *Sunday News.*

The idea was that virtually all expatriates would be out in two or three years, replaced by Tanzanians who were not only journalistically but also politically ready to carry on the development of a socialist newspaper. Journalism training was combined with political orientation both in the classroom and on the job. Newspaper training was preceded on most days by political and current affairs lectures. Strongly socialist in orientation, they were given by members of TANU, the staff of Dar-es-Salaam University or high level outsiders.

Intensive daily post-mortems of the previous day's paper were held in which politics and journalism played an equal part. A number of the African journalists felt that the whole approach to the training programme was too heavily weighed towards political orientation and one meeting of the editorial staff, when grievances of this nature were aired, went on all night. As a result the training programme was revised and Nyerere came to see the staff. A number of the Africans repeated their grievances to him. A new training programme was begun, but again the staff was unhappy and it died slowly through non-cooperation.

Frene Ginwala added to her news agency intake, which on nationalisation was solely from Reuters, Associated Press from America, Hsin-hua from Peking and Tass from Moscow. It put a considerable strain on the sub-editors, for this often entailed four reports of the same story from four different sources. The subs were flummoxed. Which one to use? Frene Ginwala solved the problem by saying that no reports should be used straight. More and more news agency stories were rejigged. 'Viet-Cong' became 'Liberation Forces' and words like 'thugs' 'terrorists' and 'mob'—when used in a political context—were replaced by words biased the other way—'demonstrators', 'freedom fighters' 'crowds'. All this involved an enormous amount of re-writing and a degree of sophistication which the African staff was hardly up to and anyway rarely in complete sympathy with.

Both Reuters and Associated Press were far from happy when they found out what was happening to their service. They told Frene Ginwala that their contracts with the newspaper specified there should be no re-writing. She replied by pointing out another clause which said they should provide impartial news and if they insisted, for example, in calling the Government of South Vietnam—that is the Provisional Revolutionary Government which Tanzania recognised—rebels, then that was not impartial news. When Frene Ginwala gave a vigorous lecture along these lines to the A.P. man who had gone to Dar-es-Salaam to complain, a slightly glazed look came over his face. He duly reported back to New York.

Richard Gott figures prominently in this reorientation of the news. A political situation would be selected from any part of the world, but particularly from those parts in the news, and an explanation given to the staff as to where Tanzania stood in relation to it. Terminology lists were issued for the guidance of the sub-editors. But it was difficult to keep abreast of the vast moving international scene. Late one night a sub turned to Frene as she walked through the newsroom and asked 'What are we calling these chaps who are blowing up buildings in Venezuela?'

She recalls: 'We slipped up sometimes.' There was a difficulty about when to call Rhodesia Zimbabwe or South West Africa Namibia. For a readership, of which the great majority were poorly educated, it was hard to make the switch without confusing everybody.

Terrorism ceased to exist. Everyone was a freedom-fighter. Nothing was spared. Even captions of agency pictures were re-written. All the time the newsroom operated on the basis of 'Now what is the Government's policy on this?'

Nyerere was nominally editor-in-chief, but the amount of time he could spare was naturally limited. There were constant 'phone calls from the newsroom to State House and all the Government ministries. A drama developed over Laos when the vital battle for the Plain of Jars took place. From State House to the newest recruit on the subs desk, nobody was quite sure who were the goodies and who were the baddies. Gott was the font of knowledge on the more obscure issues. Directives would be issued to the subs on the lines of: 'For X substitute Y. For A substitute B.'

At the morning post-mortems, everyone and everything could be called to account. A reporter could challenge a sub on the changes made in his story. Frene herself could be challenged on something she had written in the editorial column. Sometimes she was challenged over something she had written on a specific Presidential directive. But she never felt she could say that she was following Nyerere's instructions. She says she felt it would have changed the character of the paper had she revealed this. As this was a Government paper with the President himself as the editor-in-chief, it seems a curious attitude.

A year after the nationalisation, at the end of January 1971, Idi Amin overthrew Milton Obote in neighbouring Uganda. This created shock waves which were never to subside completely. Obote fled to Dar-es-Salaam and Nyerere refused to recognise Amin. There was almost a state of war between the two countries. Amin began to make the extraordinary speeches which led to his international reputation as probably the most bizarre leader in the world. In one of these, at the height of tension between Uganda and Tanzania, Amin declared that he would marry Nyerere if he were a woman.

The Uganda crisis marked a turning point in the *Standard*'s links with State House. Nyerere just did not have the time to attend to the *Standard* in the old way. The paper did not call Amin President; it merely used his military rank—then a Colonel. Obote was still referred to as President. Finally the reality of the situation had to be recognised, and Nyerere issued a long statement which said that Obote did not have the support inside Uganda that his friends claimed. This was a major change of policy and clearly a very big news story. Frene Ginwala was so surprised that she rang State House to confirm it. She published the story in full, but the essential change in policy was rather buried in the wordiness. On another paper, she admits, she would probably have elevated the news point to the first paragraph, but in the *Standard* it was printed as State House issued it.

But there were a lot of other news stories about Uganda that were printed without Presidential guidance. The *Standard* was the first newspaper anywhere to publish the massacre stories from Uganda. These were first read with scepticism by the outside world, and then, as the foreign press confirmed them, accepted with horror. Frene had an excellent source of news direct from Uganda that was smuggled through to her.

It would be totally false to convey a picture of the *Standard* and the *Sunday News* of those times as a press servile to the Government. Time and time again both papers would set their sights on some aspect of Government policy, often some individual up to Cabinet level, which they felt should be considered. The old colonial *Standard* had never dared do this. Not even Nyerere himself was to be entirely free from criticism, though as editor-in-chief it was something more than delicate to criticise him.

The body that controlled the common services shared by the three East African territories—the East African Community—was, in the final resort, directed by the Presidents of the three states. When Barclay's Bank was given a big role in the Community's financial affairs, Frene Ginwala felt that Barclay's help in financing the Cabora Bosa Dam in Portuguese-ruled Moçambique made them the wrong partners. The *Standard* said so. Nyerere is said to have read the oblique criticism of him, tightened his lips, then smiled and shrugged his shoulders.

Frene Ginwala resisted letting her loathing for White South Africa affect the policy of the paper. As a South African exile dedicated to the overthrow of White rule in South Africa, and as a Marxist opposed to capitalism, it rankled that the head of the mighty Anglo-American Corporation, Harry Oppenheimer, had *carte blanche* to come and go to Tanzania to inspect one of the diamond mines in his empire. But she rationalised the fact. If the Government allowed it and it was not kept secret, then she would not criticise it.

But the pressures were mounting, and she was running out of time faster than she had allocated herself to Tanzanise her own position. In retrospect, it is clear that her nature and her whole background was one of an opponent. Although Nyerere's Charter for the *Standard* had been specific—the *Standard* was to be no mere mouthpiece—it was nonetheless the major arm for projecting Government policy. She would probably have been happier producing the TANU party paper, the *Nationalist*. She began to realise more and more the contradictory position the *Standard* was in: on the one hand speaking for the Government, and on the other questioning and even criticising Government policies.

She ruffled many establishment figures. One issue concerned tourism. Tanzania was in a classic ideological dilemma. Next door Kenya, which was vying with Nigeria as the most capitalist state in Black Africa, was creaming off the rich tourist trade built around its wild-life and beaches. Tanzania had better of both, and in an effort to attract some of the foreign visitors had built an international airport on the foothills of Mount Kilimanjaro to receive the German, Scandinavian, American and British tourists on their hard-currency package tours.

TANU's Youth League published a paper questioning the whole concept of tourism. There were two levels of argument. One was whether Tanzania's emphasis on high-cost tourism, with the head-hunting capitalists of the western world after its trophies, was not contradictory to the kind of socialist state Tanzania was trying to build. The *Standard* printed the TANU paper, saying it was something that should be discussed and invited leaders to give their views. Not unnaturally the Minister of Tourism, who only existed to promote foreign visitors to the country, attacked the *Standard* in vehement language in Parliament. He was not interested in an ideological student debate; he was after the Deutschmarks and dollars which would buy the much-needed foreign imports Tanzania required, including newsprint for the *Standard*. The Minister, in his wrath, talked about the need to Africanise the *Standard*.

In the 'Readers Forum' column of the paper came a letter asking, 'What does the Minister mean by Africanisation? The editor is a South African and therefore an African. Does the Minister mean by any chance that she is an Asian? In which case, he is a racist and should not be a member of TANU'. This was all fuel to the fire that was beginning to scorch Frene's sari.

All the time she was going as fast as she could with Africanisation. Every company in the country had to have a phased programme of Tanzanisation. When she discussed the *Standard*'s plans with the Minister of Labour, he said: 'You can have ten years. That's what Lonrho had.' But she replied, 'No. Give me five years but we will do it in two'. In fact events were to beat her deadline by six months.

The great sacred cow of the state was the National Development Corporation which ran all manner of businesses. The *Standard* questioned whether Tanzania really had socialism or state capitalism. It questioned the way many of the para-state organisations were being run (the *Standard* itself was one of them).

Nyerere continued to give Frene a lot of rein. The truth probably was that he just did not know what to do about her. Looking back on the papers she produced at that time, it seems clear that the fine polemics and socialist dialectics were much too sophisticated for a desperately poor state with a literacy rate among the lowest in Africa. Her arguments were fine in the debating halls of Western universities, but constantly beating the wrong note at the wrong time in the wrong place in down-town Dar-es-Salaam.

As managing editor she had more than just editorial problems on her shoulders. Nyerere wanted the paper to survive on its own profitability rather than on Government subsidies, but the realities of socialism worked against newspaper viability. The wholesale import sector was nationalised and this meant, for example, that whereas Tanzania had once imported eleven different makes of refrigerator, they now imported only three. Seven potential advertisers were therefore lost. This pattern was repeated with many commodities, and advertising revenue fell swiftly away. Frene Ginwala would have liked to see a merger with the big printing and packaging corporation which had also been owned by Lonrho and which was a money spinner.

She embarked on a major reorganisation of distribution of the papers. Tanzania, mile for mile, has poorer communications than almost any other country in Africa—certainly any other country attempting to produce a national daily serving the whole nation. Like almost every other daily in Black Africa, the *Standard* had previously been very much the paper for the urban elite. Nyerere was desperate to de-centralise. He was already planning to move the capital from Dar-es-Salaam on the coast to the arid interior plains of Tanzania. In an effort to give the paper a greater national character, Frene appointed correspondents in as many regional centres as she could, with staff men in the three or four main centres away from the capital. Suddenly, news from places like Mwanza hundreds of miles in the interior, began to occupy almost as much space as news from Dar-es-Salaam.

In 1964, Tanzania had formed a federation with the turbulent island of Zanzibar just off the coast, but it was a very tenuous union. It was the *Standard* which broke a story that went all round the world, the story that the rulers of the island had changed the marriage laws so that children could be married without parental consent. At the time nobody took very much notice of this. In fact, Frene Ginwala thought it was a progressive step and welcomed it as such. But the truth was not long in coming. An announcement from Zanzibar said that 'if society demanded a marriage' it must take place. Frene's liberated ears prickled when she heard this. She wrote an editorial in the *Standard* saying that though the first measure was a good socialist step, the second announcement was reactionary.

Stories began to filter over from Zanzibar to the mainland that forced marriages of young Persian girls were taking place. Not only had the parents of the girls opposed the marriages, generally to very much older members of the Zanzibar Revolutionary Council, but the young girls themselves had been virtually dragged screaming from their homes. The *Standard* printed the stories, and in spite of denials from Zanzibar which created enormous political difficulties for Nyerere, the newspaper substantiated the stories with chapter and verse. It says a great deal for the moral character of Nyerere that he allowed this newspaper campaign full play. Frene Ginwala had many critics even on the mainland over these stories. These took the line that she was taking up the cause because she was an Asian woman, but the great majority of decent Tanzanians, including many of those she had brushed with in print, respected her for the stand she took.

Then, in the intrigue which began to develop, the *Standard* became the victim of a set-up. A story, well authenticated, it appeared, was carried about a young Persian girl who had been taken from her home as a bride-to-be for a member of Zanzibar's Revolutionary Council. But, said the story, the girl had escaped and made her way secretly to the mainland. The story was false. It had been planted to discredit the *Standard*. Frene Ginwala immediately printed a retraction, but the incident had left a nasty mark and Frene knew that it had brought her day of departure that much closer.

There is a familiar similarity between this planted story and the report in the *Nation* of the 'finding' of James Kariuki, the missing Kenyan MP. Both editors received the stories from 'reliable' sources. Both the Kenya Government and the Tanzania Government were in a tight corner because of the truth behind the stories.

Yet both stories appeared in newspapers edited—though ideologically poles apart—by single-minded, strong characters who rarely temporised with any politicians except the presidents of their countries.

The sands were running out for Frene Ginwala. There was to be one more spin of the hour-glass before it finally emptied.

There was growing discontent within the office, not only from the reporters and subs as they battled to digest the political reorientation required of them, but also between Frene Ginwala and her principal White aide, Richard Gott. Their political differences grew sharper. Finally Frene went to Nyerere and said she could no longer work with Gott. Nyerere, weighed heavy with innumerable problems of state and trying desperately to pull one of the Continent's most poverty-stricken nations up by its own bootlaces, had little time for office politicking and personality clashes. Right, he said, Gott would go, but so would some of the others she had brought in. Two other ex-patriates had already resigned.

In May 1971 there was a coup—or what appeared to be a coup—in the Sudan. President Numeiri was overthrown, but the revolutionaries led by Mohammed Mahgroub, a Communist, made the fatal error of not killing him, a curious oversight in a land so soiled with blood. The news agencies began feeding in the story of the coup to the *Standard*, and though the reports of the four agencies varied in perspective, it seemed clear at first that the coup had succeeded.

It had not. Forty-eight hours later Numeiri had been returned to power by loyalist troops. The *Standard* had taken no side editorially at this stage but then, following Numeiri's restoration to power, reports began coming out of the Sudan of secret military trials followed by executions. One of the leaders of the revolutionaries, Joseph Garang, had been a member of the Communist Party with which Numeiri had been constantly at logger-heads.

When news of Garang's execution came over the *Standard's* teleprinters, it set Frene Ginwala's blood bubbling. Here was the classic revolutionary scene; coup, counter coup, executions, secret trials. And a good Red dead. The *Standard* came out with a strident editorial. It said, in effect, that if you were going to stage a coup, then it was better to kill off the head of state than to leave him alive. Frene was later to say that this was 'perhaps not the best way to have started'. It was one thing, she believed, for the leaders of the attempted coup to be executed; but the fact Numeiri had seized the opportunity to carry out a wholesale purge of the Communist Party was something else.

In fact, although she had not written the editorial, she had always accepted responsibility for it. Tony Hall says it was written by Richard Gott.

The editorial itself was likely to cause trouble; however the situation was made worse. Early on the morning of publication, Radio Tanzania, in a broadcast called 'From the Editorials', quoted some of the material which, though not quite out of context, was put forward in a style which was not a true reflection of the leader as a whole. The crunch, though, unknown to Frene, was that Numeiri was shortly to pay a state visit to Tanzania. She was sacked that evening by the man who had appointed her just eighteen months earlier. She left the paper, but not yet the country. The full circle was about to be joined.

A few streets away from the *Standard* building, the offices of the South African National Congress in exile welcomed her back. The majority opinion in the newsrooms of the *Standard* and the *Sunday News* was of satisfaction. But now, years later, she is remembered with a mixture of irritation and affection. The *Standard,* now merged with the *Nationalist* as the *Daily News,* is a very different newspaper from the one she produced. It is certainly duller. Whatever one's views about her political ideology, while Frene Ginwala was running the *Standard,* it was that rare thing in Black Africa—exciting, controversial, argued about, sought after.

The new editor of the *Standard* was a Black Tanzanian, Sammy Mdee, and the whole operation became visibly stabler and calmer, if less exciting and controversial. Until the TANU party paper, the *Nationalist,* merged with the *Standard* to become the *Daily News* on 26 April 1972, the *Nationalist* became the much more radical voice, while the new editor of the *Standard* and his staff were recovering from the hurly-burly of Frene Ginwala's reign.

There was healthy competition between the two papers, even though the fountain-head of both was the same. On one occasion the news editor of the *Nationalist* wrote a letter to the *Standard* fiercely attacking another correspondent for belittling Marx, and saying that Communism was irrelevant to TANU's socialism. Communism did lie at the end of TANU's socialist path, insisted the *Nationalist's* news editor.

Time will tell whether this happens in Tanzania, but as in so many other African socialist states, Marx must be turning in his grave at the policies propounded in his name.

There are very few Zanzibari journalists and the best of them, Ali Hafidh, has been under sentence of death by firing squad since May 1974. Hafidh has been a journalist since before leaving school. As a student he used to spend his holidays and evenings helping out on the daily bi-lingual *Adal Insaf*. When he left school he became a sub-editor and later joined the Zanzibar News Service, where he rose to become assistant director. He spent three years at Long Island University in the United States, and further training included a course at the Thomson Foundation Editorial Centre in Britain.

He was working for the government information services on the mainland in April 1972 when Zanzibar's strong man, Abeid Karume, who was vice-president of the Union under Nyerere, was assassinated in an attempted coup. Mass arrests followed the coup attempt, both on the island and on the mainland. Hafidh was lying down in his room after lunch when a five-man contingent of secret police burst in, the leader wielding a Chinese-made sub-machine gun.

It was the beginning of 105 weeks in Ukonga maximum security prison nine miles from Dar-es-Salaam, crammed full with prisoners, all alleged coup-plotters. Each cell measured nine feet by nine feet, each contained three prisoners. Nyerere refused to hand them over to the authorities in Zanzibar, and the deadlock stretched the never very strong union between the island and the mainland to the limit.

Hafidh was released on 1 May 1974 as suddenly as he had been arrested. Ten days later he was tried in his absence by a three-judge court in Zanzibar and sentenced to death by firing squad. Hafidh found his way to Kenya, and two years later picked up the threads of his career when the *Standard* in Nairobi gave him a job as a sub-editor.

7 Central Africa

Even though Britain's three former possessions in East Africa, Kenya, Uganda and Tanzania, have as independent states gone their very different ways, they are still to a large extent one entity, 'East Africa'. This oneness will probably disappear if the East African Community which controls many of the three nations' public services breaks up.

If and when that day comes, Tanzania may forge political links with the Central African state of Zambia. A whole variety of reasons will be responsible for such a Federation. Tanzania's leader, Julius Nyerere, is a close personal friend of Zambia's Kenneth Kaunda. They are both relatively young men, and though there are differences in their political philosophies, there is great common cause between them. If such a union does come about, then the principal hand in the architecture will have been Chinese, for the railway line which they constructed with remarkable speed from the Indian Ocean coast into the very interior of Africa to link the two states is swiftly becoming both an emotional and an economic bond.

One can see a considerable parallel between the newspapers of the two territories, and the sort of press pattern which may emerge. In Tanzania the colonial, White *Standard* was first sold to Black Africa's only major White entrepreneur, Lonhro's 'Tiny' Rowlands, and in turn Rowlands' operation in Tanzania was taken over by the State. Tanzania's other daily, until it was merged with the Government paper, was owned by the ruling political party.

In Zambia the old colonial owners of the press, the South African Argus Company, retreated hastily in the face of Black nationalism. The operation they left behind was in turn acquired by Lonrho. Kenneth Kaunda has not yet found it necessary to totally nationalise their newspaper, *The Times of Zambia,* but to all intents and purposes it is a Government paper projecting the Government's voice with its editor appointed by Kaunda.

As in Tanzania, until the merger, the Zambian Government *Times* is published in tandem with the ruling Party's *Daily Mail.*

As the eastern side of the continent had a paucity of African newspaper publishers compared with West Africa, so did Central Africa, in turn, have an almost negligible African press.

Zambia, as the pre-independence colony of Northern Rhodesia, was a curious appendage of its White Southern neighbour, Southern Rhodesia. It was the last outpost of Cecil Rhodes' nineteenth century empire. There were one or two missionary news-sheets in Northern Rhodesia, but nothing serious appeared until the *Livingstone Mail* was founded in 1906. But this was in every sense a White man's paper, owned by a White man, Leopold Moore, and designed to be read by the White men who were beginning to filter up from South Africa and Southern Rhodesia. An early editorial in the *Mail* declared: 'We shall consistently oppose the employment of natives where they compete with . . . . White men. It is better to pay a White man three times as much as a native than to run the risk of evolving a native—as contrasted with a White man's—state'.

Moore went on to become one of the leading—and in European eyes—most respected figures in the country, eventually knighted by the British Government for his services to the territory.

It was not until the 1939–45 war that the *Mail* had any competition, and this was to be more than five hundred miles away when a young Roy Welensky, who had recently climbed down from the locomotive footplate to enter political life, launched the twice-weekly *Northern News* at Ndola on the edge of the Copperbelt.

Although it was Welensky's partner who was the editor, the *Northern News* was Welensky's mouthpiece from first to last. It was not taken seriously by the British colonial administration, and African nationalism was at such an early stage that it did not even offend the 'natives'. But it did offend a remarkable Scotsman, Alexander Scott. Scott had been a doctor in Livingstone, and though not particularly liberal in the sense the word came to be used a decade later when political tempo increased in Northern Rhodesia, he was a great humanitarian. He knew nothing about newspapers but to counter Welensky's *Northern News,* he founded in 1948 the weekly *Central African Post* in Lusaka. The early issues of the *Post* were very amateurish affairs, both technically and editorially. There was no sub-editing at all. Scott would scribble out his news and views, generally so entwined as to make it impossible to separate the one from the other, and hand them to the linotype operator who would set them as a grey mass of type, headlined in the same size as the stories themselves. Scott had friends in various parts of Northern Rhodesia, an assorted bunch of settlers and colonial civil servants, and these became his district correspondents. When their envelopes began to appear on his desk, he would peer at the postmarks and then take the letters unopened to the linotype operator with the instruction 'These are the Fort Jameson notes' or 'This is old Mrs Brown's stuff from Abercorn'.

Often the correspondents' copy included all sorts of little personal details which had been meant for Scott's own edification. Many of them ended up in print.

The *Central African Post* was a remarkable hotch-potch, but though turgid and dull to look at, it had a personality which was positively effervescent. Issue after issue hammered away at Welensky, who was now the leader of the settler group in the colonial Legislative Council. Welensky's *Northern News* prospered in a modest way on the Copperbelt and in 1951 the Argus empire, centred in Johannesburg, reached out and acquired it. But it continued very largely to serve Welensky's political purposes. Scott employed a young Englishman from Britain and some of the rougher, amateurish edges were knocked off the *Post*. It began to have headlines that fitted and made sense, and the little personal notes from Mrs Brown or the other district correspondents were separated from the news.

The *Post* began to do something unheard of in 'White' newspapers in any part of tropical Africa: report African news, and even more revolutionary, publish letters from Africans. As word spread that African letters were being printed, a regular flood began to arrive, from Africans all over the country and further afield, many of them written on any pieces of paper available, with toilet paper the most common.

An early correspondent of those days was someone who signed himself 'H. K. Banda'. His letters were postmarked from London. Years later the same man was to appear, having served his political apprenticeship with Kwame Nkrumah on the Gold Coast, as the middle-aged fire-brand who became Malawi's first President.

From Kenya a letter came one day from an African who merely signed himself 'Kimathi'. He was to be hanged by the British as the now legendary Field-Marshal Dedan Kimathi, one of the leaders of the Mau Mau rising.

When a young crop of African politicians just beginning to emerge, including a short-trousered, bare-footed young man named Kenneth Kaunda, realised they could get into print, the *Post* found itself in confrontation not only with White settlers but often with the colonial government. The *Post's* English editor was sent for by the colonial government's Chief Secretary and asked 'Whose side are you on?'

The Argus turned the *Northern News* into a daily in 1953, and the *Post* became a twice and then thrice-weekly as it moved as fast as it was able towards daily publication.

Though it had not a fraction of the resources of the *Northern News,* the *Post* constantly beat the Ndola daily to all the big political news that was beginning to brew. More and more the fledgling African nationalists, soon to take wing, looked to the *Post* to give a fair show to their views and, increasingly, editorial support in its leader column. Scott, who had gone into politics as the only independent member of Parliament of the Central African Federation which was supposed to create Britain's eighth dominion out of Northern Rhodesia, Southern Rhodesia and Nyasaland, was striving to find the backing to turn the *Post* into a daily. Britain's big provincial Westminster Press Group came near to acquiring an interest but finally Scott went into partnership with a Salisbury company, Kachaloloa, which was owned by Bernard Paver. Kachalola acquired the majority shares of the *Post*. Scott was to say many times afterwards that he rued the day he met Paver.

Paver had been the prime mover in the creation of the South African Bantu Press in 1931 which, notwithstanding its name, was White-owned, White-managed and very much concerned with the *status quo* in Southern Africa. The original project envisaged a chain of newspapers for Africans, managed from the centre, whose policy would be to 'prevent irresponsible exploitation and benefit individual papers by supplying an organisation capable of maintaining a guiding policy in both political and commercial development'. The Argus Company, although with a minority shareholding, was to be deferred to in matters of editorial policy and they had a seat on the board. Among other shareholders in the 1950s was the mighty Anglo-American Corporation, bedrock of the Oppenheimer gold mining empire.

Shortly after the Second World War, Bantu Press had a chain of thirteen weeklies from the Cape to Salisbury. Most of them were in African vernacular languages, but some of the larger ones were published in English. In the post-war years it established papers in all three of Britain's High Comission Territories, Basutoland (Lesotho), Swaziland and Bechuanaland (Botswana).

When Paver sold control of the *Central African Post* to the Argus Group in 1957, Scott was very nearly a broken man. His staff, Black and White, had worked seven days a week for years in an effort to establish the *Post* to the position it now held as the pre-eminent liberal voice in Central Africa—and now it had been sold over their heads. But by 1958 Scott was back in business with most of his old staff on a new paper, the *African Times*. Although a brave attempt to produce a voice supporting the radical African nationalists as they struggled to break the Central African Federation and obtain independence, the *Times* was several years before its time and hopelessly under-capitalised. It finally died when the print-works which produced it had pressure put on it by its biggest customers, behind whom were the White leaders of the Federal Government in Salisbury.

Still Scott was not beaten, and in February 1960 he formed an alliance with David Astor, editor of Britain's prestigious Sunday *Observer*. The modest off-set presses which had been bought to produce the *African Times* began turning out the weekly *African Mail*. This was a turbulent period in the political development of Northern Rhodesia. The Federation was splitting at the seams and a bewildered British Government in Whitehall acted with ineptitude, at first trying to prop up Welensky's Government in Salisbury. Welensky's reaction to African nationalism was in the long tradition of British colonial rule; lock up the political agitators and trust that support for them from the masses will wither away. It had never worked in any part of Britain's empire, and it never looked for a minute that it would be successful in Central Africa. Kenneth Kaunda was imprisoned in Salisbury, and many other prominent Northern Rhodesian African nationalists were placed in restriction in the bush. When Kaunda was released from Salisbury prison he, too, was 'rusticated' (the quaint term invented for the exercise), hundreds of miles away from any centre. He nearly died. All these tactics were later to be repeated by Welensky's successor three of four times removed, Ian Smith, as the White leader of the settlers in Southern Rhodesia.

In this atmosphere and with David Astor's money, Scott started the *African Mail*. The subsequent story of the man he chose to edit it, Richard Hall, shows the hopelessness of even the best intentioned White man of trying to edit an African newspaper in an African state. The *Mail* appeared shortly after the African nationalist movement had split down the middle; one faction was led by Kenneth Kaunda, who was eventually released from rustication, and the other by the father-figure of African Nationalism in Northern Rhodesia, Harry Nkumbula. The *Mail*—which after two years changed its name to the *Central African Mail* in an effort to spread its circulation over the border into Southern Rhodesia—tried to steer an independent line between the two. This was difficult enough, but when the Federation was abandoned on the last day of 1963 Britain threw in the towel and the Europeans of Northern Rhodesia, their nerve-ends tingling as the Africans scented power, caused Hall as much trouble as the warring African factions.

Zambia's great mineral wealth on the Copperbelt had for thirty years attracted that rare thing in tropical Africa, a White artisan class. Most of the recruits for the mines came from South Africa, though after the War and during the fifties large numbers were also attracted from Britain. Many of these White miners were doing jobs which Africans could easily have done. Almost all of them were hard right-wingers and race relations were on a knife-edge throughout the Copperbelt.

There were numerous incidents which created situations for the *Mail* which were not merely difficult but often highly dangerous. On one occasion a White copper miner's wife, Mrs. Beryl Burton, was killed when her car was stopped and set alight

by young hoodlums of the African United National Independence
Party (UNIP). This was a great trauma and there were fears of
a White back-lash. When the UNIP youths were caught, tried
and hanged, a prominent senior UNIP leader, Sokota Wina,
who later became a cabinet minister, said that the hanged youths
were martyrs to African nationalism.

The *Mail* came out with a front page editorial headline:
'Don't Talk Such Rubbish Mr. W'. Sokota Wina never forgave
Hall for this. Hall felt that it was invidious for a White man to
be the editor of a paper which was propagating African
nationalist views, so he appointed as editor one of the few
Africans in the country with any real experience of journalism,
Titus Mukupo. The editorial staff was entirely Black except for
Hall's wife, Barbara, who ran a highly successful correspondence
column for African women called 'Tell me Josephine'. This gave
tropical Africa its first taste of a form of journalism found in the
tabloids and women's magazines of the West.

The Whites, whose own standards of morals in the high-
salaried and servanted colonies were hardly of a standard to be
followed, were indignant that Africans should be allowed to air
their personal problems in print. Northern Rhodesia's European
politicians, mostly of a particularly low calibre, were desperately
trying to cling on as Whitehall made it abundantly clear that
their days were numbered. They became exceedingly hostile to
the *Mail*. They saw it as fanning of nationalism, which is exactly
what its policy was. Hall's children had notes put in their satchels
at school saying things like 'Your father's a Kaffir boetie'
(Afrikaans for 'lover').

The colonial civil servants were more sympathetic to the *Mail*.
They had nothing to lose and, in fact, a considerable amount
to gain by Black Government. The younger ones would be
transferred to other colonies, the older ones pensioned off on
generous terms, and all given substantial 'golden handshakes'.

In 1961 Roy Welensky, who was presiding over the creaking
Central African Federation, sued Hall for libel. Britain had
created a new constitution for Northern Rhodesia. When
Welensky studied it, he realised that UNIP had a chance of
obtaining a majority in the coming elections. This was anathema
to Welensky. He put tremendous pressure on the Colonial Office
in London to have things altered just enough to swing things
against this possibility. Northern Rhodesia's Governor, Sir
Evelyn Hone, came back from London very unhappy with the

change. Kenneth Kaunda immediately grasped the significance of what Whitehall had done. It was in character with all that had gone before and everything that was to come afterwards in British Central Africa—broken promises. Kaunda sat in his little mud-house in the African location on the outskirts of Lusaka which is today a national shrine and, shaking his head in bewilderment, told Hall: 'I can't understand why Ian has done this'. 'Ian' was Ian McLeod—the British Colonial Secretary.

The *Mail* ran a double page-spread on the constitution and headlined it: A Constitution like a Pit Latrine—the Deeper you Dig into it the More it Stinks.

The hard-core of UNIP was enraged at the changes London had made. It wanted a physical confrontation to bring things to a head. Kaunda was in a dilemma. He was a Christian and dedicated to a peaceful transfer of power. He could not sanction violence, but equally he could not speak against it.

There was a major insurrection by Africans in the sparsely populated Northern province bordering on Tanganyika. Welensky sent the Federal Army in and a state of emergency was declared.

Hall wrote another front page leader. It said: 'For the bloodshed and destruction, Welensky is guilty. For the death and misery, Welensky is guilty.'

Underneath, in large type, Hall listed half a dozen searing denunciations of the Federal Prime Minister. As the one-eyed Congolese compositor in the *Mail's* print-shop set up the headline, he shook his head morosely at Hall and said 'Ah, Bwana, we are all going to prison'. Hall wasn't sure he might not be right.

Next day the writ for defamation came in from Salisbury. This was a civil action, but later Hall was to learn that the Federal Government were trying to get the Northern Rhodesia Government to bring a charge of criminal libel which carried imprisonment. Hall knew well when he wrote the *Mail's* front page story that he was putting both himself and the paper in a dangerous position, but, increasingly angry as Welensky's Federal troops moved into the territory, he felt he had to hit out.

Welensky was not the only person incensed by the story. The Whites of the territory, especially the copper-miners, were up in arms. Hall contacted David Astor in London and told him he had better get somebody out quickly to take over the *Mail* in case he was locked up.

In fact, the Northern Rhodesia Government had no wish to bring an action for criminal libel. The authorities realised this would only heighten the drama, with reaction in London and probably questions in the House of Commons. Also the colonial civil servants of the North were by this time thoroughly disenchanted with Welensky and his Federal Government in Salisbury.

UNIP said they would lay a line of pennies from Lake Tanganyika to Victoria Falls (more than a thousand miles) to pay off Welensky if he won his libel action against the *Mail*. The Archbishop of Central Africa agreed to give evidence on Hall's behalf, and also his Catholic counterpart. They were both willing to be seen as freedom fighters in such a respectable battle-ground as a court of law. But eventually the case fell away.

This incident gave the *Mail* tremendous prestige among Africans, but the hard core of UNIP was still not happy with the paper. They wanted all or nothing.

At the Northern Rhodesia general election of 1962, the two rival factions of African nationalists formed a temporary alliance to keep Welensky's Federal Party out. They gave the *Mail's* commercial printing side all their election manifestos to produce. But they never paid the bill.

The *Mail* was still a weekly but Hall had it very much in mind to go daily as soon as possible. Production problems were enormous. The offset machines which printed the paper were little better than glorified office equipment models, and as circulation rose from 10,000 to 35,000, with twenty-four tabloid pages, they were run pretty well seven days and seven nights a week. Collating was done by hand, with dozens of little boys all over the floor putting the pages together and then folding them up.

Northern Rhodesia became independent as the Republic of Zambia in October 1964 after the Central African Federation had fallen apart. Financially the *Mail* was kept going by monthly injections from David Astor in London who had a family trust aptly named Cushion Trust.

By now the standing of the *Mail* was very high. Advertising was booming as the wind of change over Zambia swept in a new and confident era.

Then something happened in London which was to change everything. This was the middle sixties when London was billed as 'swinging'. Astor, who curled his lip when Roy Thomson had launched a give-away colour magazine in London's *Sunday Times*, now realised he had been wrong and the quicker he produced one too, the better. But he knew it would be a costly operation, and his accountants told him to trim his sails. He decided to get out of Zambia.

He felt, justifiably, that he had contributed something very substantial towards the African cause and that now was as good a time as any to withdraw. His investment up to then had been something like £100,000 over five years. Astor's decision to withdraw was a body-blow to Hall. He believed that the *Mail* was just on the verge of getting into the black, and that Astor could expect not merely to get his capital back but also a substantial interest.

Hall flew to London in January 1965 to urge Astor to retain his interest. It was the time of Winston Churchill's funeral, and all the Commonwealth leaders were there. The same hotel, the Dorchester in Park Lane, housed Roy Welensky, Ian Smith, whose star had not yet risen to the unilateral heights which were soon to put him on the front pages of the world's press, and Kenneth Kaunda, now President of Zambia.

Zambia's independence had created a highly sensitive situation for two unrelated companies in Zambia. One was the *Argus* group, with its links going all the way back to Johannesburg, and the other was owned by a South African of German extraction named Hans Heinrich, who had made a fortune out of brewing beer for the Copperbelt's African miners. African beer is made from maize and has a consistency like porridge. It is almost a meal and the name of it in Zambia is *chibuku*. Heinrich had made so much money out of his brewery that he had branched out into several other ventures.

Titus Mukupo had quarrelled with Hall during the 1962 elections and left the *Mail*. He persuaded Heinrich that he needed a newspaper to keep in with the new Black establishment. Heinrich built a newspaper plant at Kitwe in the middle of the Copperbelt, big enough to run a fair-sized daily newspaper in

Britain or the United States. The rotary machine he bought to produce it came from such an improbable source as *Die Transvaler*, the Afrikaans nationalist organ in Johannesburg. Heinrich started a Sunday called the *Zambia News* and this was quite successful. The Argus Company, which still had the *Northern News*, did not mind this competition too much. By then they were looking over their shoulders and preparing for the trek back South to the sanctuary of White Africa. A few years earlier they would have pulled out all the stops to have killed such competition.

The *Zambia News* had a mixed staff of White free-booters from Britain, South Africa, Rhodesia and even Australia, with a sprinkling of Blacks.

But Heinrich soon realised that the economics of newspaper production did not allow for a press working just an hour or two on Saturday afternoons while standing idle the rest of the week. So he started the daily *Zambia Times*.

He was very soon totally out of his depth, and even the Copperbelt's well-paid African miners could not drink his *chibuku* fast enough to subsidise the new daily. Heinrich panicked and looked around for a way out and the road back to South Africa. Providentially there then appeared on the scene the redoubtable 'Tiny' Rowlands of Lonrho. He sniffed Heinrich's *chibuku*, knew he was on to a winner, and was prepared to take Heinrich's losers to get it. He brought everything Heinrich owned.

At this stage in his career, Rowlands was not interested in newspapers, which he knew were rarely money-makers anywhere and never in Black Africa. But as they were part of the Heinrich package, which also included hotels, he took over the Sunday *News* and the daily *Times*. Rowlands was still pushing north, as Cecil Rhodes had done a century before, except that Rhodes had run out of steam and Rowlands had no intention of doing anything of the kind.

Rowlands' first inclination after buying Heinrich out was to close the daily paper down, but when he added up the figures he realised he would be in the same position as Heinrich had been, with a press in use for only a short period on Saturday afternoons in an expensive building and doing nothing the rest of the week.

He approached Hall and asked him if the *Mail* was for sale. He wanted Hall to put together a publishing package providing the experience and expertise that would be required. Hall explored the project, but it was clear that it would not be viable to run a weekly in Lusaka and another weekly in Kitwe 200 miles away. Hall was also determined that Astor should get his £100,000 back. Then the new Zambia Government approached Hall about buying the *Mail,* and so Rowlands turned his attention to the still surviving and still profitable *Northern News* in Ndola, forty miles from his own newspaper plant in Kitwe.

It made more sense to bring together his Sunday paper and the viable, long-established *Northern News*. The Argus were delighted to get out and hurry back across the Zambesi. Rowlands closed the *Zambia Times* in Kitwe and re-named the *Northern News* the *Times of Zambia*.

Meanwhile, the Government had agreed to buy the *Mail* from Astor, who had told them that all he was interested in was an assurance that he would get back the £100,000 he had put in. This was really an insignificant amount for the enormous prestige which the *Mail* had won over five years. The *Mail* was also just on the verge of becoming viable. The Government appointed an auditor to go through the *Mail's* books, and he came up with a figure of something less than half of what had been agreed between them and Astor. No account was taken of good-will which was, of course, enormous. Hall was stunned at the Government's offer of £50,000 to Astor. He wrote to Kaunda saying that for years everyone connected with the paper had been breaking their backs, that the *Mail* had consistently supported African nationalism, and that Astor had continued to pour money into the venture when many of his advisers had felt it was unwise. Now, said Hall to the President, the Government's promise on the price was to be broken.

Kaunda was sympathetic but nothing was done. It was clear there were people in the new Black Cabinet who had not liked the fact that during the pre-independence period the *Mail* had not been in their pockets.

Hall urged Astor to refuse the offer, but by now the *Observer's* colour magazine had started and Astor, disenchanted with Africa, just wanted to get out. Hall bitterly denounced the colour magazine as being 'something for the trendies of Hampstead'. It made him sick that this latest toy for 'swinging Britain' was the governing factor in a drama going on in Central Africa. But there was even greater irony to come, for four years later Hall was to find himself seated in the editor's chair of that colour magazine planning what to serve up on Sunday mornings to 'the trendies of Hampstead'.

He says of this twist of fate: 'It was as though the system had beaten me twice over'.

When the Zambian Government bought the *Mail,* Hall prepared to leave. He had been offered a staff job by the London *Guardian* as their Africa man based in Nairobi. Then Rowlands offered him the overall managing editorship of his new publishing package. Hall moved to Ndola and did a major re-design of the paper. The editorial staff was still predominantly White. There were just two Black reporters. Rowlands gave Hall no brief, no political or economic policy to follow. All he wanted of the papers was that they should pay. UNIP was especially suspicious of all this activity. Here was a latter-day Cecil Rhodes from White Africa buying up almost everything in sight and installing as editor of the newly-independent state's only daily newspaper a White man who had crossed swords with many African politicians who were now in power.

On his first day, Hall told the staff he proposed to embark on a programme that would make the editorial and print-shop 80 per cent Black within ten years. Everyone thought this was tremendously daring, and some of the old White hands winked at each other. Even Hall, as close as he was to events and totally in sympathy with the idea of Africanisation, had not yet learned, as no Whites ever learned in any African state during the early years of independence, that when making estimates of change you had to think of a number, half it and then half it again. And you were still likely to be wrong.

In fact, the *Times* and the Sunday *News* were 90 per cent Black within five years and with a Black editor-in-chief in three.

There was a good spirit on the paper, with some genuine White liberals and all the other Europeans trying hard to accommodate to the new ways. But, as Hall says, they frequently got the tone of things wrong when they wrote about Africans. Paternalism, which was exactly what Hall did not want, often came through. Stories would be written about 'the African' as though they were a separate species. It was never 'us'.

One by one many of the Whites left, treading that well-worn path to the White South. This at least hastened Hall's Africanisation programme, but often the quality of the replacements were dubious. They were not so much journalists as people who had been disappointed in politics or who had not fitted into the picture when the spoils of independence had been handed out to UNIP Party faithfuls. The style of the paper began to change. It was considerably less professional but much more African.

What new White staff Hall did recruit, he brought out from Britain. He made it clear that they were all on short-term contract and must expect to go as soon as Africans were ready to take over. He was very careful to choose a breed of Englishmen who understood that the Union Jack no longer flew in Zambia.

It is interesting to reflect what would happen in Britain, the United States or similar democracies if a journalist were to be questioned at a job interview about his political beliefs and particularly his views on Blacks.

But Hall had to do it. Gradually, and then increasingly, this paid off. The paper began to win the same sort of respect as the old *Central African Mail* had done. Rowlands never interfered, seldom ever came near the paper. Hall bent over backwards to demonstrate that the *Times* and the *News* were not White capitalist playthings.

The sanctions which the United Nations with Britain's urging had applied to rebel Rhodesia meant that land-locked Zambia was suddenly denied three-quarters of its access to every sort of commodity. Fuel was the most serious shortage and a seven hundred mile pipeline was to be built carrying oil from Dar-es-Salaam to Zambia. The contract for the job was worth £17 million. Lonrho made a bid for the contract, but the *Mail* supported a rival bid by an Italian group. When a letter to the editor came in accusing the *Mail* of being 'a capitalist, imperialist, fascist and reactionary' agent for Lonrho, Hall printed it in a box saying the *Times* neither knew nor cared about the opinion of Lonrho on any subject.

During colonial times, the Copperbelt had been the centre of power since it was here that the mining industry was based. Mining managers ruled like kings over their domains. Lusaka was the sleepy little administrative centre, largely serving the colonial civil servants, who ran the territory sucking briar pipes and wearing white topees. But with independence and Black Government in Lusaka, things quickly changed. Now, although the Copperbelt was still the industrial and money-making centre, with Kaunda and his Black Government in Lusaka cracking the whip, the capital became the fulcrum upon which everything else hinged.

Thus Hall, two hundred miles away in Ndola, was to a great extent out of touch with what was going on in the capital. He spent half of his time on lengthy telephone calls trying to assess the political temperature in Lusaka, and very often driving or flying back and forth to see ministers and senior civil servants.

Sanctions meant that newsprint supplies, along with almost everything else, had to come in through Portuguese Angola on a long rail journey clogged with a mass of traffic it was never equipped to handle. On one occasion, the *Times* ran out of newsprint but in the nick of time found some rolls of green paper, very old and brittle from the tropical heat. It made for a very novel-looking newspaper, and when ordinary supplies were available again, many readers wrote in saying they wanted 'a green paper'.

Hall, too, liked the effect and fancied working on a 'coloured' newspaper. Today he works on London's *Financial Times*, which is published on orange-coloured newsprint.

Slowly Hall began the most difficult task in any African newspaper inherited from European ownership: Africanisation of the sub-editor's desk. There was great competition all over the Copperbelt for any African able to sub. The rich mining companies had a whole range of house publications, and with the new vogue of the times, were anxious to be seen to be using Africans. So many of Hall's subs were lured to the richer and less troublesome pastures of the mines.

The telex room of the *Times* was Africanised, but Hall ran into a very African problem in that department. There was jealousy among the operators about the post of the telex room manager. When an African was appointed to this job the other operators said they would put witchcraft on him. Hall put up a notice on the wall which read: 'Witchcraft must cease in this office. By order'. One particular operator was doing most of the bewitching, putting obscure but highly emotive objects under the manager's seat. Hall called in the offender, told him directly that he would never get the manager's job, and asked him to desist. A few days later when Hall went to see his doctor to get some sleeping tablets, the doctor, a European, said that one of Hall's staff had just been in with his family who were very concerned about him. Hall asked who the man was and what was wrong with him. The doctor said it was the telex-room manager. He was not sure what was wrong, but, he said, 'It's almost as though he's bewitched'.

Bewitched or not, the unfortunate telex room manager died. The bewitcher was despatched by Hall to the Livingstone office five hundred miles away and warned not to do it again.

The rich tabestry of Africa, as they say, touched the paper in other ways. All the linotype operators were Black and all were Rhodesians, where there had been a long tradition of Black printers. One day one of the operators failed to turn up for work, and another man told Hall he had been taken 'by the army'. Hall was dumbfounded, and asked 'For God's sake, what army?' In the man's clock-in slot, he found a note. He had been 'taken away to train for the Zimbabwe army'. This was very much an unofficial body of guerillas operating at that time as a hole-and-corner outfit in Zambia. The professional guerilla army which was to range war against Rhodesia several years later had not yet been formed.

Hall was very much in sympathy with the liberation of Rhodesia, but he felt that this was hardly the way to go about things. He went to the Government's Resident Commissioner on the Copperbelt and asked angrily. 'Who is running the country, you or them?' He demanded to have his linotype operator back. After three weeks of negotiation, the missing man emerged from the bush, looking somewhat bewildered, and sat down at his machine to recommence setting. Hall asked him what it had been like in 'the army'. The operator, furtive eyes casting nervously round the print shop, whispered hoarsely 'Terrible, bwana'.

Insignificant and amusing though this incident was in itself, Hall believes it demonstrates the great void between Black and White in Africa. 'This is where the White liberal is found out' he says. 'I've never been any more than that—that and a White socialist. But after independence what these countries needed were either White mercenaries or people so dedicated to the African cause that they would follow blindly, never questioning. The role of the White liberal falls away with independence.'

Hall believes that in newspaper terms, this means that freedom of the press is something superfluous in Africa. 'Any newspaperman reared in the ordinary journalistic school sees the role of the press as helping to keep authority on its toes', he says. More and more it became obvious that this was something not acceptable in Zambia, as it has not been in any other Black state.

The pressures mounted, and the difficulties of running a newspaper along the lines that Hall believed in became greater daily. There was a spate of sabotage on the Copperbelt, almost certainly the work of Whites sympathetic to Rhodesia, which by this time was an illegal state. There was a big fire at an oil refinery in Kitwe at a time of acute oil shortage. It later turned out that the fire had been an accident; someone had left a tap on, the oil had leaked and ignited in the tropical heat when sparks from a dropped piece of iron struck it. But the local UNIP Party boss seized on this, and insisted it was sabotage. At a time of increasing unemployment, UNIP's Youth Wing, with time on their hands, began to stone cars and anything else within range. It was the Beryl Burton story all over again.

The car of an Afrikaner miner who was out driving with his wife was hit and the woman killed. Hall wrote another front page leader denouncing the stonings and accusing UNIP of stirring up emotion. White miners were needed, he said, and this sort of thing was not going to help them to stay.

The local police chief, a Pole, at a time when Africanisation of the higher ranks of the police force had not been completed, produced a report showing the oil fire to have been an accident. He was sacked and later left the country. It did not ease matters when Hall printed the police report in the *Times*.

It was now the middle of 1966. Hall had taken out Zambian citizenship. He felt it was difficult enough being a White man and editor of the national daily, but too much also to be a foreigner telling the country every morning how it should run its affairs.

Another link in the long and increasingly heavy chain that was eventually to drag Hall down was an editorial in which he attacked students in Lusaka who had demanded that beer and spirits be available in their canteen. The students, incensed, produced a huge banner which they paraded through the streets. It read: 'Richard Hall is a crypto-neo-colonialist.'

One of Hall's African photographers took a picture of it, and Hall used it as his Christmas card that year. It did not go down too well with African politicians who read it, but President Kaunda had it on the mantlepiece in the drawing-room of State House over the festive season.

The *Times* and the *News* blossomed and almost bloomed. They were both making money and this was all Rowlands asked for. Circulation of the daily went from 15,000 to 35,000 in two years and was later to double again.

In Lusaka, Hall's old paper, the *Mail* had a lot of money spent on it by the Government but inevitably it had lost its old sparkle and began to be recognised as the voice of authority, the very antithesis of what had made its reputation. It was now 1967, and the last chapter was about to be written for Hall in Africa. It was known as the 'rotten chicken episode' and has become part of modern folk-lore in Zambia, recounted by Europeans—when they are alone—as a high point of those early years after Black independence when anything could happen and often did.

There was an Italian butcher in Lusaka called Carlo Ottini. He was the capital's fashionable butcher, and most of the new Black establishment bought their meat from him. One such customer was Mrs Reuben Kamanga, wife of the Vice-President. One day in March 1967, she sent her servant to Ottini's to buy some meat. Ottini had in his cold store half a dozen turkeys left over from Christmas, now three months past. Apart from being very cold and thus slightly blue, they were perfectly good. When Ottini saw that the African was the Vice-President's servant, he produced one of the birds and said: 'Give the madam a turkey with my compliments.' He handed over a prize, if slightly blue bird. The servant took the turkey home and put it in the refrigerator. Mrs Kamanga knew nothing of this, But later in the day, when she opened the refrigerator, she saw the turkey, thought the servant had bought it, and took a dislike to the blue bird. She removed it, drove straight down to the butchers, and throwing it across the counter, told an aghast Ottini: 'I don't want your rotten chicken.'

At first Ottini was lost for words. His Latin temperament rose but he controlled himself sufficiently to restrict his rejoinder to: 'Madam, that is no chicken, that is a turkey.' The Vice-President's wife, to the delight of the other shoppers, replied loudly: 'Don't be so stupid.'

This was an interesting phrase to come from the lips of an African, in as much as they were almost certainly the most commonly used four words by Europeans to Blacks in colonial Africa. Mrs Kamanga had been a quick pupil. But it was too much for Ottini. He drew himself up and announced with a flamboyant Italian gesture: 'If you call me stupid then you are stupid too.'

He might just as well have gone home and packed for Italy there and then.

Mrs Kamanga stormed out of the shop. Her parting words hurled at Ottini left no doubt that the matter was far from over. The next day the Mayor of Lusaka, a man called Witson Banda (who had achieved some minor fame in the struggle against colonialism when he was accused of urinating on a White woman's car in the capital's main street), sent a Health Inspector along to the butchers. He closed it down.

Ottini went to a White lawyer who obtained an injunction from the High Court enabling the butchery to re-open. He posted the injunction on his window and renewed business. This was meat and drink for the local UNIP Youth Wing, and the next night one of Hall's African reporters saw a Youth League van going round the African township outside Lusaka with a loud hailer urging 'All out for a big demonstration'. The reporter went to investigate, and at the Youth League offices found three lorries loaded with bricks and other debris. He climbed aboard with the eager Youth Leaguers, and off they set to Ottini's butchery. There they began to heave the rocks, and for good measure had a go at an adjoining shop owned by Asians (who are always fair game when Youth Leaguers in any East or Central African state are demonstrating). The reporter phoned Ndola and Hall was called. Appalled, he flew at once to Lusaka, saw the damage for himself and verified the story. Another front page leader was due. In it he demanded to know who was running the country, the UNIP Youth League or the High Court judge who had granted the injunction. There was a national furore. Judges threatened to resign, but in the event none of them did. Lusaka's Mayor was prosecuted for contempt of court but the case fell away. The UNIP official, a man named Mumba, who had led the attack on Ottini's butchery, was sentenced to six months' imprisonment.

A week later Hall was in his office when the President's Press Secretary, Dunstan Kamana, telephoned him. Kaunda wanted to see Hall at once, and he was to come straight to Lusaka. Hall went immediately. In State House an embarrassed

Kaunda told him: 'I wanted to tell you, Dick, that I am letting Mumba out.' Kaunda said his Presidential powers allowed him to overrule the judges. There was little Hall could do. What he did say to the President was: 'I don't know where it's going to end.' Dunstan Kamana, who stood nearby during the interview, was to remember and recall those words a little later in his own career.

Hall returned to Ndola beaten and almost broken. There was one more front page leader to write. In it he quoted Julius Nyerere, greatly respected in Zambia and a close friend of Kaunda. The leading article recalled that Tanzania had suffered a mutiny, and that many of the officers who took part were given very lenient sentences in the face of a public and Party demand for very heavy ones. But Nyerere had said: 'One thing we must never do is to overrule the judges.'

Hall quoted this at the top of the leader which went on to attack Kaunda for letting Mumba out.

Now all the big guns at State House turned their fire on Hall and the *Times*. The attack was led by Mainza Chona, Minister of Home Affairs. He accused Hall of being part of a conspiracy based in London to destroy Zambia. For a decade or more after independence, it was always a safe bet for African politicians in former British colonies to talk about a London-based plot to destroy the nation. The same thing never happened in the Francophone states about Paris and therein lies an interesting field of study. The Zambia Government had a taped broadcast made attacking Hall in the most virulent terms. Every time Hall switched on his radio it seemed to be coming out. It continued four times a day for a month. It had a totally demoralising effect on Hall, his wife and his four sons and there were very real fears for their lives. A police guard was put on his house, but this would have been scant defence against a determined gang of UNIP Youth rowdies on the rampage.

Throughout all this, Rowlands supported Hall. Hall was not only concerned for his own and his family's safety but also for the survival of the paper. A friend in the Attorney-General's office warned him that the law officers of the Government were going through the small print of everything they could find with a view to banning the paper. Hall knew well that even if they were not able to come up with anything legal, it was a simple matter for the paper to be closed by Government or Presidential decree, and if that happened it would be useless to fight in the courts.

Hall knew it was vital to cool the situation down. He had already taken the leading articles off the front page of the *Times*, but as the attacks continued he told Rowlands he thought he should take a year's leave of absence. Rowlands nodded. He was probably torn between losing his editor, who had made the paper what it was and who was virtually irreplaceable, and the realisation that the whole existence of his publishing group was at stake. He merely said prophetically to Hall: 'You won't come back.' Hall was too worn out to do more than shrug. Rowlands wrote to Kaunda telling the President of Hall's suggestion. Kaunda replied agreeing.

Thus, living on pills, nerves shot to pieces, on the verge of a nervous breakdown, Hall boarded the London-bound plane at Ndola and left Zambia never to return.

He travelled to Britain on his Zambian passport at a time when tens of thousands of Asians in East Africa waited destitute and abandoned by Britain, which though it had given them British passports, would not admit them to the United Kingdom. Hall had no trouble passing through immigration at London airport. Hall was a White man, and in the New Commonwealth, though that was no longer a qualification in Britain's former colonies, it was the *open sesame* for admission to the shores of the motherland.

Two years later Hall applied for, and got his British citizenship back.

With Hall's departure from the *Times*, Zambia's Black hierarchy were determined that the next editor was not merely going to toe the line but be bound hand and foot to it. Lonrho was told that the next editor should be a Zambian who was acceptable to the authorities'. In plain language, this meant the editor was to be one of the President's men. Kaunda looked around to see who was available. He did not have to look far. In the next office to himself sat Dunstan Kamana, his Press Secretary whose job it had been to summon Hall for his last interview with Kaunda. Kamana was appointed as editor-in-chief, and everybody thought that was the end of the *Times* as anything other than a straight Government mouthpiece. The joke in the bars and cafes over Dunstan Kamana's appointment was that the next step would be to re-name the *Times* the Government Gazette.

But it did not work out like that at all—not, at least, for some time. To the astonishment of the whole nation and the dumb-founded anger of the Cabinet, Dunstan Kamana not merely picked up the reins Dick Hall had dropped, but he buckled on a pair of spurs which soon had the Kaunda establishment bucking vigorously.

It was not just his questioning of some aspects of Government policies that caused trouble, but the way he tried to enliven the pages of the *Times* with something more than turgid official communiques and reports of interminable speeches by politicians. He began publishing pictures of pretty girls wearing mini-skirts which had then reached Central Africa. These were attacked as 'un-Zambian', though as eight out of ten young African women in the urban centres of the country were sporting them this was rather a curious accusation. Crime stories, too, were attacked for 'not being in the public's interest'. With Zambia's Copperbelt representing the biggest industrial complex in Black Africa and producing all the problems of such a society, it was hardly possible to ignore crime as a source of news.

Almost immediately on moving into the editorial chair, Kamana began to take issue on a whole range of things dear to the Government's heart. What could State House do now? For years Kaunda's advisers had preached the gospel that only a Zambian—a Black Zambian—could edit the country's leading newspaper. Well, Kamana was clearly that. He was also a dedicated nationalist and a man with a proven record of Party service and loyalty. He had seemed an ideal choice. But he was also something else, something that the establishment had not considered a qualification for editorship; he was a newspaperman at heart. Not, it is true, a seasoned and experienced one, but none the less one with all the zest and belief of a good newspaperman. As a young schoolboy he had set his sights on becoming a reporter, and during the school holidays had gone looking for odd jobs at the old colonial *Central African Post*.

At the end of 1971, Kaunda was under pressure yet again from his inner Cabinet to get rid of the editor of the *Times*. With the continuing Rhodesian crisis on his door-step, and Zambia virtual-ly abandoned by Britain who said they could take no action against 'Kith and Kin' in Rhodesia even though they had created treason, Kaunda had to bow to the pressures to have Kamana removed. He 're-assigned him' to the general management of the

Dairy Produce Board. Now the bar jokes were about Kamana being 'put in cold storage'.

An editorial in the paper as he left said that '. . . few readers could understand the pressures he had experienced from all quarters in order to bring the newspaper into the reputable position it enjoys today'. And, said the leader, 'Dunstan Kamana has set an example that will be hard to emulate'.

The Government was going to make very sure next time that Kamana's example would not merely be hard to emulate, but impossible.

A few days after he was removed, Kamana spoke at a party given by the Ministry of Information for Zambian Pressmen. He said there was 'mutual distrust' between Government officials and the press which led to lack of co-operation, denials and counter-denials. He accused the Government of using the press 'as a kind of fire-brigade'. Newspapers were kept out of the picture about Government plans, and when they found out things on their own they were often vehemently denied only to be confirmed later. 'Yet when there is trouble the Government always turns to the press for help', he said.

Kamana was as broken in spirit as his White predecessor had been. He did not take up the dairy job, but went instead on what has become known in Africa as the diplomatic roundabout. Troublesome party members who are too senior to leave sitting around are often found such jobs. Kamana went to Moscow, later to Peking, and then to the United Nations as Ambassador for his country.

He was replaced on the *Times* by Vernon Mwanga who was Ambassador at the United Nations. Mwanga's instructions from Government were clear as he moved into the *Times* editor's chair: straight, no-nonsense, no-questioning Party line. As an experienced diplomat, Mwanga knew what was expected of him. A Zambian journalist who still works on the *Times* put it this way: 'We were told "This is a Zambian paper, so how can you write against Zambia?"'

No definition of 'against' was called for.

Vernon Mwanga did a sound enough job as editor to gain promotion to the Cabinet as Foreign Minister. He was replaced by Milimo Punabantu who had been Permanent Secretary in the Ministry of Information.

Meanwhile, the *Mail* in Lusaka, which had been bought by

Government, had been turned into the official Party paper for UNIP. When Dick Hall had left it and moved on to the *Times*, Kelvin Mlenga took over as editor. But he found himself in precisely the same position as Dunstan Kamana was when he, in turn, replaced Hall. For Mlenga was an African who had replaced a *muzungu* (White man), and if there is anything more precarious than a *muzungu* editing an African newspaper it is the Black man who replaces him.

A reporter on the *Mail* during Mlenga's time says the new editor became so frustrated at the never-ending interference of politicians and civil servants that he finally quit. He was replaced by an Englishman, William Dullforce, and if that seems illogical then one should not look for logic in the African media scene. The theory behind the appointment of Dullforce was that it was one thing to have an old colonial *muzungu*, but something else to have a sort of hired mercenary who would serve his new masters unquestionably.

Dullforce arrived in Zambia at a time when Kaunda was officially adopting the policy of 'humanism' as the national creed. This was a religious and political philosophy, largely invented by a Yorkshire Methodist minister, Colin Morris, who had fought the good fight in the cause of African nationalism, taking Zambian citizenship. He then finally left the country and like Hall regained British citizenship.

An African reporter who worked under Dullforce at the time says that he 'plugged humanism like it was the very stuff of life'. A lot of readers got sick of it. One morning Dullforce picked up the rival *Times* to see what they were using that day, and read that he had been dismissed from the *Mail*. His strange epitaph (from one of his ex-reporters) is that in trying so hard to please his masters he ended up displeasing them. Or more simply, if you are a White editor in Black Africa, you cannot win.

All these upheavals within the Zambia Press left the journalists of the country bemused. They just did not know what was expected of them—except total subservience which they were reluctant to accept. So Kaunda mounted a seminar lasting two full days to spell out to them exactly what was required. He made three major speeches, and at the end of the second day no one was left in any more doubt.

In case anyone missed the significance of the message, it was spelt out in simple terms: Misbehaviour by journalists would be severely dealt with.

There was only one newspaperman left who was to continue to resist. He was William Saidi. Saidi was much too intelligent not to know the odds facing him, but he was simply almost physically incapable of toeing the rigid line Kaunda had drawn for the newspapermen of Zambia. He had already been fired from the *Mail* after it had been taken over by the Government, and for months he was out of work, doing a bit of free-lancing here and there. When Dunstan Kamana moved into the editorial chair at the *Times,* he could not see so good a newspaperman as Saidi walking the streets and took him on. At first he sent him to the branch office in Livingstone, a sort of Zambian Siberia, 500 miles away on the Rhodesian border. Then he moved Saidi back to Ndola as news editor at head office. When Kamana himself was sent off, not to any tropical Siberia but to much nearer the real thing in Moscow, Saidi became assistant editor under Milimo Punabantu. His rapid promotion was a case of a thoroughbred asserting his superiority in a stable-full of cart-horses. When Saidi spoke to graduates at a centre training religious journalists in Zambia, he said: '. . . journalism for me is the endless search for the truth. Newspapermen should be prepared to be knocked down for the sake of the truth.'

He was just about to be.

More and more Saidi clashed with authority. Punabantu gave him as much rope as he dared, but as Saidi stuck to his professional standards it became clear that the rope was running out.

As the man seeing the paper away every night, Saidi, by a typographical trick here, a telling headline there, was able to give a punch to many stories which by themselves would not have created trouble. The evil eye from Lusaka fell on him. Because he was not a Zambian by birth, having been born in Rhodesia, this was one stick with which to beat him; another was that as he had not been appointed by the Government (though, of course, he had been appointed by the Government's editor), he was really serving the interests of Lonrho.

Now everything Saidi wrote was pored over in Lusaka. When he did a light-hearted piece on mini-skirts saying it seemed some people in high places could not see beyond them, this was seized upon by officialdom to illustrate 'un-Zambian attitudes'.

Making fun of Governments is as dangerous, and even more rare, than actually challenging them in Africa.

The refugee Rhodesian nationalists based in Zambia were constantly causing trouble for Kaunda. Like the nationalists of Zambia itself, they were split into two factions and there was frequent physical confrontation between them. On one occasion the leader of one of the factions had his car blown up and was killed. Both sides were issuing press statements almost daily.

The Rhodesian issue and its great overspill into Zambia was for years the major story in the local press. Even the best newspapermen in the country knew they were walking a tightrope every time they dealt with the issue. It was easy enough when they were told specifically what to do and what not to do, but with the fast-moving events of these times—and these times were to continue for years—time and time again things were happening that called out to any newspaperman worth the name to do something about it.

Kaunda, to all intents and purposes abandoned by the British and desperate to prevent Central Africa being turned into a blood-bath, was spending almost every minute of his 18-hour day grappling to find some chink that he could prise open and let sanity in. Suddenly the London papers carried a story that Zambia had sent an emissary to Salisbury to have talks with one of the imprisoned black nationalists held by Ian Smith. Obviously this could only have been done with the sanction of Kaunda himself and it was thus clear that there must be some links between Salisbury and Lusaka. In point of fact, during this period there was a good deal of undercover diplomacy going on at various levels. The Zambian press avoided these stories. It would have been political dynamite for it to have got out that Kaunda, the great black humanitarian, was doing any sort of business with Smith, who in this period was seen as the biggest white ogre in southern Africa—bigger, in the emotions of the hour, even than South Africa's Vorster, who at least was internationally recognised as a legal entity.

From London, Reuters picked up the story of the Zambian emissary's journey to Salisbury and put it out with their general service. Bill Saidi, champing at the bit as any good newspaperman would be under the circumstances, could resist the temptation no longer. He printed the story of the mission to Salisbury in the *Times*. Here was arguably a case where Saidi's 'search for truth' ethic should have been shelved in the cause of Kaunda's efforts to settle the Rhodesian situation and the race war it threatened.

Kaunda, whose every nerve now must have been ragged and torn all through those years, was furious.

But he tempered his wrath by adding that he was ready to forgive if an 'honest error' had been made. On 5 November 1975, the biggest story on the front page of both the *Times* in Ndola and the *Mail* in Lusaka was the instant dismissal by President Kaunda of William Saidi. The *Times* printed President Kaunda's letter to Saidi. This said: 'I have followed very closely your work as a journalist. I have been particularly concerned about your misconception regarding your approach to nation-building in this country. As you know I have given you every opportunity to reform. Regrettably I find no improvement in your performance. On the contrary, the evidence clearly demonstrates a deterioration. Consequently, your performance continues to be inconsistent with the philosophy and spirit of the paper which must be the mouthpiece of the Party of which you are a leader. I am, therefore, now left with no option but to fire you with immediate effect.' The President ended his public dismissal of Saidi: 'I wish you luck in your future endeavours in any field of your choice.'

Zambian radio and television played the story big. It meant, almost certainly, that Saidi would never work again as a journalist. But nothing is ever certain for the newspapermen of Zambia.

A few weeks after Saidi had found himself front-paged, he was in the bar of Kitwe's Edinburgh Hotel, another part of the Lonrho empire, when one of his old reporters from the *Times* came in. 'Hi Bill! How are you doing?' asked the reporter.

Saidi nodded. 'I sleep nights' he answered.

The reporter knew what he meant. But he had a rejoinder that is the epitaph of many an otherwise good newspaperman in a score of African states.

'Sure' he said, 'but I eat days'.

But by the beginning of 1977 it was time for President Kaunda to reshuffle the Zambian newspaper pack. On 13 January both the *Times* and the *Mail* announced that 'the Party' had appointed John Musukuma as editor-in-chief of the *Times*, replacing Milimo Punabantu. Musukuma was a former assistant editor of the *Mail* before taking over the biggest trade paper in tropical Africa, the *Mining Mirror*, serving Zambia's huge copper mining industry.

As his deputy, the Party appointed William Saidi, with

the formal title of deputy editor-in-chief—virtually what he had been at the time of his removal by Kaunda because his 'performance continues to be inconsistent with the philosophy and the spirit of the paper which must be the mouthpiece of the Party . . .'

Besides the removal of Punabantu, four heads rolled in the switch. The Party's announcement said that they had 'terminated the services of one assistant editor, one chief reporter and two senior reporters'.

In June 1975 it was announced that the *Times* and its Sunday sister, the *News*—by now renamed the *Sunday Times*—had been nationalised, but late in 1976 the staffs were still being paid by Lonrho, and the local Lonrho chief in Zambia, Tom Mtine, was still responsible for administration.

There was only one White left in the newsroom, Marta Paynter, who had survived from the colonial days when the paper was called the *Northern News*. The subs' desk had been totally Africanised with the exception of a woman from Sri Lanka.

But Whites still ran the management, advertising, accounts and the print-shop.

The editorials of the *Mail* in Lusaka are believed to be written in the Ministry of Information.

There is a line that non-Africans find difficult to trace between the ruling Party in Black states and the Government. Although there are variations of the theme, it is generally true to say (certainly in Zambia) that what the Party puts out cannot be questioned by the Government. This frequently leads to difficulties for the press which might report what a Cabinet minister has said—only to learn after publication that what he said was contrary to Party policy.

It is a Catch-22 situation.

One of Zambia's most professional journalists, Timothy Nyahunzvi, who left newspapers first to teach journalism and who is now in public relations, says he believes a large part of the problem people like himself face is that they learnt their craft during colonial times on papers which had often been outspoken against authority, albeit only to a nuisance degree.

'The set-up was such in those days that unless you actually broke the law nobody minded very much what you did', he says. 'Old habits die hard, and now that things have changed so much with independence, these journalists are bound to find themselves out of step almost any time—with all that entails.'

Both the *Mail* and the *Times* now have Party Committees, and all the editorial staff (from junior reporters to editor-in-chief) are expected to be familiar with the philosophy of humanism.

Once in a very long while events will move so fast or become so complex that there seems to be a superficial freedom in the newspapers of Zambia.

When Angola's civil war began, even before the Portuguese left and the warring African nationalist factions there began to battle it out, the *Times* tended to support one side, UNITA, while the *Mail* was for the MPLA. But when the Cubans quickly achieved victory for the MPLA, Kaunda was forced to see the reality of the situation and both papers were pulled into line in formal recognition of the MPLA. Christopher Parker, a long-time British foreign correspondent serving a number of Western papers and broadcasting stations from Lusaka, but who finally got out when life became virtually impossible, says it was useless attending official press conferences. If you tried to ask a pertinent question, you were shouted down by UNIP Party officials who were always present along with senior civil servants, the heads of foreign diplomatic missions and the managers of the Government para-statal organisations who were always summoned on such occasions.

Such press conferences always begin with the singing of the national anthem. Occasionally the press is still able to ask embarrassing questions, but it is an acquired skill to know just what sort of issues can be questioned.

If the state schools are as good as they are claimed to be by the Government, ask the newspapers, why do many of the country's leaders send their children to be educated privately? Until they were abolished, private hospitals came in for the same sort of questioning by the press. There is a complete parallel in this situation with Zambia's erstwhile imperialist masters in Socialist-governed Britain, where cabinet ministers go into private hospitals and send their children to private schools.

Both papers also ran a successful campaign against a steep rise in the price of essential foodstuffs. The outcry by the public was fully reported and readers' letters in the strongest terms were published. As a result prices were reduced to their former levels. They went up again in the Budget later in the year, and because this was now official policy the papers were unable to return to the subject.

If this somewhat bizarre state of the press in Zambia can

hardly be described as healthy, there is still more room for manoeuvre by newspapermen than in almost every other black state, bar Kenya. This is due in the last resort to the stature of Kenneth Kaunda, a complex and often misunderstood man but never less than a great humanitarian who was abandoned by Britain at the time of the Rhodesian UDI crisis while a handful of white racists were able to commit treason against the Crown because, as the Labour Government of Britain unembarrassingly explained, they were 'kith and kin'.

While it is easy to make out a strong case against Kaunda's handling of the Zambia Press there is something unique in Black Africa—at least as strong a defence. For with his personal position imperilled and his country economically strangled by the Rhodesian situation it is surprising that Kaunda has not been obliged to turn the screws even tighter.

Final judgement must be reserved until the Rhodesian situation is resolved and the economic and political threat to Kaunda removed.

MALAWI: THE PRESIDENT'S PRESS

If there was ever such a thing as a Scottish colony it was Malawi. Scottish missionaries were there even before the English colonisers came. It was David Livingstone's favourite territory outside his native Scotland, and as the early morning mists come down from the mountain which lies above Blantyre—named after its Scottish counter-part where Livingstone was born—it even looks like Scotland.

Scotland's missionaries were active there in the middle of the nineteenth century when the country was merely known as British Central Africa, with no properly defined borders.

Its first newspaper was founded by a Scot in 1895 and was called the *Central African Planter,* the plant in question being the little tea bushes which for a long time were the bedrock of Malawi's economy and which to a great extent still are.

Soon after the turn of the century, the *Planter* changed its name to the *Central African Times* (the 'Cat'), and although it was geared to a White readership among the small but steadily increasing number of settlers who were beginning to arrive from Britain, it was benevolent and fair towards the Africans.

When the country was formally re-named Nyasaland, the *Central African Times* became the *Nyasaland Times.*

One of the editors in the early sixties was Donald Trelford, later to become editor of Britain's Sunday *Observer*.

He recalls that some of his African reporters were straight out of Ben Hecht's '*Front Page*'. 'They must have picked up their notion of a journalist's life-style from bad Chicago films of the 1940s which reached Africa in the 1950s—hard-living, fast-talking types with snap brims worn at the back of the head', he remembers. One of the youngsters Trelford took on was Austin M'madi. When Trelford asked him about his qualifications, he replied: 'My mother is Kachasu, Queen of Zingwangwa'. Kachasu was the local gin, highly potent and highly illicit.

Trelford realised that the young man thus came from a family of great influence, knowledge and wealth. He hired him on the spot. As things were to turn out a decade later, it would have been much better for young Austin M'madi if Trelford had sent him back to his mother's illicit still.

In the early sixties the *Times* came under the eye of another Scot—Roy Thomson's No. 1 man in London, James Coltart. At this period Thomson was empire-building all over the world. His West African investments had not yet gone sour. In 1962 he bought the *Nyasaland Times*. For almost ten years Thomson ran it well and profitably as a bi-weekly, but in 1972 he sold out to the Edinburgh-educated Hastings Banda.

The venture, though never a high-flyer, had been profitable and relatively trouble-free. Banda met Thomson's figure for compensation, and was still paying the instalment terms at the end of 1975.

Hastings Banda, like Nigeria's Nnamdi Azikiwe and Ghana's Kwame Nkrumah, had made his way as a young man to the West to acquire not only an education but a taste for politics. All three were to become presidents of the countries they left behind them, all three newspaper proprietors.

What more natural when Banda bought out the *Times* from Thomson than that he should import a Scot to be the editorial linchpin.

Norman Cattanach seemed an ideal choice. Not only did he have an excellent newspaper background in Britain, but he had been working for some years for the Thomson Foundation which Roy Thomson had established to train Third World journalists and radio and television personnel. With the intensive programme of Africanisation that Banda required for his newspaper, Cattanach's teaching experience was invaluable.

During the run-up period to independence, Banda's Congress

Party had started a weekly paper, the *Malawi News*, and Cattanach's brief was to turn that into the week-end newspaper and the *Times* (now called the *Malawi Times*) into a daily as quickly as possible.

Cattanach's letter of appointment from the Thomson left-over who was managing director, David Burnett, said that the *News* '. . . will still be slanted in a way which could describe it as an organ of the Party'.

Cattanach had no qualms about working for what his letter of appointment had called 'an organ of the Party'. In theory he was what Zambia's Richard Hall described as the new man who was better able to accommodate to African newspapers than the Whites who were still there when the Blacks came to power. The practice, though, was very different.

'I didn't see that it was really part of my job to change a Party paper around' he says. 'It was there for a specific purpose and my job was improving its technical quality not changing its policy.'

Of the *Times*, which as the country's only daily was to be Cattanach's principal operation, Burnett's letter said 'The *Times*, on the other hand, will be essentially an international paper . . . and will not, in the accepted sense of the word, be a vehicle for direct political propaganda'.

This was to prove not so much an under-statement as a travesty that became, for Cattanach, a nightmare. Cattanach arrived in Malawi in November 1972. Banda wanted to see him at once and he was hurried to the Presidential office. Banda dismissed everybody else in the room and greeted Cattanach genially. 'I'm very fond of Scotland', he began and then reminisced about his years there and his studies at Edinburgh University. He even tried to impersonate a Glasgow accent and laughed uproariously at himself.

Banda told Cattanach: 'My concern is Malawi. I am out to make the people of Malawi stronger, richer and better.'

This is one side of Hastings Banda, Malawi's 'Kamuzu', completely civilised, rational, highly intelligent, even warm-hearted. The other side is of a man easily enraged, wide-eyed, quivering lips, wielding a heavy walking-stick and genuinely terrifying to many who cross his path while he is in this mood.

Banda produced a map of Malawi and Moçambique. Before he had left Britain, Cattanach had been told to expect to find the President ailing, with poor eyesight and in generally bad health. But as Banda gave him a run-down on the delicate military situation then beginning to develop in Moçambique, he was able to point out remote spots on the map without even putting on his glasses. Cattanach could barely see the tiny name places with his glasses on.

Banda showed Cattanach where FRELIMO, the Moçambique guerilla force, was operating within Malawi and said there was nothing that could be done to stop them.

His final words to Cattanach at that first interview were: 'Remember, this is Africa. This is not Aberdeen, Glasgow, Dundee or Edinburgh. This is Africa. You must tell people that.' Cattanach was not sure what Banda meant. He was soon to understand rather more clearly.

The amalgamation of the *Times* and the *News* produced what Cattanach described as 'complete chaos'. It brought together two groups of people who had been sworn enemies. The staff of the *Times* had represented the old White planter viewpoint; the *News* was the rabid Black nationalist organ created solely for the purpose of overthrowing the planters.

Neither paper had journalists in any real sense of the word. Cattanach recalls: 'They were people who had picked up a little bit of experience here and there'—typical of the majority of the African press all over the Continent.

In a very short time Cattanach did a remarkable job, not only bridging this divide between the editorial staffs of the *News* and the *Times*, but even creating the beginnings of something like a sense of adventure and *esprit-de-corps*.

The best local journalist was a serious-minded, intelligent man named Al Osman. He was one of the few journalists from his country to have received any proper training. He had attended a three-month course at the Thomson Foundation Editorial Centre in Cardiff.

He was given the title of editor of the *Times* as it was politically important that a Black man should be seen to hold this position. In fact, Cattanach was in every sense the real editor.

Within a few days of Cattanach's arrival, an incident occurred, seemingly trifling but the tip of the iceberg which was soon to start surfacing.

A Portuguese army officer in Beira, the Moçambique port which Britain was then blockading in an abortive attempt to enforce sanctions against Rhodesia, made a statement saying that FRELIMO, which two years later became the Government of Moçambique, were finding sanctuary across the border in

Malawi. The correspondent for the South African Press Association in Beira had filed the story to SAPA's head office in Johannesburg which passed it on to Reuters in London.

Cattanach got the Reuter story over the office teleprinter. He pursed his lips, sensing problems. He took it to David Burnett who read it, poured two double gins and said: 'I've been here a lot longer than you, old boy, and I'd advise you to forget it.'

Cattanach replied that he did not think he could do that. What he wanted to do, he said, was to carry the story with a denial from the Malawi Government.

When Burnett became what Cattanach describes as 'quite heavy', Cattanach was even more determined that the Reuter story should appear.

'We had another double gin. Then he became avuncular. I said "Look, the BBC Overseas Service is broadcasting this news every hour on the hour and we have got to do something about it".'

Burnett, now mellowed by a mixture of Scots persuasion and London gin, agreed that the story should be used but that a denial should be carried.

During this period, as the curtain began to rise on a period of great uncertainty in that part of Africa, Banda was in a very tight corner. White Africa, in the shape of Rhodesia's rebellious settlers, was immediately to his south. He was also heavily involved with South Africa, and Prime Minister Johannes Vorster had lent him a number of Afrikaner civil servants to help organise a number of Malawi ministries.

Black Africa was to his north, and though Banda had little time for the posturings of the Organisation of African Unity, he could not afford entirely to queer his pitch with Zambia's Kenneth Kaunda and Tanzania's Julius Nyerere, just across two of his most important borders.

But most worrying of all for Banda was his eastern flank. The FRELIMO guerillas, who had been fighting their war of liberation for more than a decade, were pushing down from the north of Moçambique with greater and greater speed. Portugal's colonial Army was showing less and less stomach for the fight. Banda was trying to keep a foot in both camps, not wanting to be seen as opposing FRELIMO, but equally desperate not to offend the Portuguese, who were his only outlet to the coast.

Banda was frantic that the outside world should have Malawi's formal denial of the Reuter story.

For two days the Ministry of Foreign Affairs, the Ministry of Information and sundry other official bodies drafted, tore up, redrafted, threw away and got into a hopeless mess about how to word such a denial. It was a fairly typical example of the ineptitude of new African governments in dealing with what was hardly an earth-shattering event, and the inability of untutored bureaucrats in composing a one hundred-word statement.

Finally, officialdom turned to Cattanach. He was rushed to the President's house and Banda told him to write the denial. Cattanach, though no diplomat, had enough Scots canniness to know that a flat denial of the Portuguese officer's statement would fly in the face of Malawi's delicate and important relations with Lisbon, the most vital element of which was the fact that Beira was Malawi's only outlet to the sea.

Cattanach told the President he felt sure the Portuguese Government in Lisbon would certainly apologise for what one of its colonial army officers had said, but only if Malawi left the door sufficiently open to allow them to do so gracefully. Cattanach told Banda that the best tactic was to do what everybody else did in such situations—he quoted the Americans in Vietnam— and that was to blame the Army and not the Government.

Cattanach suggested that the sort of phrases to be used in the Malawi denial should include things like 'very foolish officer', and 'after all it is impossible to define just where the borders are' and 'nobody even knows who really goes in and out of the borders'.

Banda was delighted with this, and it was the sort of statement eventually issued. Sure enough, the Portuguese authorities in Lisbon jumped at the chance to cool down the situation and issued a statement to the effect that the Beira officer had been speaking without authority and was unaware of the true facts.

This had happened within a few days of Cattanach's arrival and it demonstrated in the clearest terms just who the boss was in Malawi, right down to dotting the i's and crossing the t's. Banda was handling an enormous amount of Government business, and it may well be that the strain upon him was responsible for his behaviour during these years.

Cattanach's title was editorial director of both the *Times* and the *News*. In fact he soon found he was also advertising manager, circulation manager, publisher, transport controller and almost tying up the bundles of newspapers as they came off the seventy-year-old, broken-toothed flat-bed press. This meant any-

thing up to an eighteen hour day, six and a half days a week.
Cattanach had no complaints on that score.

But then the pressures began; subtle suggestions, advice in the
form of 'If I were you' or 'I've been here a long time'.

Cattanach went along with this. He did not want to be diverted
from what he saw as his prime aim; turning out two technically
and editorially worthwhile papers with an improving staff of
Black Malawians who would acquire both the professional skills
and the professional approach of newspapermen.

At first there was great suspicion towards the new venture,
even from among his own staff. Colonial editors were still recent
enough to cause distrust.

Slowly, then rapidly, 'the weird things' as he called them
began. It was one thing to go along with the political philosophy
and ideology of Banda as he contorted his nation so as not to
offend either the FRELIMO guerillas, the Portuguese Government, Ian Smith and even the Government of South Africa, home
of the ultimate in White devilry.

This tight-rope Cattanach was prepared to tread. But there
were a score of other issues, trifling to an absurd degree,
which began to grind him down; issues like Presidential decrees
which were conducted as national campaigns and launched by
Banda sometimes in seemingly interminable speeches before an
exhausted Parliament unable to move while he was on his feet.

Banda's decrees were enforced by the bully-boys of his Congress
Party, who were liable to pounce with big sticks and heavy boot
at anyone they considered to be breaking them.

One such campaign was against mini-skirts. These were
banned, and many was the Malawian miss who felt the full
wrath of male chauvinism if her skirts, meticulously measured
at street corners, were a fraction higher than the Kamuzu's decree.

Another was hair length. In Africa nature prevents the neck-
long locks favoured among the youth of many societies. But
there were still enough Europeans around among the foreign-aid
workers and tourists to keep the Congress watch-dogs busy.

In an effort to boost advertising revenue, Cattanach organised
a supplement in the *Times* about one of the main department
stores. It worked out well but on the morning of publication,
before breakfast, an official of the Ministry of Information
telephoned him and roared 'This is a racist publication'.

Dumbfounded, Cattanach asked what on earth he meant.

One of the pictures in the supplement had shown Europeans

among the shoppers in the department store. That was what was wrong with it. The feature had been written by a Malawian, the pictures taken by a Malawian, and the layout done by a Malawian.

On a more serious level was Banda's campaign against the religious sect, Jehovah's Witnesses. Banda persecuted them unmercifully. Finally he banned them. His hatred for the sect appeared to be that they preached a doctrine in which Jehovah was number one.

There was only one number one in Malawi.

But then, suddenly, he had something of a change of heart. On New Year's day 1973, Banda addressed the nation on radio. He spoke for an hour, and it emerged from his speech that he was allowing back the 17,500 Malawian Jehovah Witnesses who had fled the country. Banda said they could come back provided they became 'loyal and faithful members' of his Congress Party. Jehovah was thus to be put in his place in Malawi.

This was obviously a first-class story and a happy one in a land where there was very little joy. Cattanach told his staff it was to be the front page lead. Banda's speech ran to about 5,000 words, but Cattanach told his subs: 'Cut it down to 750 words'. He remembers the effect this had as being equivalent to his having announced: 'We are going to blow up State House tonight.'

The subs and the reporters who heard Cattanach's instructions were appalled. There was near panic in the office. Nobody would cut the President's speech.

To the awe and terror of his watching staff, Cattanach sat down at his desk, read through the speech, ticked off the bits he wanted, put up an intro and duly typed out the 750 words. As nobody else in the newsroom would be associated with any part of the operation, he also had to sub it, write the headline and hand it to the very unhappy linotype operator to set.

His staff went home that night unnerved and frightened. They expected swift and forceful retribution as soon as the paper appeared. If you could be beaten up for having your skirt a centimetre too high, what was likely to be the price for subbing the President?

Malawi journalists are not alone in this respect. All over the Continent reporters and sub-editors are learning to accept presidential speeches as holy writ.

But when Cattanach's story appeared not a word was heard

from official quarters. Cattanach had won an important battle, even though he was shortly to lose the war. A precedent had been set; the President could be subbed, cut down—at least to editorial size.

'We never had any disagreement over this sort of thing', says Cattanach. And he makes a point that again and again has been demonstrated all over Africa. 'The trouble was that many of the people around the President tried to anticipate what he would like or not like. You had to battle with all these people, often without knowing quite who they were.'

By now his African staff were much more willing to follow Cattanach. His obvious professionalism and his transparent sincerity persuaded them that he was a White man who had their interests at heart.

Both the daily *Times* and the week-end *News* made tremendous headway, though all the time a steady stream of trivial or serious issues arose which kept undermining morale.

One incident was the publication in the *Times* of a photograph of Oliveira Salazar, the former President of Portugal, which was incorrectly captioned as the new President, Marcello Caetano, who had replaced him. The mistake had occurred because the zinc block in the newspaper library was simply labelled 'The President of Portugal' without giving a name. This would hardly rank as a catastrophe in any normal newspaper office, but it was more than enough to give the heavies of Banda's court the opportunity to lean threateningly on Cattanach and his staff.

Banda himself was enraged at the mistake. He summoned Cattanach, Burnett and Osman to State House.

The trio sat apprehensively in the President's office waiting for the wrath to descend. The door was flung open and Banda came storming in. He ignored Cattanach and Burnett completely, and began a tirade against Osman. All the unfortunate editor could do was nod limply and mumble a series of 'Yes Sir', 'I agree, Sir', 'I am very sorry, Sir'.

There were a series of such incidents and the cumulative effect was debilitating to the whole newsroom. It meant raw nerves for everyone on both papers.

The crunch came in May. It was another report about the Portuguese Army and FRELIMO. A story broke that the Portuguese Army, in hot pursuit of a band of FRELIMO guerillas, had crossed the Malawi border where a clash had occurred between them and the Malawi Army.

Cattanach checked the story out and was satisfied it was not true, at least regarding the vital part about the Portuguese Army clashing with the Malawi Army. Cattanach established that as soon as the Portuguese Army had realised that they were in Malawi, they had withdrawn back across the unmarked border.

Like the earlier story from Beira, this one had been picked up by the South African Press Association who had given it to Reuters. Reuters had put it out on their service, but qualified it to the extent that it said there had merely been a report of a clash. They did not confirm that one had occurred.

Cattanach, in his other role as diplomatic watch-dog, again issued the Government's denial and this went out of the country via Malawi Radio. But everyone wanted to know who had sent out the original story of the 'clash'. The unearthing of this source became the principal Government business for weeks.

It could hardly have been a European, as every White correspondent had long since departed from Malawi. Or, then again, could it? If it was a White man, then Cattanach was the obvious subject. But not even the fanatics of the President's court really thought it could be him. Such a canny Scot as Cattanach was not going to stick his neck into that noose.

Thus, it must be a Black man. But who, and how to find him? Banda himself, livid at what he considered an act of treachery, supervised the search. The Malawi Special Branch dropped everything else to find the guilty man. Their plan of detection was simple; pick up any and everybody known ever to have had links with any outside publications or news agencies.

Top of the list was Austin M'madi, the mild-mannered son of Malawi's gin-queen, who for several years had been the stringer for Associated Press. But AP, well aware of the delicate positions of their Black stringers all over the Continent, had long since told M'madi that all they expected of him was that he should file the official Government handouts. They did not want him to do anything which would remotely endanger him. Nevertheless, he was the first one arrested. But it became obvious he was not the guilty man when other Black journalists began being picked up. Altogether eight men were arrested, five of them on Cattanach's staff, including the deputy editor of the *Times* and the editor of the Party paper, the *News*.

Joseph Wadda, a naturalised British subject who had been born in the Gambia, was Director of News Programmes for the Malawi Broadcasting Corporation. He was given seventy-two hours to leave the country. No reason was given, but a British official who saw Banda on the same day said he was seething with rage. He had clearly told his Special Branch to pick up all the Malawians who could conceivably be responsible and deport any foreign journalists. Wadda came under the second heading.

John Borrell, a British free-lancer who was visiting Malawi, was asked by Reuters in London to check the report about the clash between the Portuguese and Malawian troops. No sooner had he filed his story, including the denial, than he was picked up by the Special Branch and interrogated for forty-eight hours. He was continually asked why he had filed a story using the words 'reports of fighting', even though the story went on to deny that such a clash had taken place. Borrell was driven to the point of exasperation trying to explain that it was impossible to deny something without saying what you were denying.

A number of bodies like the International Press Institute, the Commonwealth Press Union and Amnesty International sent protests to Banda about the arrests, but these probably did more harm than good. Banda told Parliament that Malawi was an independent country and would not be dictated to by outside organisations.

He then brought in legislation to deal with what he called 'lying journalists'. This Act was passed two months after the detention of the newsmen, and it provided that journalists could be charged for publishing misleading information. In fact, none of the imprisoned journalists were ever charged or brought before any court.

So frantic were the Special Branch, almost hourly under the whip from Banda to find the culprit, that they even arrested a man who had written an occasional piece about Malawi's sportsmen for foreign magazines.

To this day Cattanach does not know who sent the story out of Malawi, and it is highly improbable that anybody else knows either. He never saw any of the imprisoned journalists again. Because Banda has effectively sealed all information channels out of Malawi, what became of these men remained unknown for four years until, unexplained, they were released.

Cattanach tried to get messages through to those of his staff who were locked up but he doubts whether he was successful.

Banda dropped the Reuter service, complaining that it was employing 'pseudo-journalists' in Malawi to send out false reports about the country. A Reuter salesman hurried out from London, and eventually the service was resumed. To this day all Reuter correspondents entering Malawi have to carry special authorisation.

The crunch was near for Cattanach. His staff was now both decimated and demoralised. One Sunday morning at eight o'clock he was working in his office when a Special Branch inspector arrived. He told Cattanach: 'I have a warrant for your arrest.' Cattanach looked over his typewriter and answered: 'Do you put the handcuffs on or not?'

He had no idea what was happening. Was it a genuine arrest? Was it just more pressure? Was it intimidation? Was it even a joke?

Such 'jokes' are not uncommon when African Special Branch officers are fencing with Europeans.

The Special Branch man patted his pocket, laughed, and said: 'I must have left the handcuffs in the office' and he walked out of the newsroom. Cattanach sat alone in the office. He had had enough. He went home, talked things over with his wife and decided it was time to go.

'I realised that I was wasting my time; that I would never be able to produce either decent newspapers or decent newspapermen', he was to say later.

Cattanach had been in Malawi five months. 'It was like five years', he says. 'There was a kind of madness there.'

The unfortunate Al Osman now became not only editor in name but in fact. Morale on both papers was at rock bottom. Almost every day Banda was making speeches describing journalists as third-class and fourth-class citizens. He said the press in Malawi was 'highly uninformed'. Osman did the only thing possible in the circumstances: total surrender. Virtually every word that went into both papers was now checked and double-checked with authority.

There were a dozen-phone calls or visits to various ministries every day to ask 'Do you think this is alright?' Eight times out of ten, the answer would be 'No'. No civil servant wanted to stick his neck out.

News of upheavals in other parts of Africa were especially taboo. But as state after state changed hands at the point of a gun, it became impossible not to make some reference to the changes. So a 'softly-softly' plan was devised which was to ignore news of any coups, but weeks or even months later, as reports came in from such countries, there would be vague references inserted in the papers about 'the recent change of administration' in Ghana, Nigeria, Uganda, the Sudan or whatever.

There are many well-educated people in Malawi to this day who, denied all access to information from the outside world, believe that these 'changes in administration' came about through the ballot box.

A British doctor who worked in Malawi was approached at a cocktail party by a senior civil servant who unblinkingly observed: 'Isn't it surprising how many soldiers are getting elected all over Africa these days?'

Even with the ultra-care Osman impressed upon his staff, things could go wrong. A story appeared about a visiting African fortune-teller, quite famous in his own way, who was passing through Malawi from Kenya.

It is difficult to imagine a more harmless report, but within an hour of the paper appearing, what had now become known as the Banda-sound-barrier broke. To this day nobody knows what was objected to, although one view is that the fortune-teller might have started seeing things in his crystal ball about the future of Malawi. The Ministry of Information eventually explained that it had been an insult to put the fortune-teller's picture on a page in the paper before that which carried the obligatory picture of Banda.

The Special Branch were frequently sent to the office to question the staff, but generally they had no idea why they had been sent and finally became quite sympathetic towards the journalists.

Unlike African journalists almost everywhere else on the Continent, Malawi's newspapermen have never been politically motivated. They are a true cross-section of the better-educated people of the country, pleasant, mild-mannered, courteous, and at one time full of humour. But not any more.

Since the arrests, no journalist has been sent abroad for training and no outside agency such as the Thomson Foundation or the International Press Institute has conducted training within the country. Some of Malawi's more enlightened officials are greatly concerned about the deteriorating standard of the press.

On the whole, the Department of Information is sympathetic to the position of the journalists. The officials feel that they are in very much the same sort of spot, but they must watch the press as they know that in turn they are being watched. This is the position in virtually every walk of life; everyone is being watched or watching.

And on top of it all is the Kamuzu himself, now in his eighties, watching over not only his nation but, it seems almost, into the very minds of everyone in it.

There are many Big Black Brothers in Africa but Banda is in the very top league. He is totally unpredictable—more so than even Uganda's Idi Amin or the self-proclaimed emperor of the Central African Empire, Jean-Bedel Bokassa, who at least have the dubious distinction of being consistently ferocious towards any vestige of opposition.

Totally unpredictably, in the middle of 1977, Banda released more than one thousand political prisoners, including the eight journalists rounded up in 1973. No announcement of their release was ever made. and news only reached the outside world when one of them, Victor Ndovi, who had been on the *Times* of Malawi, reached Britain. He revealed that most of the political prisoners were held in Mikuyu, ten miles from the former capital, Zomba, in an area infested with malaria-carrying mosquitos. The prison had been built there against medical advice. The four sections of Mikuyu Prison were known as Sections A, B, C and D. 'A' was for those who were said (never charged) to have been making military preparations to overthrow Banda; 'B' was for foreigners— for the most part unfortunates from neighbouring Tanzania and Zambia who had crossed the border either intentionally or accidentally; 'C' was for those who had been detained before, and Block 'D' was for anybody who fell outside the previous three categories. This is where the eight journalists spent four years. The warders were thugs who rushed the prisoners through barely edible slop meals. Many prisoners suffered serious malnutrition and some died. There were virtually no medical facilities. A good many of the prisoners became paralysed, blind or went out of their minds. All the eight journalists survived, but apart from Ndovi, there have been no news of the rest. They will certainly never work as journalists again, and are probably unlikely to work at anything else.

Many of the journalists who survived the 1973 purge have now left journalism to go into public relations or some other form of alien employment. One or two have managed to get out of the country. A few are listed as 'missing' but they have probably just gone back to their villages to grow maize and beans and sit in the sun wondering whether their years in the city were not a daydream—or a nightmare.

Ten years ago there were, give or take, about fifteen Black journalists in Malawi. Today, seven of the eight detainees could be anywhere, and three more are out of the country.

The *Times* and the *News* have been re-staffed, for the most part by graduates from the University of Malawi, who although of a much higher educational standard, are hopeless as newspaper-men. There is no one to train them. Osman himself has long since left Malawi. The graduates are all too aware that one false step could turn them into prison inmates.

There is also a huge cultural gap between them and the people they are writing for, plus a total ignorance of the technicalities of newspaper production. A story designed to fit six inches of single-column type is often two or three times that length. When the pages are being locked by a disenchanted printer, he merely throws away the surplus.

Headlines are written with no thought as to whether they fit or not.

With Banda now in his 80s and showing some signs of his years, but still capable of summoning up the vigour of a man half his age, less is heard of his long tirades about the press of his country being a disgrace. But it still is.

8 Portuguese Africa: From Fascism to Marxism

So often in Africa, it is the men with the guns who change the course of history. In Portuguese Africa, there was an ironic twist to this pattern. Though in both Moçambique and Angola there were plenty of Black men with guns trying to rewrite history, it was White soldiers thousands of miles away in Lisbon who on the morning of 25 April 1974 were to set in train events which not only ended four hundred years of Portugal's African Empire but were to bring the threat of an international confrontation to White Africa.

The end of Fascism in Portugal with the overthrow of Marcello Caetano, the man who had succeeded Antonio de Oliveira Salazar when the Portuguese dictator became too ill to carry on in 1968, was greeted by a tiny handful of Moçambique newspapermen as the coming of the New Jerusalem. For three quarters of a century under one of the most vicious regimes in the world, the press in Moçambique had always been distinguished by two or three courageous publications.

During the forty years of Salazar-brand Fascism, while the newspapers of Portugal itself were being beaten into servility, a handful of journalists in Moçambique had somehow managed to keep the idea of democracy alive.

So when the Portuguese Army, equally disenchanted with the never-ending colonial war in Africa and the dog-fighting among politicians which began when Salazar became bed-ridden took over in Lisbon, it seemed for a moment that the press of

Moçambique and Angola was about to become truly free for the first time.

In fact the tiny flame of freedom which successive generations of colonial newspapermen had kept flickering was just about to be totally extinguished. Fascism was dead, but in the ashes were to arise Marxist regimes which in their treatment of the press were to make the old times seem almost paternal.

Moçambique was much the more important of Portugal's two southern African territories. Vasco de Gama called in on his voyage to India in 1498, and the first Portuguese settlements were founded there early in the sixteenth century. The first daily newspaper in Moçambique was established not by the Portuguese and certainly not by the Africans. The large English-speaking community of the capital got together in 1905 and put up the money for the *Lourenco Marques Guardian*. It was the embodiment of British communities in hot foreign lands everywhere, insular, self-centred and arrogant in its attitudes to everybody else. For more than half a century, it continued to publish exclusively in English, and almost exclusively news about England. It was nicknamed the *Littlehampton Gazette*, a snide commentary on the British parochialism which people considered was represented in that minor English seaside resort.

There was a sudden change in 1956 when the Roman Catholic Archbishop of Lourenco Marques bought the *Guardian*, changed its name to *Diario* and began publishing in Portuguese and English. The Archbishop was one of the most reactionary men in the country, many degrees to the right of the colonial administration. It was said of him that he conducted himself as though he were the right hand of God, and the small, liberal community of the capital used to add 'the extreme right hand'.

In contrast with the reactionary Archbishop of Lourenco Marques, the country's second port, Beira, had an enlightened and courageous Bishop. It was chiefly his support, both moral and financial, which created *A Voz Africana*, a weekly, in 1932. The editor was an African, but the Bishop was believed to be behind the highly literate editorials. There was constant friction between the Bishop and the Archbishop in Lourenco Marques, including a row on the steps of the cathedral after service one Sunday in 1935, when the Bishop raised a clenched fist in the face of his superior, and then, at the last moment, unclenched it and turned the gesture he was making into a sweeping sign of the cross.

In defiance of the Archbishop, the Bishop founded a daily in Beira in 1950, *Diario de Moçambique* which was the expression of liberal thought in the northern part of the country. It spent as much time struggling for survival with the Roman Catholic hierarchy as it did with the colonial administration.

Noticias da Beira was started as a bi-weekly in Portuguese and English in the early twenties to counter the liberal voice of the Bishop's weekly, *A Voz Africana*. It was backed by the major trading company of the port, Companhia de Moçambique, and took a hard, uncompromising right-wing stand. When the Bishop brought out the daily *Diario*, publication of *Noticias* was increased to match it, with heavy support from the banking and financial circles of Beira.

Although with nothing like the resources of *Noticias*, *Voz Africana* held its own for many years, and within the confines of the colonial administration was able to keep the voice of liberalism alive. But by the end of the sixties, the financial interests behind *Noticias* finally got the upper hand and bought it out. A few years later, in July 1974, the colonial administration took over control, and within a month of putting its own men in, had the embarrassing experience of having to charge *Noticias* for violating the new press laws imposed by Lisbon. The Government itself was obliged to pay the 150,000 escudos (£2,500) fine when the paper was found guilty of not publishing the entire speech of Portuguese President Antonio de Spinola, and for criticising the pilots of the Jordanian Air Force.

During the early nineteen thirties, there were a handful of newspapers, for the most part poorly produced, aimed specifically at non-Europeans. The most important of these was *O Brado Africano*, a weekly established by the Associacao Africana, the Coloureds organisation, in 1918. In its heyday it was selling nearly 40,000 copies, but after censorship was imposed in 1933 and political reporting and commentary was all but forbidden, it became largely emasculated.

The outstanding liberal organ of the country, *Tribuna*, was only founded as late as 1962 at the height of Salazar's power. To staff the newsroom the major shareholder, Joao Reis, gathered together a group of liberal-minded Moçambicanos, Black, White and Coloured. The struggle to get the paper going was enormous, and by the time it came out it was virtually owned by the

Portuguese National Bank (Banco Nacional Ultramarino) which
had guaranteed Reis's overdraft.

The staff of *Tribuna* were paid exactly the same terms regardless
of colour, something unique in newspapers anywhere in Africa.
Beside the small editorial staff, there were a number of liberal-
minded part-timers contributing. One of these was Rui Knopfli,
a pharmaceutical salesman whose subsequent story would be very
near the front in any anthology of the fates that have befallen
Africa's newspapermen.

Towards the end of the 1950s a group of political moderates
started a weekly, *A Voz de Moçambique.* This was published by a
group of Whites born in Moçambique who had formed themselves into an organisation called Associacao dos Naturais de
Moçambique which was concerned with the political, economic
and social problems of the territory. *Voz* was never more than
moderately outspoken, but for a few years the colonial administration allowed it an increasing amount of rope. Though the
authorities described the staff as 'dangerous left-wingers', the
higher echelons of the colonial administration, and particularly
the Army, whose officers were beginning to grow disenchanted
with Lisbon, allowed *Voz* to continue. But in 1964, with the
guerilla war gathering pace in the northern end of the country,
Voz was in repeated conflict with the censor and was taken over
by the Portuguese National Bank.

The biggest Moçambique paper, *Noticias,* was founded in 1926
by a retired army captain, Manuel Simoes Vaz. Vaz was a hard
right-winger, and in those pre-Salazar days, even further to the
right than Lisbon. Thus when the Fascist era came in 1933
Noticias merely moved a little to the left, and from then on
to all extents and purposes it became the official Government
paper in Lourenco Marques, with both morning and evening
editions.

Liberalism was kept alive during the Salazar regime's rule in
Moçambique through three associations representing Whites,
Blacks and Coloureds. These were the Associacao dos Naturais in
Moçambique (Whites born in Moçambique), Associacao Africana (mixed-blood Coloureds) and Centro Associativo dos Negros
de Moçambique (Black). Though nominally cultural organisations, they were virtually political parties.

While in the rest of White Africa anyone of mixed blood
suffered all the indignities of racial discrimination, the Coloureds
in Moçambique were in a very different position in spite of the

ruthlessness of the colonial regime.

The Portuguese aristocrats, much more so than their British equivalents in other parts of settler Africa, not only cohabited fairly openly with the local women but allowed their progeny to take their names. The probable explanation is that White women in Britain's colonies were much freer with their fancies, and much less inhibited by the Church than the White Colonial Portuguese women. Many famous names appear as members through the years of the Associacao Africana, among them journalists, writers and poets.

After the Second World War Salazar, embarrassed by the defeat of German Fascism, thought he had better make a gesture to the world by undoing some of the tighter screws of his regime, and in 1949 'free elections' were held which led to Portugal joining NATO and being admitted to the United Nations.

All this liberal shadow-boxing in Lisbon sent out ripples to the colonies which gave false hope to newspapermen like Joao Reis and his friends. There were to be a number of false dawns for the liberal newspaperman of Moçambique over the next quarter of a century, ending in the darkest dawn of all when FRELIMO came to power.

By 1964 it had become obvious that the insurrection of Africans in the northern end of Moçambique was something more than a rising of 'rabble natives' as Lisbon described them. FRELIMO was the best organised and most dedicated African nationalist movement in tropical Africa, and more than a match for the dispirited Portuguese Army. There was a total parallel with what was happening in Vietnam, and Lisbon was getting as jittery as Washington.

The immediate reaction was to get even tougher. Hard-line generals were sent to Moçambique. The colonial administration in Lourenco Marques was told to pull in the reins until the bit bled.

In the middle of the year, Joao Reis and many other liberals were arrested. A few months later Luis Bernardo Honwana, editor of *A Voz Africana* in Beira, followed him to prison. Not long afterwards, in April 1965, Domingos Arouca, editor of *O Brado Africano*, was also picked up.

The guts of liberal journalism had been torn out of the press of the two biggest cities, Lourenco Marques and Beira. The administration was too busy with the war formally to take over the press, but the Banco Nacional Ultramarino moved in for them.

Noticias and *Tribuna* were taken over.

The bank, which already had a licence to print money, now acquired a licence to print newspapers. The head office of the bank in Lisbon was politically dominated and used as a haven for former Salazar ministers. They saw to it that there was no more liberal nonsense coming out of Lourenco Marques. The Bank put in their own editor-in-chief to supervise both *Noticia*, and *Tribuna*. He was a hard line right-winger, Antonio Maric Zorro. He closed down the morning edition of *Noticias*, and in effect *Tribuna* became the evening edition of the morning *Noticias* Some of the *Tribuna* staff who had served under Joao Reis resigned. The rest did what newspapermen all over the Continent—and the world—learn to do when such changes come grit their teeth and keep their heads down.

Zorro drastically changed the tone of *Tribuna*. When Jean-Pau Sartre won the Nobel Prize for literature, Zorro refused to publish the news. He told the staff 'I hate that son of a bitch'

But Zorro was finally to go the way of all hard right-winger serving the Salazar colonial regime, and years later when FRELIMO came to power, he was back in Lisbon—the city that Jean-Paul Sartre had once called 'that most ignoble of towns'

Having got rid of liberal journalism in the capital, the authorities turned to their northern trouble-spot, Beira. Again the bank was used as the front to move in, and by the end of the year *A Voz de Moçambique*, the brave little creation of the Bishop, was another official mouthpiece.

When Salazar became too ill to continue in office in 1968 and Marcello Caetano succeeded him, the official description of this change was that it was 'a renovation in continuity'. Those teeth gritting newspapermen in Moçambique who had survived the 1964 arrests were at first elated as Caetano gave tentative sign of liberalisation. But this was not to be for long.

Fascism was in its death throes in Lisbon, but the convolution were to continue for another six years as Caetano was replaced by General Antonio Spinola, followed by General Costa Gomes followed by General Vasco Goncalves. The overseas empire could barely keep track of what exactly was happening and in Moçambique, with FRELIMO now sweeping down from the north at a frightening pace, the Lourenco Marques administration resorted to the tactics they understood best: repression.

Public opinion, still virtually the prerogative of the Whites was becoming divided between accepting the inevitability of what was happening in Lisbon and in the north of the country as FRELIMO got closer and closer to routing the rift-ridden Army. An enlightened minority were for facing reality and preparing to come to terms with what the future clearly seemed to hold. But the majority of Whites, their backs to the crumbling wall, felt betrayed by Lisbon. They could do nothing about what was happening there, but they lashed out at any sign of what they considered treachery in Moçambique itself.

Zorro had seen the writing on the wall and gone. Rui Knopfli, the pharmaceutical salesman turned journalist who had survived the 1964 arrests of liberal newspapermen, was now editor of *Tribuna*. Under his direction, the paper began to resume something of its former shape, but this roused extremist White anger. The paper began getting telephone calls threatening reprisals 'for supporting the cause of FRELIMO'. On 15 August, 1974 right-wingers planted bombs at the printing works and wrecked the press that printed both *Noticias* and its afternoon, *Tribuna*.

Then came the Lisbon coup of 25 November by the far-left. Four hundred years of Portuguese colonialism was at an end. The new rulers in Portugal told the administrations in Moçambique and Angola to hand over control to the Africans as quickly as possible and then come home.

There was near pandemonium in the colonies. The right-wingers started packing and the left-wingers came out of hiding. Rui Knopfli and a dozen newspapermen like him went to mass and thanked God that at last real freedom of the press was at hand. The reactionary *Diario*, bi-lingual creation of the Archbishop, closed.

There is often a moment of total disillusionment in the life of newspapermen, the moment when they accept that in the last resort, after all the fine phrases about ethics and conscience, a newspaperman is just a hired hand who does what he is told to do or quits.

The final disillusionment for Rui Knopfli came right at the end of the Portuguese story in Africa as the victorious leaders of FRELIMO were casting off their jungle greens and moving into the Government ministries in Lourenco Marques.

Graham Greene, who had been one of Our Men in Lourenco Marques during the Second War, could hardly have invented a more bizarre plot for the final chapter in the career of Rui Knopfli and the ending of his family's four generations in Africa.

There were three principal characters besides Knopfli: a Scottish convict on the run, an Irish solicitor doing a deal, and a Portuguese admiral on the way out.

In neighbouring Rhodesia, where the illegal regime of Ian Smith was struggling against sanctions, Kenneth McIntosh was sent to prison early in 1974 for 'economic espionage'. McIntosh, aged thirty-five, was the investment manager of a Rhodesian merchant bank. He had pleaded guilty to charges under the Rhodesian Sanctions Counter-espionage Act, and in sentencing him to five years imprisonment, the judge at the trial, which was held *in camera*, said that McIntosh had planned to export documents that could have endangered the Rhodesian economy 'at a stroke'.

McIntosh had, in fact, already sent some documents to his brother-in-law who was the headmaster of a school in Aberdeen. These documents were passed to the *Sunday Times* in London, but before they could be published a Mr. D. P. R. O'Beirne flew in from Salisbury and said he had an offer to make on behalf of the Deputy Attorney-General in Rhodesia.

O'Beirne travelled on an Irish Passport, and in 1974 he was still a member of the Irish Bar. He had been around Africa a long time. In the late fifties he was prosecuting counsel against the Mau Mau in Kenya. He was a partner in the firm of solicitors who had defended McIntosh at his trial. He told the *Sunday Times* that immediately after McIntosh had been sentenced, he had been summoned to meet the Deputy Attorney-General and a number of CID officers. They had told him that additional charges could be brought against McIntosh for which he might receive a further five or six years' imprisonment.

O'Beirne told the *Sunday Times* that if the Rhodesian authorities got the documents back, and if no further publicity was given to the matter, the prosecution would drop the fresh charges. It subsequently emerged that a reduction in McIntosh's sentence of five years was also possible if the *Sunday Times* would agree to the deal. Two and a half years was mentioned as the likely period McIntosh would have to serve in prison. O'Beirne said the deal also depended on the *Sunday Times* persuading the British Foreign Office not to take the matter further.

The *Sunday Times* asked O'Beirne if the Rhodesian authorities would provide a written guarantee of the shortened sentence McIntosh would have to serve or an official statement of intent

O'Beirne said he was not authorised to offer this.

Harold Evans, editor of the *Sunday Times*, told O'Beirne that the newspaper could not agree to the deal he sought.

Ten months later in February 1975, McIntosh escaped from his cell. It was a big story, not only in Rhodesia but in Britain too. When he was not re-captured after a number of days, it seemed that he had got clean away. Stories even appeared in British newspapers that he was in Europe. In reality he was living rough in the Rhodesian bush trying to make his way across the border into Moçambique. After eighteen days on the run, he finally made it and was found in pretty poor shape by a Portuguese Army patrol sixteen miles across the border from Rhodesia. He was taken to the FRELIMO barracks for identification and then to the border police post at Vila de Manica. There he telephoned the British Consul in Beira 180 miles away and told his story.

The Consul immediately contacted the Portuguese authorities, told them to hold McIntosh, and set off in his car to collect him. When he arrived at Vila de Manica he found the Scotsman had been handed back to the Rhodesians just across the border.

White liberals in Moçambique were appalled. So was the British Foreign Office. The authorities in Lourenco Marques were embarrassed. They issued a statement saying there had been a misunderstanding over language. It was unconvincing, and it appeared transparently obvious that the Portuguese guards on the border, who for years had been on first names with their Rhodesian counterparts on the same border, had simply handed McIntosh over. Later it was claimed that money and cigarettes had been used by the Rhodesians to buy McIntosh back.

Admiral Victor Crespo, the Portuguese High Commissioner who was very nearly beginning to pack his bags for Lisbon prior to the formal hand-over of the territory to FRELIMO, said the Rhodesian police at the border had tricked the Portuguese.

But Knopfli wrote a leading article in *Tribuna* condemning the Lourenco Marques explanation as 'frail'.

Knopfli said that the whole credibility of Moçambique had been put in question. Here was an illegal White Regime, after South Africa the arch-suppressor of Africans, which had been able to recover a prisoner who had fled to the sanctuary of what was now virtually a free Black State.

Admiral Crespo was incensed when he read what Knopfli had written. Even in these dying moments of colonialism, new Black State or not, no Portuguese admiral was going to be publicly reprimanded like this. He demanded an apology in print couched, it was suggested, in 'second thoughts' style.

Knopfli refused. Though FRELIMO now held the whip hand in Moçambique, none of the new Black ministers lifted a finger to help him. He drove straight from Admiral Crespo's office back to his home and started packing. The next morning he bought air tickets for his wife and children to Lisbon; not *back* to Lisbon, just to Lisbon.

McIntosh was back in his cell in Salisbury. He was tried again on the new charges and finally sentenced to fourteen years plus two more for escaping.

In the new Moçambique there is a refreshing lack of the sort of political double-talk most of Africa's new states indulge in. It is a straight Marxist government with no nonsense about freedom—of the press or anything else. Given the circumstances under which FRELIMO came to power—almost literally hacking their path through the African bush every inch of the way—it is not surprising that they have thrown out all vestiges of Western democracy. All through the long years of the war of liberation no Western state gave them either a penny or a bullet. The forces they faced were armed with weapons from NATO.

FRELIMO came to power on 25 June, 1975. It immediately introduced a series of seminars covering virtually every aspect of life to define the principles and policies it would adopt as the government of the country. The seminar covering 'information' was held at Macomia at the end of November, and the agenda is significant in as much as it reveals the place the press is to occupy in the new state. Top of the list for discussion was radio, followed by wall newspapers. Next came 'organisation of information in the villages', then such vague sounding matters as 'propaganda', 'national bulletin', 'libraries', 'documentation' and just above 'cinemas, books and records', 'the press'.

'Bearing in mind the rate of illiteracy' (90 per cent) says the minutes of the seminar, 'the press is not a priority relevant to other means of communication'. Nonetheless, it added 'The importance of the ideological influence of newspapers should be recognised'.

Wall newspapers, called 'people's newspapers', were discussed with a thoroughness and attention to detail that might have seemed finicky to an untutored Westerner. So often the well-meaning Western aid official with impressive credentials overlooks the one thing—or often the whole string of things—which will separate the failure of a project from success. The Third World is littered with the whitening bones of such projects. Graham Greene took the theme for his *Ugly American*.

FRELIMO had been taught the art of wall newspapers by the inventors of the idea, the Chinese, and throughout the war of liberation they had proved highly successful as more and more of the northern part of Moçambique came under their control. Now, with the whole country liberated, the wall newspapers were to be geared to increasing literacy and 'making the people understand the revolutionary process'.

Unity is always the watchword of new governments, and unity it was that the wall newspapers were to plug. But it was not to be all politics and polemics. There were to be different versions of the wall newspapers, virtually local editions, with the village papers emphasising the need for self-sufficiency in food, while the town editions would concentrate on calling for greater production from the factories.

The contents were largely limited to local issues, but national and even international news would also be carried 'to create a spirit of internationalism with other countries like Angola'. The seminar agreed that there was little point in referring to 'little-known countries' unless 'there is an understanding of how they relate to the class struggle'.

Portuguese was to be used wherever possible, but local tribal languages could be included 'when necessary'.

These 'people's newspapers' were to have a maximum life of seven days, with 'constant alterations', and the ultimate aim was for completely new versions every three days. They were to be displayed so that they could be read 'standing up'. Considerable thought was given to the sort of places they should be displayed at: 'near a tap or a well at markets and other meeting places.' During the wet season they should be protected from the rain with little roofs'.

If paper was not available, then other materials like wood—old cases etc'—and scrap paper from old packaging should be used ... Even alternative writing materials, such as charcoal, were recommended.

The whole project was imaginatively and intelligently con‐
ceived.

Many of the lower cadre of Moçambique's new rulers wante‐
to scrap the conventional press altogether. 'The journalisti
technique is rooted in the bourgeois concept of journalism copie‐
from the Western capitalistic model' say the minutes of th
seminar. Speaker after speaker pointed to the role the press ha‐
played during the colonial period—and not one of them ha‐
anything to say for the men who had risked their lives, ofte‐
lost their liberty, and eventually their careers, trying to produc
decent newspapers all through the years of Fascism.

The newspapers of the towns, reported the minutes, were sti
aimed at the elite. If they were to continue 'they must hencefort
cease to reflect the values of the privileged classes. On th
contrary, the Press should relate to the large masses'.

Perhaps the key sentence in the minutes of the seminar wa‐
'The press must be placed at the service of the masses withi
the direction of the political orientation of FRELIMO.'

The seminar recommended that teams of journalists should b
sent to the rural areas, particularly to the new commun‐
villages which FRELIMO was busy setting up. It recommende
that 'journalistic technique should be strictly conditioned by th
concrete realities of Moçambique and by the revolutionar
political line directed towards national reconstruction'.

Of the language to be used in the remodelled press, th
seminar condemned 'stereotyped, sophisticated language bare‐
understandable'. Newspapers should 'try to portray a vision ‐
the world corresponding to the dynamic class struggle withou
resorting to sensational journalism made up of apparently u‐
connected facts'.

It should 'reject the bourgeois concept of history as merely
succession of facts and personalities rather than the result
the constant struggle between the exploited and exploitin
classes'.

Journalists, 'with a mentality rooted in bourgeois capitalism
should be retrained and 'ultra-leftists and rightists deviatio‐
which frequently arise in the national organs' were condemne‐

The seminar did not define what it meant by wanting
greater participation of the masses in the press' but it said th‐
'the deficiencies of the press tend to reflect the deficiencies of th

professional classes who work in them, the majority of them of *petit-bourgeois* origin who have no knowledge of the life of the masses'.

The 'importance of political activity among journalists' was stressed 'so that the subjects written about have a national and international level and do not merely reflect their personal views but should be integrated within the policies of FRELIMO'.

On a rather more practical note, the seminar called for a national network of local correspondents for the newspapers 'as being the most practical way of involving the whole country and eliminating the regional character which the press tends to have'.

It struck a more relevant note for the press all over Africa— where up-country readers are likely to receive their newspaper, if at all, several days after publication—when it urged the need to transform the existing form of the press from 'immediate consumerism into a style with a longer lasting interest'. Distribution problems were to be solved through the Party network, whose cells would act as distributing agents.

Three priorities were listed: defining the role of the press in relation to the people; ways of making newspapers cheaper; how to create a distribution network to embrace the whole country.

The seminar ended with a call for the press 'to strengthen its links with the cultural realities of the nation, avoiding the improvisations to which Moçambique journalism is conditioned'.

Across the other side of the Continent, Angola had followed a similar colonial history to Moçambique; forty years of authoritarian rule while Salazar was President of Portugal. The press, though generally a servile supporter of Fascism, was always marginally decent as two generations of White, Coloured and Black newspapermen tried to keep liberalism from being completely obliterated. They had less success than their counterparts in Moçambique, and with the bitterness caused by the attack of South African forces across its southern borders, the intervention of foreign mercenaries from the West in the civil war that preceded independence, and finally the massive infusion of Cuban troops, there seems even less hope of anything but the most rigid control of the press.

The evening *Diario de Luanda* was closed by the new government, and the country's biggest paper, the morning *A Provincia de Angola,* founded in 1923 and selling 41,000 at the time of independence, had its name changed to *O Journal de Angola*.

Many Portuguese journalists left when the rival African factions began fighting amongst themselves before the Cubans established the MPLA as the winners, and after many years in the bush in charge of the MPLA propaganda machine, one of the few White Angolans who had openly identified themselves with Black nationalism, Costa Andrade, took over as editor of the new *Journal*.

From its beginnings as an untrained, ill-equipped and relatively small group of guerillas, the MPLA had as its clarion call three priorities: War, Peace. Feeding.

Having achieved the first two, the third is going to be a long haul and the press—certainly the conventional press—is as low on the Party's list as it is on FRELIMO's in Moçambique. But there are a number of influential Party members who believe that the existing newspapers must be sustained and developed. One senior MPLA member who spent some years in the West, said 'My fear is that with the thousand and one pressing problems we have to tackle, and the realisation that there may be an all-out war in Southern Africa at any time, the press will wither away for want of attention. There is also a strong feeling in the Party that because newspapers were so much a part of colonial oppression they, too, should now be oppressed. Against this there are the intellectuals who believe the press must be preserved and so far they have won the day'.

But there is no division in the Party as to what the contents of the newspapers should be. 'Educated people will find them no more edifying than educated Russians find *Pravda* and *Isvestia*. But they will serve a greater good in getting across to the masses the national message of unity.' And, he added with a wry smile 'It is better to have bad newspapers than no newspapers. After all, bad newspapers can improve.'

A national centre for journalism has been opened in Luanda, but at the end of 1976 there was still discussion on what the syllabus should be. When it gets going, it will train both radio and newspaper journalists.

As in Moçambique, the MPLA is a great believer in wall newspapers and a poster artist course has begun which is producing a lively style of graphics. The wall newspapers tend to be more *collages*, with clippings from an assortment of publications. Many organisations, from factories to ministries, have their own wall papers and they are jointly edited, though individuals are encouraged to make their own contributions once they are up. They are changed weekly.

The Army is used to distribute the newspapers outside the main towns, and this is being done much more efficiently than in colonial times.

White Angolans have been encouraged to stay and there has been no talk of settling old scores. But that is very much the pattern of independence in Africa. It is generally a decade later that the squeeze on 'foreigners' begins, as it did in Uganda, Zambia, Kenya and Nigeria.

Champions of press freedom are doubtless dismayed at what has happened to the newspapers in both of Portugal's principal African territories, but nothing less should have been expected. FRELIMO and the MPLA, who began by fighting for liberation from colonialism, had the struggle turned into a war against the West as the democracies not merely stood by, but because of Portugal's membership of NATO, armed the troops facing them.

Both Moçambique and Angola are eager and grateful for help from any outside source, and though it is the Communists who have filled most of the vacua created by the withdrawal of the Portuguese, the West—as distinct from Western standards—is not entirely unrepresented in the shaping of the news media of both states.

Shortly after it came to power and thereafter, the MPLA was being helped in developing the Angolan News Agency by Michael Wolfers, who had sympathetically reported the African scene all over the Continent for the London *Times*, and who believed that it was not enough to give lip service to helping a fledgling state, whatever its political philosophy.

In Lourenco Marques another Briton, Ian Christie, son of dedicated Scottish socialist parents, moved into the Radio Station shortly after independence and began organising the propaganda broadcasts to Rhodesia. The bulletin of the International Press Institute, watchdog of press freedom throughout the world, described Christie as 'giving treasonable advice to the African people of Rhodesia' but ignored the fact that the rulers of Rhodesia had themselves committed treason by seizing power from Britain, and that with the unilateral declaration of independence in 1965, all legal authority in the country became void. IPI's comment is interesting in as much as it reveals the often biased, even bitter, viewpoint the West adopts when it observes unpalatable events in its former African possessions.

9 The White South

Two things prevent South Africa from being a total police state : the judiciary, which though obliged to administer laws made by racial fanatics, generally does so fairly and often humanely, and the press, which though also bound by the ruthless philosophy of apartheid, still has more freedom than newspapers in any other part of the Continent.

The freedom that the South African press has is in no way due to any enlightenment on the part of the Afrikaner Government.

When that Government came to power in 1948, it had every intention of emasculating the English-language press, in the same way as it had just politically emasculated the English-language community. But so ponderous were the new rulers of South Africa, and so untutored in organising the new administrative machine, that they floundered about seeking a satisfactory way of bringing the press to heel. They finally came up with the *Suppression of Communism Act* in 1950 which empowered the State President to prohibit 'the printing, publication or dissemination' of any publication, not only of the Communist Party, but also anything 'which serves *inter alia* as a means for expressing views or conveying information, the publication of which is calculated to fit the achievement of any of the objects of Communism'.

Though year after year innumerable other laws were to follow which were to restrict the press, this Act remains the bedrock of not merely legislation aimed at newspapers, but virtually every other form of activity in South Africa.

This pre-occupation with Communism pervades all Afrikaner political thought, and in South Africa politics spills over into almost every other form of life. Though some Afrikaners have mellowed somewhat after a generation of power holding and the reduction of power of the English community—never very strong—this fear of Communism is still the power-house of apartheid.

In the early years of White Nationalism, many of South Africa's new Afrikaner rulers believed that the most effective way to handle the English-language Press was by the simple act of closing it down. But the less fanatical Nationalists cautioned against such an extreme move. They believed, and they have been proved right, that it would be enough to get the English-language Press by the throat and apply whatever pressure was necessary whenever it was necessary.

This, in effect, has been the way that the South African press has been allowed to function; often wriggling hard under the Nationalist grip and occasionally kicking out at the shins of the rulers. But never seriously threatening 'Basskap'—the policy of White is Right.

There were no such reservations about obliterating those publications which were predominantly political and openly opposed to the new rulers.

All the political publications which supported African, Asian and Coloured opposition to apartheid were obliterated. Newspapers and magazines like *The Guardian, Advance, New Age, Fighting Talk* and *The Torch* were not only banned, but both their journalists and their managers were served with notices preventing them from ever working again on any publication.

But this was not enough for the more extreme of the extremists ruling South Africa. They were still after the blood of the important and much more influential string of morning and evening newspapers in all the major cities of the country. So in October 1950 the Nationalist Government appointed a commission to look into the 'discipline, self-control and character of (a) editors, journalists and correspondents serving local newspapers and periodicals, (b) correspondents of overseas newspapers and periodicals and (c) free-lance journalists serving the local or overseas Press'.

The idea behind the inquiry was to turn up enough evidence

to justify either the closure or seizure of newspapers which the Nationalists felt were opposed to apartheid. The Commission was a fiasco. It slogged on for an incredible fourteen years and became a bad joke even among the Government supporters. It was finally dissolved with only two-thirds of its agenda completed.

But by now the unsophisticated politicians who had come to power from farming backgrounds in 1948 had begun to learn some of the tricks of government. They also felt much more secure as in election after election their grip on both the national and local governments of South Africa became greater, with the inept English-speaking community unable to produce intelligent political alternatives in a land where everything was seen in stark Black and White.

Although the anti-Communist message was still the strident theme both at home and abroad in forums like the United Nations, there was a realisation in Pretoria that South Africa could hardly pose as the great defender of Western civilisation on the African Continent and at the same time resort to measures against the press which were in line with what had just happened in post-war Eastern Europe.

The White Nationalists, led by Hendrik Verwoerd, and after he was assassinated on the floor of Parliament, by his successor Johannes Vorster, began to realise that for all the irritating noises the English language press was making, it really did not have the slightest effect in political terms. Indeed, at every election, the readers of the English-language press were voting more and more for the Nationalists.

From its very beginnings, the press of South Africa has had a turbulent path. It is curious that though Europeans had been at the Cape for more than a century and a half no newspaper was started until August 1800 when the *Capetown Gazette and African Advertiser* became the first newspaper on the Continent, beating the *Royal Gazette of Sierra Leone* by a few months.

In no other part of the world settled by Europeans was there anything like this delay in starting newspapers. It is all the more odd in the case of South Africa since the first settlers of the Cape, the Dutch, came from a society where many kinds of publications were the order of the day. A possible explanation is that the relatively regular sea traffic from Europe to the Far East that the Dutch East India Company provided made the early Cape settlers feel adequate reading matter was available with supplies from home.

After all, until Charles de Breteuil appeared in French West Africa in the 1930s, the French community there were in a similar position to the early Cape colonists, happy enough to wait for the ship from Marseilles or Le Havre.

That first publication in Africa, the *Capetown Gazette*, was one of the very few, perhaps the only, early attempt at a bi-lingual newspaper in South Africa. It typifies what has happened to the two White communities in South Africa over the past three centuries; in the early years there was a sharing of interests between the Dutch and the English; then a parting of the ways and the establishment of virtually two White communities and now, towards the end of the twentieth century as Black Africa begins to gird its loins for the final onslaught against White rule in Africa, a coming together again to face what both communities see as the common enemy.

Although no daily newspaper or any other major publication is yet bi-lingual, there are a growing number of weeklies publishing in both English and Afrikaans and this trend may be expected to accelerate.

After almost thirty years of an educational system which obliges the two European groups to learn each other's language, South Africa is nearer to real bi-lingualism than any of the other handful of countries in the world which have more than one official language.

The first in the long succession of conflicts between press and Government in South Africa began in 1823 when two applications were made to Lord Charles Somerset, Britain's tyrannical and corrupt Governor of the Cape, to start newspapers. One of the applications was from Thomas Pringle, an Englishman, and his partner, the Rev. Abraham Faure, a missionary. Pringle and Faure were concerned about the way the natives were being treated at the hands of the Boers. Somerset said no to the venture. The other application came from another Englishman, a printer named George Greig. He wanted to publish a periodical which, he assured Somerset, would exclude 'all discussion of the policy or administration of the colonial government'.

He, too, was given a firm no. Then Greig discovered there was a loophole in the law concerning publications, and that in fact permission was only required for periodicals and not newspapers. In January 1824, with Thomas Pringle and James Fairbairn as editors, Greig hand-pulled the first issue of his *South*

African Commercial Advertiser off the old wooden press borrowed from a mission.

The *Advertiser* quickly began to turn over many stones at the court of Lord George Somerset and to report on what crawled out.

Somerset told Greig that if he did not stop he would be deported from the Colony. Greig refused and waited to see what would happen. Somerset began demanding to see proofs of what was to be printed, and every evening before the *Advertiser* was due to appear the next morning, he would send a messenger to the works with a note demanding the proofs. Greig refused to hand them over, and after several confrontations came out with a notice on the front page of the *Advertiser* declaring that 'we find it our duty as British subjects under these circumstances to discontinue the publication of the said paper for the present in this Colony until we have applied for redress and direction to his Excellency the Governor and the British Government'.

Greig sailed for Britain and sought redress. He had powerful friends including Thomas Barnes, editor of the *Times*, and others at the influential London Missonary Society. They advised him to return to the Cape, start publishing the *Advertiser* again, but to go easy in his criticisms of Somerset. Greig sailed for the Cape and began turning out the second, somewhat muted version of the *Advertiser*.

When Somerset suppressed it again in May 1827, this was too much for London and on 30 April 1828, a new Colonial Secretary sanctioned a Press law for the Cape based on the Law of England. Under this law publishers were to deposit £300, plus another £300 in guarantees with the authorities. They were then free to publish, subject only to the law of libel.

Thus the principle of press freedom was established in South Africa. It is significant that the battle had been won by a White man who was able to bring influence to bear in the corridors of power of Whitehall. During the very same years as Greig was fighting for these rights, the first generation of African newspapermen emerging in Britain's West African colonies were struggling to establish their freedom to produce newspapers unhindered by the constraints of their colonial masters.

Greig's victory produced a whole spate of other newspapers all over that part of South Africa which was settled by Europeans. The Afrikaners had not yet started the great trek into the interior.

The Dutch community in the Eastern Cape started its own paper, *De Zuid Afrikaan*, in 1830. The policy it adopted towards the Africans was hardly to be varied by the Afrikaans language Press of South Africa for the next 150 years; that the White man is a superior being and has a natural right to rule Blacks.

It was not until 1875 that Afrikaans, which was still evolving as a language distinct from the original Dutch, was used in print. This was when *Di Patriot* appeared as the voice of the Society of True Afrikaans and its policy was to 'stand up for our language, our nation and our people'.

All the little settlements in the Cape were producing newspapers. In Grahamstown the *Journal* appeared in very much the same shape as the small newspapers of Britain which the Eastern Cape's colonisers had left. The British settlers were great writers of letters to the *Journal*, and the surviving early issues are among the best records of contemporary life in South Africa as the Whites asserted themselves over the Blacks.

The continuing theme of the letters' column was for the authorities to do something about 'the troublesome caffres'. Another paper founded in 1850 in Grahamstown, *The Friend of the Sovereignty*, thumped the Land of Hope and Glory note. When it moved into the hinterland, to Bloemfontein, it announced that this was 'to further the march of civilisation north'. But it added, in rather more materialistic vein 'and boom real estate'. *The Friend*—long since shorn of its Sovereignty—thrives today as the biggest daily in the Orange Free State.

In 1854 the Robinson family founded Durban's first daily, the *Natal Mercury and Commercial Shipping Gazette*, and it has remained in the same family's hands ever since, though it is now known as the *Natal Mercury*. It was as fiercely British as the English settlers who settled in Natal Colony.

A high point in the history of the press of South Africa was the publication in 1857 of the *Cape Argus*, followed by the *Cape Times* in 1876. These papers, the *Argus* an evening and the *Times* a morning, were the genesis of the great newspaper empires which came to predominate in South Africa and, in the case of the *Argus*, in the hinterland to the north which became known as Southern Rhodesia and Northern Rhodesia.

Although the *Cape Argus* was started by another Englishman devout in his belief in all things British (and preferably English), Bryan Henry Darnell, the *Argus* soon came under the control of its printer, Saul Solomon, who, although without the Oxford-educated background of Darnell, was one of the earliest humanitarians at the Cape. His belief in decent treatment for the non-Europeans earned him the label of 'negrophilist'. The *Cape Argus* became the first newspaper in Africa to use the new telegraph facilities, and the attainment of full self-government for Cape Colony in 1872 was largely the result of Solomon's campaign in and out of the columns of his newspaper.

The liberal tone of the *Argus* began to change when Solomon appointed Francis Joseph Dormer editor in 1877. The paper continued to develop and largely because of the need for new capital to keep up with its expansion, Solomon went looking for money. Dormer had some, but not enough. Dormer went to see the son of an English country parson who had come to South Africa to give his weak chest a better chance in the sunshine, Cecil John Rhodes. Rhodes, probably the greatest Empire builder of them all, and certainly its sharpest operator, knew a good thing when he saw it. He put up the money Dormer needed to expand the *Argus*. Solomon sold out.

Thereafter there was no more championing of the African's cause.

From their beginnings, both the Cape newspapers and virtually all the other major English-language publications that followed, adopted the British pattern of newspaper production. London's Fleet Street not only set the standard, but until after the Second World War, Britain was the place where the South Africans recruited their editors, and many of their other employees.

When gold was discovered in the Transvaal in 1886, the *Argus* opened a branch office there. Three years later it bought out the *Star* which is today the biggest daily newspaper on the African Continent.

The *Star* had been started in Grahamstown, hundreds of miles away in the Eastern Cape, and was transported by ox-wagon to the gold-fields of the Transvaal in 1887. With the purchase of the *Star*, there came into being the Argus Printing and Publishing Company. In the 1890s shareholders included many of the biggest names in the minefields, men like Solly Joel, Barney Barnato and, of course, Cecil John Rhodes. Rhodes had already made one fortune—he was to multiply it several times over—in the diamond fields. When he bought into the Argus Company, he was busy consolidating his political career, which had begun when he entered the Cape Parliament in 1880, shortly after putting up the money for Dormer to buy the Cape *Argus*.

The *Star* had changed from twice weekly to daily publication, and with men like Rhodes behind it, began to spend a lot of money to establish itself as the highly professional and businesslike operation it remains to this day. The new cable link had just been laid between South Africa and Europe, and this enabled the *Star* to take the Reuter service from London. With the mining industry now established as one of the world's great centres of industrial wealth, the innovation of a daily news service which included financial news from the City of London, gave the *Star* a unique position in the Transvaal. By 1893 the *Star* was being produced on a rotary press with linotype setting.

The Afrikaners, who had trekked north from the Cape in ox-wagons to get away from the aggravations of the arriving British, were incensed at this new intrusion. To them, the *Star* seemed to represent all that was worst among the English-speaking community of South Africa with its pre-occupation on wealth and mammon.

Paul Kruger, God-fearing President of the Transvaal Republic, gave a State subsidy to the *Standard and Diggers News* in Johannesburg and *The Press* in Pretoria, which though English-language papers, were sympathetic to the Boers and their concern at what was happening to the country at the hands of people like Cecil Rhodes.

The *Star* was banned when one of Rhodes's men, Leander Storm Jameson, led a band of privateers against the Boer Republic in an attempt to seize total control of the gold fields.

When the Jameson raid failed, Kruger accused the *Star* and its backers of being involved in the plot. But the *Star*'s lawyers were more than a match for Kruger, and the day after the banning order was made a new newspaper, *The Comet*, appeared. A year later the Boer War broke out which was to finish Kruger, re-establish *The Star*, and sow the seeds of mistrust between the two White tribes of South Africa.

The rest of the history of South Africa, until Black Nationalism flowed down from the north to its borders, was to be steeped in this White mistrust.

When the Boer War finished in 1902 a new daily appeared in Johannesburg, the *Rand Daily Mail*. Its first editor was Edgar Wallace, one of the most popular British novelists of his day, who had gone to South Africa as an officer in the British Army fighting the Boers.

In 1906 the *Mail* was bringing out a Sunday edition, the *Sunday Times,* which was to become the biggest seller on the African Continent, with a circulation in 1977 of 500,000.

After the Boer War, South Africa began to attract settlers from many parts of Europe and North America, and the Argus Group became busy enlarging its grip on the evening paper readership of the country. By the end of the First World War it had bought the *Natal Advertiser* in Durban, which later became the *Natal Daily News, The Friend* in Bloemfontein, the *Diamond Fields Advertiser* in Kimberley in 1922, and the *Pretoria News* in 1930.

The Argus Group was now the biggest newspaper publishing company in South Africa—indeed, in the whole of Africa—and it was to continue to expand. In an effort to counter the influence of the Argus, some of the leading morning newspapers (the Argus papers were mainly afternoon papers) got together in 1932 to form the South African Morning Newspaper Group, sharing news gathering facilities and even some staff. This co-operation led to the creation of a company called South African Associated Newspapers (SAAN) with membership made up of the *Rand Daily Mail,* the *Sunday Times,* the *Natal Mercury,* the Johannesburg *Sunday Express,* the *Eastern Province Herald* and the *Evening Post* of Port Elizabeth. The SAAN was designed to provide a counterpoint to the powerful Argus Group, which in addition to its newspapers, controls an impressive range of annuals, specialist magazines, mining year-books and financial publications.

In the middle seventies the Argus increased its holding in the Central News Agency, the major newspaper distributing company in the country, to 37.75 per cent.

Until recent years, when the political power of the Afrikaners began to manifest itself in the business life of the country, the Afrikaans Press of South Africa was no match for the English-language Press. From the beginning, more than was the case with their English counterparts, the Afrikaans press was geared towards achieving political influence. The two great architects of apartheid, Daniel Malan and Hendrik Verwoerd, rose through the ranks of Afrikaner nationalism to become prime ministers via the editorial chairs of their party's Cape and Transvaal organs, *Die Burger* and *Die Transvaler.*

Die Burger was launched as the first Afrikaans daily in 1915.

It has remained the Nationalist Party's most prestigious newspaper ever since. Malan became Prime Minister when the Nationalist Party won the 1948 general election.

Twenty years after the appearance of *Die Burger*, Malan and fourteen other Nationalist leaders met in the Cape university town of Stellenbosch to consider ways and means of expanding the newspaper voice of Nationalism in the Transvaal. The Party leaders knew that unless it made headway in the Transvaal, the Party had no hope of one day coming to power. Of its nineteen members in the 150-seat House of Assembly, the Party had only one representative from the Transvaal.

With financial backing from a wealthy farmer in the Cape, Pieter Neethling, and assistance in the form of public contributions from the readers of *Die Burger* and *Die Volksblad* in the Free State, a company named *Voortrekker Pers Beperk* was created. The articles of association defined the political policy of the paper proposed for the Transvaal as '. . . the furtherance of National interests of the land and the people . . . to help the Afrikaans-speaking section . . . it will seek to lead our volk along the Christian-National road . . . It will help interpret and fulfill the general principles of the National Party . . . to plead for the establishment of a free republic on Christian-National foundations'.

Hendrik Verwoerd completed his year as professor of sociology at Stellenbosch University and moved to the Transvaal to start *Die Transvaler*. He applied himself with singlemindedness and dedication, travelling all over the Transvaal canvassing for subscribers for the new paper and setting up groups to collect funds for *Voortrekker Pers*.

On 1 October 1937 the first issue of *Die Transvaler* appeared on the streets of Johannesburg, Pretoria, and throughout the industrial Reef. It reeked of racialism. Verwoerd had a six thousand word article on 'The Jewish Question'; another prominent politician wrote on 'The Asiatic Flood in South Africa', Johannes (Hans) Strydom, the Party's sole MP in the Transvaal, and a future Prime Minister, dealt with 'The Maintenance of White Civilisation'. A report of a speech by a lecturer at Potchefstroom University attacking liberalism and warning of the dangers Jews threatened in South Africa was headlined: 'Liberalism carries Germs of Future Disaster; Leads only to levelling of natural differences; Creates dangerous friction regarding Jewish Question.'

Verwoerd edited *Die Transvaler* from 1937 until the Nationalists came to power in 1948. Throughout the Second World War, his editorials consistently condemned the Allied cause as a British imperialist venture. In the early days of the War when the English-language press was anticipating the German invasion of the Netherlands, *Die Transvaler* ridiculed the suggestion. On 18 November 1939 Verwoerd editorialised: '. . . from the beginning *Die Transvaler* has exposed the falsity of British propaganda about the so-called threatened German attack on Holland. The purpose of this propaganda was to panic Holland into war on the British side.'

When the Germans bombed Rotterdam to the ground and overran Holland, *Die Transvaler* of 11 May 1940 said: 'Attempts will be made by Smuts (Prime Minister) to use this sympathy for neutral, small nations for local political gain. Everything will be used in this way to parade Nationalists on the side of Smuts and the British Empire. Does the Nationalist belong there now, or not? The answer is an unequivocal NO!'

A South African judge said that Verwoerd had turned *Die Transvaler* into a 'tool of the Nazis'.

The Afrikaans press is now divided between the two major Afrikaans political groups, representing the Transvaal wing of the Nationalist Party and the Cape wing. On the boards of both groups are several cabinet ministers.

The Afrikaans press is solidly pro-government, but in recent years there has been a growing tendency for newspapers to indulge in general criticisms of the Nationalist policy.

After more than a quarter of a century of Afrikaner rule, the National Party is deeply divided. The upheavals of Angola and Moçambique and the guerilla war in Rhodesia has brought Black Africa's front line to South Africa's northern border and eastern and western flanks. The split between those sections of the Party who believe that some sort of *détente* must be reached with Independent Africa and those who believe that such moves will encourage South Africa's own Blacks to seek a share of political power has led the more intelligent sections of the Afrikaans press to begin to say things unthinkable a decade ago.

As the interminable threats of Johannes Vorster continued against the English-language press, in an article entitled 'Thus Have the Afrikaans Newspapers Failed', Dirk Richard, editor of the Sunday *Dagbreek*, asked his fellow Afrikaner editors how well they had run their own affairs. Time was, he said, when it had been necessary for Afrikaners to stand together in politics, cultural affairs and the press. Because of this the Afrikaans press had supported every Government action 'when it could sometimes very fruitfully for South Africa and the National Party have come forward with constructive criticisms'.

Similar murmurings have been heard from the editors of *Die Burger* and the Transvaal's *Die Beeld*, another morning launched in September 1974.

The story of the non-European press in South Africa is the story of the non-European peoples themselves: frustration. Before the turn of the century, there were a number of African-language publications voicing African aspirations. The most important of these was *Imvo Zabantsundu Ntsundu*, founded in 1884 by John Tengo Jababu. The South African Native National Congress, which was the earliest and most important African political organisation, was responsible for a spate of African-language papers in many parts of the country but these were all to fall away, for the most part suppressed, as White Nationalism began to assert itself more and more vigorously.

Though South Africa's Indian community, almost entirely settled in Natal, has been an important economic force in that part of South Africa, it has rarely been interested in the press as anything more than keeping in touch with events in India. Mahatma Gandhi founded *Indian Opinion* in 1906 in Durban, but its principal policy was the defence of Indian traders in Natal. When he went back to India, the paper continued under his son, Manilal, and, when he died, under his widow.

Today there is no African newspaper in South Africa owned or controlled by Africans. There have been many attempts to launch a truly non-European press, but these have all failed in the face of the political and economic realities of South Africa.

After the Second World War, the White newspaper groups, realising the economic potential of the non-European races, turned their attention to the lucrative market that was appearing. The most celebrated publication aimed exclusively at the non-European market was the monthly magazine *Drum*, which from modest beginnings in 1951 grew, under successive British editors such as Anthony Sampson and Tom Hopkinson, to become the most potent journalism, Black or White, South Africa had ever seen. It was owned by Jim Bailey, the son of a contemporary of Rhodes, Sir Abe Bailey, one of the country's legendary mining millionaires.

Drum gave opportunities to African journalists and photographers that had never existed before. During the fifties and early sixties, it achieved a power that caused great concern in political establishment circles. Besides describing the rip-roaring social society of the Africans and Coloureds and the often mysterious world of the Asians, it ran exposures on a score of issues such as the farm prisons of South Africa, the brutality of the prison staff in their dealings with non-Whites, and the suffocating restrictions of the laws of apartheid.

Before they were banned shortly after the Afrikaners came to power in 1948, many of the left-wing publications like *New Age*, *Spark* and *The Guardian* were running similar exposes—but it was much more difficult for the Nationalists to dab *Drum* with the same Red brush that they had used against the purely political papers.

Under Tom Hopkinson, *Drum* was to spread beyond the borders of South Africa and set new standards of magazine journalism in Central, East and West Africa. Originally entirely controlled from Johannesburg, the editions in other parts of Africa were eventually obliged to become separate companies as the links between South Africa and newly independent Africa became more and more tenuous.

A sister publication to *Drum* was *Post*, a weekly tabloid newspaper with three separate editions catering for the three non-White groups of the country, Africans, Coloureds and Indians. Unlike *Drum*, *Post* concerned itself less with campaigns against the injustices of apartheid, concentrating far more on sex and crime.

To compete with *Drum*, and to present a very different picture to urban Africans, an Afrikaans publishing house brought out *Bona* as a monthly, with separate editions in three of the major tribal languages Xhosa, Zulu and Sotho. The Government bought up large numbers which it distributed freely in African schools.

Jim Bailey became financially overstretched. He was badly advised about the purchase of an expensive Italian gravure press which needed to be worked for longer hours than those provided by either *Drum* or *Post*. He was obliged to cut back, and the Argus group were very glad to snap up *Post*, which was the market leader for the urban Africans, particularly those around Johannesburg. But under Argus control, *Post* became a shadow of its lusty, former self and circulation plummeted.

Bailey tried hard to find someone to share the financial strain on his operation (brought about by the purchase of the new press) but there were no takers either in South Africa or Britain. Among those who turned him down was Rupert Murdoch, the Australian newspaper magnate who had turned the setting *Sun* into the highest flyer in Fleet Street. He unencouragingly responded to Jim Bailey's South African overtures by asking 'When are you having your revolution?'

Drum, too, fell away, almost burnt out, during the late sixties and early seventies, but by 1976 it was beginning to show signs of recapturing some of the market, if not the glory, of its great days. *Drum*'s East and West African editions, at first controlled from London but then as separate companies, thrived with independence in the states it served; but in 1975, the Nigerian edition was sold out to interests in Lagos though the London office continued to produce it under a service contract.

South Africa's first daily newspaper for Africans appeared in 1963 when the Argus Group bought up *The World* and turned it into an evening in Johannesburg. The masthead announced that *The World* is 'Our Own, Our Only Newspaper'. It was hardly that, but the White management and White editorial director served up a heady brew of crime, violence and sex. It avoided politics, because, said its White general manager, Clive Kinsley, 'there was apparently very little interest in it among the Bantu'.

In a country where entering the wrong door or sitting on the wrong park bench is a political act, Kinsley could hardly have been more wrong and a few years later, in 1977, the 'very little interest' the Africans were supposed to have in politics became for the *The World* the biggest story it was ever to run. Also the last. Although the puritanical Calvinism of the Afrikaner church often erupts in condemnation of the sort of lusty diet the *World* and *Post* served up, in fact this formula suits the Nationalist Government very well. It is happy to see the Africans identified with a somewhat lurid, crime-ridden and sex-dominated way of life as this picture supports the propaganda South Africa trades on—that the Blacks are a long way from being ready to assume any real responsibility in the country. Early in 1975, *The World* switched to twenty-four hour printing, with three daily editions, and made immediate gains in circulation at the expense of the *Rand Daily Mail*.

In recent years more and more Black journalists and photographers have been employed by the 'White' publications, and though papers like the *Rand Daily Mail* have adopted this policy as a matter of principle, it has, to a large extent, been forced upon management by the exigencies of apartheid. Since White reporters are not normally allowed into non-White townships, Black journalists have played a predominant role in reporting stories like the wave of rioting throughout the African and Coloured townships of Johannesburg, Cape Town and Port Elizabeth during much of 1976.

But for the stories and the pictures produced by Black journalists, little of what has happened in these non-White areas (other than official police communiques), would have reached the outside world. Police reaction to the reports and photographs from Black journalists was predictable; assault and arrest. Between June and September 1976 fourteen Black newspapermen were picked up by the police and held without trial or explanation. *The Rand Daily Mail* alone lost five Black reporters and photographers. Peter Magubane, South Africa's best-known news photographer—originally from the *Drum* stable—was twice viciously assaulted by the police. The second time his nose was broken when he was bashed across the face by a White police officer's revolver. Almost every time he was seen in Soweto, the huge Black township which serves Johannesburg with its non-European labour force and which produced the worst rioting, Magubane had his films and cameras confiscated by the police.

Magubane was due to attend a police identification parade to point out his assailants, but before it took place he was arrested. During the sixties and early seventies, he was in detention for 586 days and several times after his release restricted to a small area of his Black township, which meant he was unable to work.

Some of the best reporting of the Soweto riots came from Nat Serache of the *Rand Daily Mail*. His copy heightened suspicions that some of the Africans in the township were being encouraged by police to take action against student militants and their families who were protesting against apartheid. Having entered one of the township hostels disguised as a resident, Serache reported that he heard the police chastising some of the Africans who opposed the militant students for attacking property as well as the students. He quoted a policeman as saying 'If you damage houses we will be forced to take action against you. You have been ordered to kill only these troublemakers'.

Another Black reporter who became a key target for the police during the rioting was Joe Thloloe of *Drum*, though he was detained more for what he represented than for anything he wrote; he barely had time to put paper into typewriter before he was picked up. As president of the Union of Black Journalists (UBJ), Tholole was a prime target for the police.

The UBJ is part of the broadly-based Black consciousness movement in South Africa which seeks to promote Black pride and self-sufficiency. It has its origins in similar movements in the United States, and South Africa's Minister of Police has referred to it as 'a prime political enemy'. Almost all its leaders have been detained. The implications for Black pressmen who were leading members of the UBJ was obvious. The UBJ *Bulletin* carrying the account of the clashes between the armed police and the township students took a much more critical line against the authorities than any of the South African newspapers. It indirectly raised the question of the extent of press objectivity in reporting the unrest. Official reaction was swift. The offending issue of the *Bulletin* was banned and future publication forbidden.

Influx control, another provision of apartheid, means that Black journalists are severely restricted in their movements about the country. A Johannesburg-based reporter cannot take a job on a Durban or Cape newspaper, and it is against the law for Africans to be away from their home towns for more than forty-eight hours without permission. Thus, a reporter sent from Johannesburg to report a story elsewhere can be prosecuted if he is away more than two days.

It is hardly surprising that a number of African journalists have become so frustrated that they have sought ways of escaping from the claustrophobic existence of apartheid. Three from the *Post-Drum* stable, Can Themba, Nat Nakasa and Lewis Nkosi found different ways out. Themba, at his best one of the finest feature writers in the country, drank himself to death—quite consciously. He told friends that he had thought about other ways of taking his life, but as the stupification of racialism had virtually reduced him to a state of permanent bewilderment anyway, it seemed a natural step to finish things off in the ultimate miasma.

Nat Nakasa, a casting director's model of the fast-moving, fast-talking city reporter, graduated to becoming a first-class columnist. Many of the pieces he wrote for the *Rand Daily Mail* have found their way into collections of African writing. In 1964 he was awarded a Nieman Scholarship at Harvard. After battling with the authorities in Pretoria, he was given permission to accept the scholarship provided he did not return. He was torn between the opportunity to breathe some fresh, free air and improve himself in the United States, and leaving his homeland for good. He finally left South Africa, but in the agony of exile threw himself from the window of his fourteenth storey hotel room in New York.

Lewis Nkosi provided a foot-note to South African history when his lawyer unearthed a never-used statute entitled the Departure from South Africa Act. It said that if you took no business assets with you and signed a document saying you would never return, you would be allowed to leave the country. There was nothing about Black or White in the Act. Nkosi applied to go. When his application was turned down, he announced that he would appeal to the Supreme Court. Astonishingly, back from the Ministry of External Affairs came his exit permit—what became known as the one-way tickets which many more South Africans of all colours were to receive in the years ahead.

The probable explanation was that Nkosi's case brought to light a situation which had never been known to the authorities, and while their initial reaction had been to refuse, it then occurred to them that this was a way of getting rid of undesirables who needed constant watching.

It is not a fool-proof escape route for all opponents of apartheid, as Robert Sobukwe, leader of the banned Pan African Congress was to discover. Sobukwe had been locked up for many years on the notorious Robben Island off the Cape coast. When he was finally released, he was not freed but served with an order confining him to a small 'magisterial limit' around the township in which he lives.

Yes, said Pretoria, when Sobukwe applied, certainly you can have an exit permit. But as he cannot leave the 'magisterial limit', he cannot get to Johannesburg Airport to catch the 'plane out to freedom.

Lewis Nkosi is remembered in South Africa not merely for how he got out of it, but for a piece of effrontery which the State Prosecutor despite great effort was unable to bring before a court.

In the affluent White society of Johannesburg, 'the servant problem' is second only to apartheid as a talking point. The small advertisement pages of all the 'White' newspapers are full of *situation vacant* ads couched in these sort of terms: *Clean living Bantu wanted by Northern Suburbs' business couple. Good opportunity for decent girl.*

Nkosi was pondering the vacancy columns at his desk in *Post* one day when a devious thought occurred to him. He wrote out an ad and sent it round to the *Star,* never imagining that it would get beyond the girl on the desk, perhaps giving her and her friends a little food for thought. But the ad got further than the *Star* counter. It blazoned forth in that evening's edition, and when word got round to the White population of Johannesburg there was a small run on the paper.

Nkosi's ad read: *Clean living European wanted for two African writers. Good opportunity for decent girl.*

There was even one reply—from a girl who said she would like the job very much but doubted if she would be able to 'live in'.

There was one more response—in person, and in the shape of a large White police sergeant. Nkosi had broken no law, it seemed, but 'you'd better watch your step my lad' was the admonishment, accompanied by much finger-wagging.

South African policemen are great finger-waggers when dealing with Black newspapermen, that is when they are not bashing them across the face with their revolvers.

In the tragi-comedy of South Africa, there is much bitter humour to lighten the darker side of apartheid, but journalists employing it must always be wary. Anthony Delius, the wittiest political columnist in the country, was banned from the Press gallery in Parliament after a light-hearted quip in his column in the *Cape Times,* which was adjudged to have 'connected a member of the floor of the House with a stranger in the gallery'. This quaint phrase, ringing of Westminster mystique, referred to a paragraph in his column which said that Prime Minister Vorster had been watched by Big Brother in the public gallery—which was literally true, but as George Orwell's *Nineteen Eighty Four* had escaped the banned list and was selling well throughout South Africa, there were overtones much too close for comfort. Delius, South African born, is another on the long list of journalists who has left his homeland for good.

The story of the *Rand Daily Mail* during the sixties provides a classic confrontation of a courageous editor and authority. In 1965 the *Mail* published a series of articles about brutality in South Africa's prisons. Much of the material on which the articles were based was provided by a former White political prisoner, Robert Strachan, and two ex-Afrikaner prison warders.

Strachan told the *Mail's* editor, Laurence Gandar, that while in prison he had frequently seen Black prisoners being kicked, whipped and tortured with an electrical machine.

The *Mail* took affidavits from Strachan, and sworn statements from the warders and other former prisoners. When the *Mail* published the allegations there was a storm, not only in South Africa but in many parts of Europe and North America where the articles were re-printed.

With one of his reporters, Benjamin Pogrund, Gandar was prosecuted by the Government under the Prison Act, a law which makes it an offence to publish false information about prison conditions. Security Police raided the offices of the *Mail* and seized documents and tape-recorders.

Strachan and the other informants were charged with making false statements and found guilty. Strachan was sent back to prison.

With the informants legally discredited, the Government had laid the groundwork for its next move against the *Mail*. Prosecutor Hendrik Liebenberg said at the opening of the trial of Gandar and Pogrund that the freedom of the press was not at stake. He accused the two newspapermen of running a campaign to vilify the Prisons Department, of publishing one-sided reports, and of rejecting information favourable to the prisons. The Prison Act specifies that newspapers must take 'reasonable steps' to check their information. It puts the onus of proof on them. 'Reasonable steps' is defined as having the allegations cleared before publication with the Comissioner of Prisons.

The *Mail* had failed to have the story so cleared, knowing full well that the Commissioner of Prisons would hardly sanction the publication of reports of torture and brutality in the prisons under his control.

The cumbersome judicial system of South Africa ground on for more than three years before Gandar and Pogrund finally came before the Johannesburg Supreme Court. *Time* magazine said the eighty-nine day trial cost the *Mail* something like 500,000 dollars in legal costs. Gandar stood by his exposés. He said that the newspaper had gone 'well beyond what most newspapers would have considered adequate in checking its facts'. Not to have published the prison stories would have been a dereliction of duty, he said, and that the exposés had been 'in accordance with the role of the free press around the world'. The *Mail*, Gandar and Pogrund were all found guilty, but the penalties imposed by the court were negligible. The newspaper was fined 420 dollars, Gandar 280 dollars and Pogrund was given a six-month prison sentence suspended for three years.

But the trial was very much more a prosecution of one newspaper and two newspapermen. The South African Government had been under pressure from important National Party branches in the Transvaal to make an example of the *Mail* as a lesson to the rest of the English-speaking press. This became clear at many points during the trial. Prosecutor Liebenberg said that newspapers must not cause 'stirs or rumpuses', not arrogate to itself rights it did not possess and 'must serve the interests not of some sections of extremists but of the majority of its readers'.

The Government was well satisfied with the outcome of the trial. It had cracked the whip and the English-language press had got the message. Certainly the directors of *Rand Daily Mail* had. They had seen the circulation drop from 125,000 in 1961 to 111,000 seven years later. Issue after issue during all these years had hammered away at apartheid and the need to bridge the racial barriers of South Africa.

The awards gained by Gandar at an international level, like the 1966 World Press Achievement Award of the American Newspaper Publishers Association, were all very fine but they did not show in the balance-sheet. Principles do not sell papers.

There was an attempt at boardroom level to have Gandar removed. He was told by the managing director and acting chairman, Henri Kuiper, that the majority shareholders had decided he should go. It would therefore be best if he prepared to leave quietly. He told Gandar that the Board was thinking of appointing Johnny Johnson, editor of the *Sunday Express,* in his place. Kuiper said the reason for these decisions was that the *Mail's* trading position was poor, and that circulation had fallen off alarmingly. It was felt that Gandar's policies were too radical for the *Mail's* readership, and that the paper was not strong enough on news. Johnson, formerly news editor of the *Mail* and later the *Sunday Times*, had a reputation as a strong newsman.

Gandar argued that his removal would look like an admission of guilt by the company if he was dismissed in the face of the court case. He also warned that the editorial staff of the *Mail* would probably baulk at Johnson who was running the *Sunday Express* more and more to the right and whose staff relations were notoriously bad. Gandar suggested a compromise formula: himself as editor-in-chief, responsible only for policy in the leading articles, and Raymond Louw, then news editor of the *Mail,* as editor in charge of news. Gandar argued that Louw had as strong a news image as Johnson and would be acceptable to the *Mail* staff. He also knew that Louw would continue the *Mail's* liberal policies whereas Johnson would almost certainly change them.

Allister Sparks, the *Mail's* assistant editor, organised a deputation of senior staff to see Kuiper and object to Gandar's proposed dismissal. The deputation urged Kuiper to prevail upon the Board to accept Gandar's compromise formula. In the end the Board did this, but there were further dramas ahead.

Gandar's proposal was accepted on a six-month trial basis. He moved up to become editor-in-chief and Raymond Louw took over as acting editor. At the end of the trial period, Louw was confirmed as editor but Gandar was told that the majority shareholders were not prepared to confirm his appointment as editor-in-chief.

By this time the *Mail* had a new chairman, Cecil Payne, who had been brought in from one of the mining houses and who was suspected by the *Mail's* editorial staff of being the hatchet man for the majority shareholders.

Again Allister Sparks rallied the senior editorial staff, and went in to do what he thought would be battle with the new chairman. To the deputation's surprise, they found Payne extremely sympathetic. At the same time they found there had been a procedural irregularity in the way the majority share-holding group had reached its decision. This information was fed to sympathetic elements on the Board. The upshot was a major row at the Board meeting, and Gandar was confirmed as editor-in-chief.

Eventually the court case against Gandar, Pogrund and the

Mail began. As it dragged on for months, it had a dreadful effect on Gandar, knowing that whatever the outcome he would be the loser, and the *Mail* a lesser paper. When eventually he was found guilty, he wanted to go to jail rather than pay his fine. Several of the senior men on the *Mail*, and his wife, persuaded him not to.

So devastating was the effect on him that he decided he wanted to get out of South Africa, at least for a long time. Friends in London, led by David Astor of *The Observer*, offered him a job setting up the Minority Rights Group. He was now fifty-seven and asked the Board of the *Mail* for early retirement. The irony was that Cecil Payne tried desperately to persuade him to stay on at the *Mail*. The two men had become firm friends and mutual admirers.

But Gandar was a broken man and determined to put distance between himself and all that South Africa represented. He went to Britain to set up the Minority Rights Group. But the stomach had gone out of him. He became increasingly disillusioned at the way governments all over the world, right and left, treated minorities. Two years later he packed again and sailed for home.

A long-time South African editor, Maurice Broughton, after thirty years editorial experience in the country, mainly with the Argus Group, had written years before:

> Freedom became secondary to the necessity of commercial and financial stability ... the outcome has been that the balance of power rests to this day with the owners through their instruments the business managers and directorates ...

Gandar's trial precipitated a threatened merger for the *Mail*. On 11 November 1968, ten days after the trial began, a group of shareholders in SAAN offered the Argus Group an option to buy a 65.9 per cent shareholding in SAAN. This would have given the Argus Group control of 60 per cent of all daily newspapers, English and Afrikaans; 70 per cent of English-language weekly papers and 77 per cent of English-language dailies.

The South African Society of Journalists condemned the move. If it went through, said the SASJ, the Argus Group would then control 74 per cent of all employment opportunities. The Argus Group ignored the protest and prepared to take up the option, but immediately Prime Minister Vorster stepped in and stopped them.

'The Cabinet feels that newspaper takeovers to this extent and which so obviously conflict with the public interest are not in the interests of the country'. he said.

In 1975 a new chapter in South African newspaper publishing opened. There had always been a sizeable section of Europeans in and around Johannesburg—mainly Afrikaners but also from the English-speaking community—who had been unhappy that the only English-language morning paper in Johannesburg was the ultra-liberal *Rand Daily Mail*. As events to the north of South Africa deepened the belief that in the near future South Africa would be the sole 'White' state on the Continent, the intransigence of many Europeans deepened. The time was right, it was felt and said, for a new Johannesburg English-language morning paper which would counter the daily breakfast diet of anti-government expression by the *Mail*.

The move to redress the balance, when it came, was a bold one. Louis Luyt, an Afrikaner industrialist who had become a millionaire manufacturing fertiliser, made a bid to buy control of the SAAN Group. Had this bid succeeded, it would have virtually removed at a stroke the entire voice of liberalism from the South African newspaper scene. The English-speaking community all over the country was aghast at the thought, and though he upped and upped again his bid for the controling shareholding, Luyt was foiled.

Luyt did not take long to regroup his forces for the next attack. After months of cloak-and-dagger activity, with the newspaper industry abounding with rumours, he launched a morning broadsheet in September 1976, *The Citizen*, in Johannesburg. The pool of journalists and advertising and circulation executives in South Africa is not large, but Luyt recruited swiftly and ruthlessly. He simply offered salaries, cars, entertainment allowances and fringe benefits no other paper could match. *Die Vaderland*, happy to watch the English-speaking side of the industry sweating at the arrival of the newcomer, published a letter which, it claimed, John Fairbairn, development manager of SAAN, had written to an advertising executive in the United States. It said that Luyt had earmarked 12 million South African Rand (£7,000,000) whose declared object was to 'knock the *Mail* for six-within six months'.

Fairbairn's letter went on: 'In the present economic climate coupled with rising newspaper production costs and commercial TV just around the corner, there is no room for two successful morning newspapers; the *Mail* does not expect to lose the market leadership it has held since 1902, but any serious loss of circulation will affect its advertising pulling power and advertising revenue and the *RDM* cannot afford this.'

Before the *Citizen* appeared, the South African *Financial Mail* estimated that if it reached a circulation of 20,000 it would be losing R150,000 a month. While Luyt was losing this sort of money, the *Rand Daily Mail* would be able to ride the storm with its 'golden goose, the *Sunday Times*'. The *Financial Mail* said that even if the *Citizen* was to reach a circulation of 40,000 or 50,000 it could still be a lossmaker.

But two months after its appearance the *Citizen* claimed it was selling more than 70,000 copies. If that was true, then it was the second biggest morning seller in the country (after the *Mail*) and ahead of long established newspapers like the *Cape Times*, *Natal Mercury* and *Die Transvaler*.

As editor of the *Citizen* Luyt recruited Johnny Johnson, the man who had been mooted to replace Laurence Gandar on the *Mail*. For all his many years with the SAAN Group, Johnson began producing a paper in almost direct contrast to the policies of the English-speaking community. The *Citizen* is strong on news, light on serious features, and unmistakably behind the Government.

A typical leading article was the one of 9 November 1976, written after Prime Minister Vorster had appeared on CBS television in the United States. Said the *Citizen*: 'What can be said with certainty is that the Prime Minister came across with an authority which gives us complete confidence in him as a statesman of international standing.'

Transvaalers had never that sort of breakfast fare served up in English before.

The Johannesburg staff correspondent of the *Christian Science Monitor*, writting in October 1977, said that many South African newspapermen believed that the *Citizen* was not merely financed entirely by Mr Luyt, but was partly under-written by the Government. The *Christian Science Monitor* also reported as issuing from 'reliable sources' that information in certain *Citizen* stories could only have come from the files of the Bureau of State

Security (BOSS), South Africa's Intelligence Service.

Looking back at the relationship between the Afrikaner Government and the English-language press since the National Party came to power in 1948, there is a clear pattern. The Afrikaner rulers continually parry with the press, keeping it on its toes. And then, every few years, the thrust comes. The Suppression of Communism Act remains the principal tool of control, but a score of other Acts have been introduced which specifically affect the press.

Even so, many sections of the English-language press have continued to anger the Nationalists. In 1962, anticipating criticism by the abortive Press Commission before it fell apart (though it still produced a 400,000 word report), the Newspaper Press Union, the managers' body, drew up a Code of Conduct. Under this Code, a Board of Reference could reprimand any newspaperman guilty of infringing the Code (which tried broadly to ensure that newspaper reports were accurate and not offensive to decency). The final clause in the Code is indicative of the nervousness of South African Press managers and reveals the shifting ground of the libertarian tradition Thomas Pringle had won when he opposed Lord George Somerset at the beginning of the nineteenth century.

This final clause reads: 'Comment by newspapers should take due cognisance of the complex racial problems of South Africa and also take into account the general good and the safety of the country and its peoples.'

Many of South Africa's editors felt that this clause gave the owners of the papers a much tighter rein on the editorial columns criticising the Government.

Many of the English-language editors, particularly those outside the Argus Group, virtually ignored this new constraint, but in six years the Board of Reference of the Code only heard fifteen complaints.

This was not good enough for the Government. Gandar's exposés in the *Rand Daily Mail* of the ruthlessness in South African prisons had proved to them that this self-regulating Code lacked teeth. Things came to a head at the Congress of the Transvaal National Party on 12 September 1973. Prime Minister Vorster told the Congress that in spite of the fact that for years in public and in private he had warned and even pleaded with the press about their attitudes, it was clear that a section, 'the opposition Press', was seeking a confrontation with the Government, 'sometimes by way of subtle attacks, sometimes by way of blatant character assassination, sometimes by remaining silent on cardinal facts, sometimes by way of half-truths, sometimes by way of lies'.

But always, declared Vorster, the motive was the same: 'to crucify the Whiteman, and by name the Nationalist Afrikaner, as a villain or exploiter and a suppressor.'

This sort of stuff made the blood of most of the managers of the English-language Press run cold. Layton Slater, president of the Newspaper Press Union, got the managers together to demonstrate to Vorster that they were ready to pull in the reins on their editors.

Under the new Code of Conduct they drew up, an offence is committed if a report merely has the 'effect' of creating hostility. A Press Commission consisting of a retired judge and two other members decides whether a newspaper contravenes the code. If it has done so, then a fine of up to R10,000 can be imposed.

When the new Code was published, there was uproar among many editors and other journalists throughout the country. At least nine editors of major English-language newspapers were totally opposed to it, though the Argus Group's editors accepted the amendments. Layton Slater was head of the Argus Group. Afrikaans-language editors also supported the amendments.

As Joel Mervis, editor of the country's biggest paper, the *Sunday Times* said: 'It will be quite impossible for any editors to agree on what constitutes material which has the effect of inflaming race relations. What appears to one person to be perfectly innocuous might appear to another to be highly inflammable'.

The general view of the opposing editors was that if the freedom of the press was to be further curtailed in South Africa, it should be seen to be curtailed by the Government and not by the press itself.

The South African Society of Journalists, which was not consulted by the N.P.U., was vehement in its condemnation of the new Code.

Having got the press to discipline itself, the Government seemed content to let the uneasy truce with the English-language newspapers resume, following the long tradition of alternate finger-wagging and big stick waving which has been the pattern since 1948.

Occasionally a line will be overstepped. One such occassion was in November 1976, when news agency reports from the United Nations in New York gave accounts of speeches made to the General Assembly by Oliver Tambo and David Sibeko, respectively representative of the banned African National Congress and the Pan African Congress. Both had spoken in the debate over self-government for the Transkei, but because both men were officially 'banned' in South Africa under the Internal Security Act, the press was not supposed to report what they had said. Hitherto there had been an unofficial working agreement between the Ministry of Justice and the newspapers that even if speakers at the United Nations were banned, they could be reported in official debates. But because the issue of self-government for one of South Africa's 'homelands' was very dear to the heart of the Nationalist Government, they were not prepared to have exiled South Africans speaking against it. The newspapers were told not to carry the Tambo and Sibeko reports.

Cape Times editor, Tony Heard, decided to risk it. He published one thousand words on an inside page. 'It is up to the newspapers to ignore intimidation', he wrote. 'But the question is, if we are not going to be intimidated, is the Government going to stand for it?' There were angry noises from Pretoria, but no action was taken against the *Cape Times*. The *Rand Daily Mail* ran a shorter version of the speeches, but *Die Burger* took the Ministry of Justice advice and did not publish.

The picture presented to the outside world of the South African English-speaking press is of a united front against White Nationalism. This is very far from reality. It is certainly united in its opposition to the Afrikaner Government, but except for a handful of newspapers, principally the *Rand Daily Mail*, the *Cape Times*, the two Eastern Province dailies, the mornir̄
Herald and the *Evening Post*, and the East London *Daily Di*
the English press is in no way an opponent of White d
over Blacks.

The powerful Argus Group with its string of even̄
the major cities of South Africa has always beeṉ
much with profit as with principles.

A pre-Second World War South African editor, H. Lindsay-Smith, wrote:

> It has been the policy of the greater part of the daily press, not omitting the Argus Group, that *ipso facto* whatever is best for the gold mines is best for South Africa as a whole, and that end is kept foremost in mind ... Before the publication of any items bearing upon the mining industry it has been the general policy of one group of newspapers to submit items in question to the mining industry, and should they clash with mining policy they are either scrapped or altered in such a way as to be inoffensive.

The wave of riotings and killings in the non-European townships of South Africa in 1976—which spilled over into the main streets of some of the White cities—produced the worst international image of apartheid since the Sharpeville shootings of 1960. South Africa has a long history of barring or deporting foreign newsmen, and in an effort to further stem the unfavourable picture of the country being filed to newspapers, news magazines and news agencies all over the world, as the Soweto riots were crushed Information Minister, Cornelius Mulder, embarked on new restrictions in the handling of foreign journalists.

Mulder brought together in Bonn, Germany, all the Press attachés from South African embassies in the most important European countries to lay down the new tough line that was to be followed. Whereas in the past it was individual journalists who were refused entry to South Africa, the new line suggested that entire newspapers would now be liable to scrutiny. Britain has traditionally been the country most interested in South Africa, and most of the international reporting of the country has been done by British reporters. Although in 1973 a work permit rule was introduced by the Department of Interior, this rule was never applied in the case of British journalists.

In November 1976, Vlok Delport, the official at the Ministry of Information in charge of foreign journalists, announced 'The days are gone when the world belongs to the British'. Henceforth, he said, British newsmen must abide by the rule covering other foreign journalists. In fact British newsmen are still in a better position than their counterparts, as their passports indicate they do not have to apply for visas, which are more complicated than work permits.

In general, the Government dislikes 'visiting fireman' journalists, as they are obviously difficult to control, apart from seizing their copy as it is handed in at post offices for transmission. By making life tenuous for foreign correspondents, South Africa feels it still has some control over them.

The Vorster-Kissinger *détente*, which led to the Geneva talks on Rhodesia, brought about a softening of the South African attitude to American journalists. The *New York Times* returned after an absence of ten years, while Lee Griggs of *Time* magazine, expelled after Sharpeville, was allowed back.

But the Ministry of Information retains its prohibited list which contains the names of most of the incisive reporters of apartheid.

Before the Second World War, there had never been a South African-born editor of any paper of substance, certainly not in the principal cities. Britons were brought out, who, although good professional craftsmen, were hardly concerned with the long-term, deeper issues which even in those days were becoming abundantly clear. They tended to think in terms of the old Imperial code and how South Africa fitted into it.

It was only after the War that a new breed of South African-born editors emerged. Victor Norton (actually born in Rhodesia) was at thirty-four the first local editor of a major South African newspaper, the *Cape Times*. From the beginning of his editorship, Norton began to speak in a voice hitherto unheard in the South African press except in the fringe political papers.

Five hundred miles away, a pugnacious little South African of Scots extraction, John Sutherland, had just started the Port Elizabeth *Evening Post*. All through the rise of Afrikanerdom, every editorial inch of the *Evening Post* has been brimful of integrity, a superb example of courageous journalism.

In the same city, where the first British settlers arrived *en masse* in 1820, a very similar type of South African, though of Irish extraction, Harry O'Connor, founded Port Elizabeth's morning daily, the *Eastern Province Herald* in 1947. This is anoth beacon of courage and decency.

Neither Sutherland nor O'Connor is much more t tall; they are known as the two gnomes of Port E. for thirty years they have towered above the sou presented by South Africa.

Not far from Port Elizabeth, in East London, another South African editor has consistently spoken out for the non-White peoples of the country to be treated as human beings. He is Donald Woods, editor of the *Daily Dispatch*.

But neither his voice nor his writings will be heard or read again for a good many years, for with the heightening drama of Southern Africa compounded by universal international odium, the war in Rhodesia, the Cubans, Russians and Chinese giving sustenance and arms to apartheid's enemies, the Whites of the Republic in the closing weeks of 1977 drew the lines of their *laager* even closer around them and Woods became one of the principal victims.

When BOSS cooly announced in September that Steve Biko, the highly-respected leader of the South African Black Consciousness Movement, a non-violent organisation, had died in a prison cell, Donald Woods wept unashamedly. Woods and Biko were probably as close as any White man and Black man in South Africa can be. Woods believed that Biko might have become prime minister of what the London *Observer* called '. . . a reconstructed, sane South Africa'.

Biko had several times been imprisoned without trial and he and Woods had made a secret pact; if he were to die in prison and BOSS claimed that he had committed suicide through starvation, hanging, suffocation or any other form, it would be untrue. Biko vowed to Woods he never would kill himself in prison, and almost as if by premonition he made Woods promise to let the world know the truth if it should happen.

The bland statement from BOSS announcing Biko's death said that he had starved himself. The front page of Donald Wood's *Daily Dispatch* on September 14 carried the headline: 'We Salute A Hero Of The Nation'. Beneath it was a black-edged coloured photograph of Biko, four columns wide and nearly ten inches deep. Woods' editorial was headed: 'Death of a Martyr', and the paper carried pages of tributes.

In the following days, Woods personally led his small team of reporters into an exacting pursuit to find out how Biko had died, pointing out the inconsistencies in the version of events issued by BOSS, and finally accusing them of murder. In a front page leader, Woods challenged the South African Minister of Justice, James Kruger, to state whether the post-mortem report on Biko (which was then on Kruger's desk) referred to brain damage consistent with severe impact to the forehead and blows to the head and internal chest injuries 'totally disconnected with hunger-strike theories'. All this was subsequently proved to be true.

The English-language *Citizen* in Johannesburg sprang to the defence of the authorities, claiming that the Black Consciousness Movement led by Biko was in direct contact with Vietnam. It said that letters signed by leaders of the group outside the country showed that negotiations had been going on with the Hanoi Government for nearly a year.

For a month Woods continued the Biko campaign and the story became an international issue, doing even more damage to the remnants of South Africa's tattered image. Then in October, Kruger had had enough. As Woods passed through immigration control at Jan Smuts Airport in Johannesburg, three BOSS men were behind him. One tapped him on the shoulder, and as he turned, he was served with a Banning Order signed personally by Kruger. The nine-page Order listed item by item what Woods cannot do for the next five years:

He can no longer edit his newspaper.
He cannot even enter the newspaper building.
He can no longer write for any other publication (he was a syndicated columnist for a number of newspapers).
Nothing he has written in the past can be quoted in any South African publication or broadcast by radio.
He cannot attend public gatherings whether political or social.
He cannot leave his hometown without special permission.
He cannot talk to more than one person at a time except his wife and five children.
If a visitor calls at his house he cannot talk to him in the presence of his family.
He cannot enter a school or factory or any area where Blacks, Coloureds or Indians live.
He cannot enter the docks area of his town.
He must report to the police once a week.

What Kruger had done was to follow the old familiar course which the Nationalists had adopted time and time again when anybody, Black or White, stepped too far over the line they had drawn; politically and professionally Donald Woods had been emasculated.

It would have been a lot easier for Kruger merely to have banned the *Daily Dispatch* but this would not, of course, have silenced Woods for he could have written in other newspapers. Personal vindictiveness is the hallmark of the frightened little men who run South Africa and the huge majority of Afrikaners and Britishers who support them. Six weeks after his banning, Woods' youngest child, five-year-old Mary, received an anonymous gift through the post. It was a child-size T-shirt carrying pictures of Steve Biko. Mary put it on, but immediately it became clear that there was something wrong. The T-shirt had been treated with acid and her eyes, shoulders and chest were immediately affected. She was taken to hospital where the T-shirt was found to contain a substance used to paralyse the cornea of the eyes.

It was this incident, more than anything else, that decided Woods to flee the country. He dyed his hair black, put on a false moustache and a German accent, hitch-hiked to the border with Lesotho, swam a flooded river and reached freedom.

He was put up at the home of the British High Commissioner and received similar VIP treatment as he made his way to Botswana, Zambia and finally Britain.

No black journalist who has fought apartheid in South Africa or brutality as bad as in many of Africa's free states had ever received such hospitality from British diplomatic missions in the Continent.

Though Woods' paper was allowed to continue publication, Justice Minister Kruger had no such compunction about *The World*, the mass circulation Black newspaper edited by Percy Qoboza. Percy Qoboza, though producing a newspaper which was mainly concerned with crime, violence and sex in the Black urban ghettos of Johannesburg, was still a good enough newspaperman to make nonsense of his White general manager's belief that Africans had 'very little interest in politics'.

When the huge Black township of Soweto on Johannesburg's doorstep erupted in 1976, and hundreds of Blacks were shot down by police in the streets, Qoboza got his teeth into the Soweto story as pugnaciously as any other newspaperman in the country.

Soweto was subdued by the initial onslaught of the police but simmered, erupted yet again, was subdued again and then for the rest of the year and all through 1977 the pattern continued with a death toll mounting almost daily. The White management of *The World* might have been right when it dismissed politics as being 'of very little interest' to Africans, but the rest of South Africa and the world at large saw Soweto as a land-mark, perhaps even a water-shed. Percy Qoboza threw out a lot of the crime and sex from the columns of *The World* and covered the Soweto story as courageously as any other journalist had ever behaved in South Africa's long history of the press versus apartheid.

Time and time again in his editorials Qoboza attacked the policies which had brought Soweto over the brink. White South Africa was as afraid of Soweto and what it threatened in terms of the carnage that could spill over into Johannesburg and then alight into the other White centres of the country as it was by the threat of the Cubans, the Russians and the Chinese who were always being presented as waiting to lead a Black liberation army across the Limpopo. For White South Africa believes it has enough military strength to handle any such threat and that should, in fact, a Communist-led onslaught ever begin, notwithstanding all the denials from the White House, the United States would come to its aid.

But a million Blacks armed with clubs, axes, rocks and probably some guns rampaging through White Johannesburg just a drumbeat away from Soweto is something else again. Kruger had told Qoboza to stop criticising Government policy or he would close down *The World*.

Time and time again BOSS men harrassed and threatened Qoboza and his staff either at his house, in his office or as the reporters went about their work, particularly in Soweto itself.

All through 1976 and 1977, Black journalists in and around Johannesburg were being roped into the BOSS net like mackerel. On 30 November 1977 alone, no less than thirty Black journalists were arrested in central Johannesburg as they marched towards John Vorster Square where the Police H.Q. is situated to protest over the detention of eleven of their colleagues.

Qoboza ignored Kruger's threats of closure and in October he paid the price. *The World* was stopped and he was imprisoned. Before he was arrested, he spoke at the University of Witwatersrand in Johannesburg. 'As the volume of public concern and protest becomes more and more muted' he told a predominently White audience, 'the number of people spirited away in the middle of the night increases annually'.

They came for Peter Qoboza just before dawn.

Though it is a bitter pill for Africans in Independent Africa to swallow, it is because of the handful of editors like Gandar, and Allister Sparks of the *Rand Daily Mail*, Norton and Heard of the *Cape Times*, Sutherland and O'Connor in Port Elizabeth, Donald Woods, now degutted in exile, and Percy Qoboza, stripped of his *World*, plus many of the reporters, Black and White, under them, that South Africa can still—just—be said to have the freest press on the African Continent.

RHODESIA; THE PRESS AND THE REBELS

As Cecil Rhodes pushed north with his dream of planting the British flag (and building a money-making railway) all the way from Cape Town to Cairo, the Argus was among his most ardent camp followers. Rhodes' men—180 Pioneers, 200 of his British South Africa Company's Police and a raggle-taggle of prospectors—reached the cool Mashonaland plains on 10 September 1890. A man named Pennefather rode ahead of the column looking for a suitable site with water, and two days later the order book of the Pioneer column records in sober and unromantic style: 'It is noted for general information that the Column, having arrived at its destination will halt. The name of this place will be Fort Salisbury ...'

The next morning the column paraded in full dress, with some of the prospectors putting on hats for the occasion. The seven-pounder canon was fired and the British flag was ceremoniously hoisted over the new settlement.

In June 1891, the Argus Company sent William Fairbridge up from Johannesburg as their representative. He did much more than just send reports of the new settlement back south for transmission to Britain; on June 27 he filled a German sausage-skin with treacle and glue, and using it as a roller, ran off the first handwritten copies of the *Mashonaland and Zambesian Times*, a crude but readable cyclostyled sheet. His office was a mud-hut, and when he ran out of paper he tore up foolscap accounts paper. Customers who had no money—and there were plenty of those—

paid for their copies in kind, with candles and jars of marmalade being the most common currency.

The launching of the *Mashonaland and Zambesian Times* is remembered and related as something of a land-mark in the history of Rhodesia; in fact it was not, strictly speaking, the territory's first newspaper at all. One of Rhodes' Company policemen, H. R. Vennell, had the curious ambition to be remembered as the man who brought the newspaper age to Central Africa. On 11 November 1890 he had produced two issues of *The Nugget* at Fort Victoria at the southern end of the territory. Ambition satisfied, he resumed his police duties.

William Fairbridge's German sausage rolled on for over a year, but the Argus imported more modern equipment by ox-waggon from the south and on 20 October 1892 the *Mashonaland and Zambesian Times* gave way to the *Rhodesia Herald*. Two years later, on 12 October 1894, the Argus started the *Bulawayo Chronicle*. The *Herald* and the *Chronicle* served Rhodes' British South Africa Company well. They supported the campaign for the continuation of Company rule over Rhodesia after the First World War, when there was growing disquiet in Whitehall that a large chunk of Central Africa which proclaimed itself British was virtually outside the jurisdiction of London and run, as a politician of the day put it 'rather like a general store by Mr Rhodes' heirs'.

In 1903 the Salisbury Chamber of Mines demanded 'that restrictions be placed on the present system of Christianising natives', and shortly afterwards the *Rhodesia Herald* declared that 'The Black peril will become a reality when the results of our misguided system of education have taken root, and when a veneer of European civilisation struggles with the innate savage nature'.

When in 1923 the settlers of Rhodesia were given the choice of joining South Africa or becoming a British colony, they opted for the Union Jack. The African people were not consulted.

Though there have been a number of attempts to break the stranglehold of the Argus Group, under its local name of the Rhodesian Printing and Publishing Company, they have all fallen by the wayside and the *Herald* in Salisbury and the *Chronicle* in Bulawayo have remained the only dailies bar an abortive attempt by the Argus itself to launch an evening in

Salisbury in 1958. Both the Salisbury and Bulawayo plants produce Sunday papers, the *Mail* in Salisbury and the *News* in Bulawayo. The *Umtali Post*, also Argus owned, serves the Eastern part of the country.

What the South African owners of the Rhodesian press have always wanted are good journeymen, sound technicians and, above all, men who knew their place. That place was several paces behind the Argus Group managers. They have almost always turned to Britain or South Africa for this sort of material and have been well served by it.

It is only since the Second World War that a home-grown brand of newspapermen has arisen in Rhodesia, and the story of two of them provide a fair commentary on both the country and the company they worked for.

John Spicer was born in Rhodesia. His grandparents are buried there; his wife is Rhodesian. He has a house in Salisbury but he chooses to live on the South coast of England. His story typifies the dilemma of the liberal Whites of Rhodesia who, during the years of illegal rule after Ian Smith declared unilateral independence, found themselves frustrated to the point where all many of them wanted to do was get out.

Spicer had worked as a reporter, and then in higher positions for the Argus Group in all three of the countries in which they own newspapers, South Africa, Southern Rhodesia and Zambia (when it was the colony of Northern Rhodesia). In the middle fifties, he persuaded the Argus Group to create a news feature service which would concentrate on bringing to the readers of their newspapers in White Africa what was happening in the rest of the Continent as the independence era dawned.

'I wanted White South Africa and White Rhodesia to understand that they shared the Continent with millions of other human beings', he says.

'Human beings' is a term rarely used by Whites in Southern Africa when they talk about non-Whites.

Spicer set up the Argus Africa News Service, and it became the most intelligent and intelligible thing of its kind anywhere on the Continent.

Spicer and a handful of reporters went all over Africa—wherever the stories and the features behind the stories were to be found. He says he was never inhibited by the Argus management, or indeed by the editors of their papers. But at the second and third level, in the newsroom, there was often a barrier against the copy his service was providing to the Argus newspapers all over Southern Africa.

This says a lot for the way the press is run in Southern Africa. Chief sub-editors anywhere are key men in the newsroom, but in Southern Africa they hold a position far ahead of their equivalents in Europe or the United States. The editorial staff is so small by comparison with similar-sized newspapers elsewhere, that the chief sub very often decides exactly what news will get into the paper. This is virtually true of the hard, running news, and totally true of the background and feature material which Spicer's service was providing. It was useful early copy for the subs to use as and when they thought fit until the harder news began to come in from the paper's own reporters and the news agencies' telex copy. Spicer's copy was useful during this early part of the morning for the Argus Group's chain of evening papers in South Africa but likely to be discarded later. On the Rhodesian morning papers it was all set long before the hard news began flowing in during the late afternoon and evening.

Thus, if the subs preparing the early pages did not like Spicer's material it never saw the light of day.

The calibre of many of these second and third level Argus journalists was such that they were totally unsympathetic, if not entirely hostile, to anything from Black Africa.

Only by the skin of its teeth did the Bulawayo *Chronicle* avoid coming out with a Spicer story from the Congo by-lined and date-lined 'Wogland, Monday' inserted by a British sub not long out from 'home'.

The illegal declaration of independence by Ian Smith in November 1965 produced the first confrontation between the press of Rhodesia and the Government. There had not been one since the hand-duplicated *Mashonaland Times* brought newspapers to Salisbury when the capital was little more than a long white pole with the Union Jack fluttering aloft.

The editors of the country's two dailies, Malcolm Smith of the *Herald* and Sidney Swadell of the *Chronicle*, were poles apart in personality. Smith, Rhodesian-born, was one of the new brand of home-grown Rhodesian newspapermen. No great liberal, he was none-the-less fair-minded and very jealous of his rights as an editor. Swadell was a mild-mannered Scot, typical of the sound British professional who had served the Argus Group well in all the territories where it had newspapers.

Neither Smith nor Swadell had very much time for Prime Minister Ian Smith. Malcolm Smith, in the capital, Salisbury, was in the more vulnerable position when UDI was declared. In those first months of illegal independence, the whole country lived on its nerve-ends and as international ostracism mounted, Ian Smith and his Cabinet, their backs to the wall, became more and more sensitive to criticism.

Malcolm Smith, to the constant nervousness of the Argus management, rankled the Smith Cabinet with almost every issue of the *Herald* he produced. Finally the illegal regime brought in censorship. Malcolm Smith gritted his teeth and flew right in the face of the controls. Every time the censor turned down a story, Smith left a white space in the newspaper equivalent to the size the story would have occupied. Sometimes column after column of the *Herald* was bare.

Ian Smith and his Cabinet, and a good many of the *Herald*'s readers who were solidly behind UDI, were incensed. The *Herald*'s empty spaces seemed a daily insult to them and, somehow, a greater indictment of the regime than any stinging editorialising.

When British Prime Minister Harold Wilson went to Rhodesia on one of Britain's several futile attempts to bring the rebel Colony back into line, force having been ruled out, the Minister of Information, James Howman, decreed that nothing at all could be printed about the visit. Ninety column inches of blank space duly appeared in the *Herald*. The regime was livid.

The offices of the *Rhodesia Herald* face Salisbury's biggest hotel, Meikles, and its famous Long Bar, reminiscent of a Wild West saloon, often with matching clientele, has been the drinking place of the capital's newspapermen for generations. UDI had brought foreign correspondents by the score to Rhodesia, and Malcolm Smith was frequently to be seen hurrying across the road, his pockets stuffed full of the proofs the censor had rejected for his own paper, which he handed out to the eager foreign press corps.

Some of the white spaces in the *Herald,* and to a lesser extent the *Chronicle*, were stories from John Spicer's service. Though these could hardly have been a threat to the security of the illegal regime of Ian Smith, the censor was not inclined to have sympathetic reports of independent Black Africa served up on the breakfast tables of Rhodesia's White rebels.

The chief censor during this period was Philip Charles Dendy, an unfrocked solicitor. Educated Africans in Rhodesia were particularly bitter about the calibre of many of the leaders of the White rebel regime, who posed to the world as 'defenders of Western civilisation'. Another of the Dendy ilk was John Gaunt, who may be remembered in a footnote to Rhodesian history for his declaration as Minister of Home Affairs that if there were any Africans who did not like UDI, 'then they should emigrate'.

Gaunt had been 'sent to the Colonies' in the fashion the British upper classes often adopted with troublesome sons between the two World Wars. He ended up as the odd job man at Broken Hill mine in Northern Rhodesia, but when the colonial administration discovered he was a British admiral's son, he was hurriedly recruited into the colonial service where he is remembered for accepting bribes from Indian traders in Livingstone.

These were the 'defenders of Western civilisation'.

Ian Smith was under pressure from the extreme wing of his extremist Cabinet to do something about the *Herald* and the *Chronicle*, and he very nearly did. He appointed the former head of the Rhodesian Air Force, Air Vice-Marshall Mulloch Bentley, as 'custodian-in-waiting' of the press. Bentley began planning the takeover of the Argus papers. Astonishingly, he asked John Spicer whether he would be prepared to assume editorial control. Spicer, who was a good many degrees to the left of Malcolm Smith, laughed in Bentley's face.

Malcolm Smith says he was never under pressure from the management during his fight against Ian Smith, but he believed that the company would either have had to move him or the Government would have taken over the Argus papers.

The reason he was never taken to court was simple. Though the magistrates of Rhodesia were very much in the pockets of the Cabinet, the High Court judges, in those early days of UDI, had not yet committed themselves. They were prepared to administer the laws of Rhodesia up to the point of UDI, but not those that had been changed or promulgated since UDI. Thus the regime knew that if Malcolm Smith appealed against the verdict of a lower court, there would be a clash between the Government and the judges, something they were anxious to avoid.

An example of the petty-mindedness of the sort of people that Ian Smith had surrounded himself with was an incident when Malcolm Smith replied to a letter from the Minister of Information, James Howman, addressing him as 'Dear Sir'. Howman sent for David Meggitt, the *Herald*'s general manager, and complained that Smith had not used the prefix 'Honourable Minister'. Howman said that this demonstrated that Malcolm Smith did not recognise his position.

Ian Smith's Government, in its desperation to off-set the international odium against UDI, issued thousands of airmailed and stamped printed letters extolling the virtues of Rhodesia, and asked people to send them to their friends overseas. Contained in this letter were the words '. . . the daily newspapers are dedicated to destroying our independence'.

Smith and Swadell sued Howman for libel. They won and were awarded £250 damages each. Smith announced that he would not touch the money 'with the longest barge-pole in the world'. Both editors gave the money to charity.

The confrontation between Malcolm Smith and his namesake Ian was now complete. He had to consider how hard and for how long he could continue to fight. He doubted he could go on much longer before the regime's 'custodian' moved in. Still in his forties, he went to the Argus management and asked for an early retirement. The regime allowed him to draw only the money he had in his current bank account, £308. With his wife and two children, he left for exile in Britain. It took a while for the bruises to heal. Then he rang up Hugh Cudlipp of the *Daily Mirror* and asked for a job. He now commutes from the south of England every day to Central London on the same railway line that carries Peter Enahoro.

In Rhodesia, John Spicer's tolerance level grew shorter and shorter. He had not endeared himself to the Government when he contributed to a book called *The Price of Freedom*, which included contributions from figures like former Prime Minister Garfield Todd, former Chief Justice Robert Tredgold, and a number of leading Africans. The theme of the book was to prevent UDI. When Ian Smith went ahead and seized power Spicer became an outspoken critic of the Government, and in the village-like atmosphere of beleaguered Rhodesia, his views immediately came to the notice of the authorities. He had been topping up his salary from the Argus as a regular commentator on both local radio and television, but the Minister of Information, James Howman, gave orders to the Director General of Broadcasting that this was to stop.

Spicer could no longer write what he wanted to in the Press; he could no longer say the things he believed needed saying on the air. He had one final shot left in his breech and he used it with devastating effect.

On Christmas Eve 1968, the Mayor of Salisbury organised a charity phone-in on Rhodesian television. A clutch of local dignitaries sat before the cameras, and viewers were asked to ring in—and on promise of a donation to the Mayor's charity fund—they could ask one of them to sing a song, tell a joke or do something equally light-hearted.

Spicer was watching the show. He picked up his telephone and got through, live, to the programme *compère*. Top of the local pop chart at that time was a song called '*I am a Puppet on a String*'.

One of the dignitaries was the Director General of Broadcasting. 'I'll pay five pounds' said Spicer, loud and clear through the telephone mike, 'if the Director General will sing "*I am a Puppet on a String*".'

Rhodesia does not have colour television but many viewers swear to this day that the Director General turned bright pink.

Spicer realised it was time to go. But where? He was a senior man in an organisation run very much on a seniority basis. He was hardly suitable editorial material for the Argus papers in South Africa. The problem was solved when Layton Slater, not an imaginative general manager but always fair to his staff, sent him off to edit a little weekly the Argus had recently bought in newly-independent Swaziland.

'All the time I was in Rhodesia, from pre-war days onwards, freedom to express yourself and write the facts were being limited', he says.

The next few years were to prove the happiest and most rewarding of his entire career.

Ian Smith gave nothing like the same amount of rope to the country's main African newspaper that prudence dictated he should allow the 'White' papers of the Argus Group. The *Daily News* was a Thomson publication which James Coltart had brought in 1962 because, he said, the Argus papers were not catering for the Africans. The Government claimed that the *Daily News*, the Salisbury evening paper, was 'pro-African' but Coltart says: 'We were not really pro anything. We were informants to the Africans.'

In Rhodesia giving information to the African population was probably the most subversive form of journalism imaginable. As John Gaunt unashamedly put it: 'What they never know they'll never miss.'

The editor of the *Daily News* was Eugene Wason, who had originally gone to Rhodesia to work for the Argus Group, but who jumped at the chance to break out of the tight managerial grip the Argus exercised over the editorial department. It was inevitable that a top-class journalist like Wason, who had been editor of a defunct Fleet Street Sunday and who was to return from Rhodesia to occupy the very nearly literally hot-seat of the *Belfast Telegraph*, should soon run into serious trouble with Ian Smith's Government. Even before the declaration of independence, the Law and Maintenance Act had been introduced to shackle anything being published in more than the most muted voice.

Wason laid down five principles upon which the *Daily News* would insist: support for the legitimate aims of the African nationalists; urge of moderation; getting across the fact that the only solution to the country's problems was a constitutional conference; setting a good moral tone; denouncing violence at every opportunity.

A sixth principle was added later when Wason realised that Ian Smith was moving towards UDI. This was to stop any illegal declaration of independence.

Violence was rife in the African townships of Salisbury and Bulawayo as rival African nationalist movements fought each other in an attempt to assert their authority. Almost every issue of the *Daily News* condemned the violence. One leading article Wason wrote was headlined 'FOR GOD'S SAKE STOP IT'.

When two small African children were burned to death by a petrol bomb, Wason filled the whole of the front page with headline type alone which said 'THE SHAME OF HIGHFIELD AND HARARE'—the two African townships where the violence was worst.

Most of the Black political leaders in the country were already locked up, but Wason sought out one who was still at large,

James Chikerema, and got him to denounce violence. The front page lead story was headlined 'Chikerema Calls For An End To Violence'.

A week later, in August 1964, the Minister of Justice, James Lardner-Burke, banned the *Daily News*. He said the paper had supported the men who indulged in violence and intimidation, and therefore encouraged violence and intimidation. When the banning was debated in Parliament, a government M.P. threw a copy of the paper on the floor and said that violence was only denounced on an inside page. The copy he threw down was the one with the front page headline: 'Chikerema Calls For An End To Violence'.

Even though the *Daily News* was silenced, Wason was taken to court when the paper was charged on three counts of false reporting. The first charge was that the *Daily News* had reported that one group of African nationalists had attacked another, whereas the prosecution claimed that it was the other way round. The second charge was for saying that the country's African chiefs had lost the support of the people, and the third that in a court report the paper had said the Crown had conceded that the police had tortured witnesses.

The paper was found guilty on all three counts and fined. A few days later Wason left Africa. The entire staff, editorial and works, of the *Daily News*, were out of work. Willie Musarurwa, the paper's news editor, was put in detention. He was to stay there, uncharged, for eleven years.

When the *Daily News* was closed, James Coltart flew from London to Salisbury to try to get the decision reversed. He got short shrift from Ian Smith and the Thomson organisation wrote off Rhodesia. Like their West African operation, their Central African safari had cost them a lot of money. But a year later, with UDI just a few weeks away, Ian Smith sent a man to London asking Coltart to re-open the *Daily News*. Smith's man said there were plenty of Africans in Rhodesia who supported the Government, and these were not being served by the Argus papers. Coltart sat with pursed lips as he listened. Smith's messenger proposed that Thomson should re-open in Salisbury but with Government control of editorial policy. It is a testimony to the total lack of understanding of the Smith regime that they believed such a deal would be remotely considered by Thomsons.

This time it was Coltart who handed out the short shrift.

Even with Malcolm Smith removed from the *Herald*, there was still an uneasy truce between the Argus Group and the Ian Smith regime and trouble was to flare up again which sent another journalist packing to Britain in 1965.

John Parker was the English-born chief sub-editor of the *Herald*'s Sunday sister, the *Sunday Mail*. A few months before Ian Smith declared UDI, Parker was shown confidential reports which revealed that both the Chambers of Commerce and the Association of Industries were wholeheartedly opposed on economic grounds to any seizure of power. It was a first-class story and Parker wrote it.

When Parker showed his story to the *Mail*'s editor, Rhys Meier, Meier said he must submit the story to both bodies and ask for their comments. Parker did so. Within an hour both organisations announced they would seek a High Court order to prohibit publication on the grounds of infringement of copyright.

It was clear that though the reports opposing UDI were true, both the Chambers of Commerce and the Association of Industries were highly embarrassed that their confidential memoranda to the Government were now to be made public. Meier decided not to publish the story.

Under normal conditions this incident would have gone no further, but with Ian Smith's Cabinet ultra-sensitive as they secretly plotted the illegal seizure of power, it was enough to set the hatchet men on Parker. The police began a campaign of intimidation and harassment. The Parker's home telephone was tapped in a very obvious way but his wife, Margaret, countered this by engaging in the most intimate gynaecological conversations with women friends. Before hanging up she would ask the unknown listening Special Branch man: 'Did that help?'

Parker was questioned for hours on end about the source of his story. He spent forty-eight hours in solitary confinement. He was eventually found guilty under the Official Secrets Act of committing 'a suspected offence'. When he appealed, he not only won, but the Court added the rider that he had been 'subjected to unwarranted persecution by police and courts'.

A month later he was deported. Sir Roy Welensky, the former Premier of the Central African Federation whose collapse had led to the political impasse Rhodesia now faced, told Parker as he was leaving: 'They did the best turn anyone has done for you in your life. There's no future in my country now.'

Newspapermen in Africa have always been obvious targets for foreign powers seeking to find out more of what is happening than is available through diplomatic channels. Russia and the United States are the principal collectors of such information. Britain, glad to be shorn of its imperial responsibilities, makes a token attempt at such intelligence activities and, probably because of its closer links with the new rulers in Anglophone Africa, often does better than the two super-powers. It certainly spends only a fraction of the amount paid out in roubles and dollars to anyone with something interesting to sell.

A reporter in an East African state who thought he had something of particular interest to the British High Commission approached the press attaché during the military unrest in Kenya, Uganda and Tanzania at the end of 1963 and the beginning of 1964. Over a drink, he asked if they could do business. Well, yes, said the press attaché, if the information was good. The journalist gave a broad outline of what he knew; the names of the politicians who were ready to support the rebel factions in the Army if it looked as though they would get away with the planned seizure of power. The Englishman was impressed. Britain, which had only recently withdrawn its troops from East Africa, but had them standing at the ready in Aden in case they were needed, was obviously concerned to know what the state of play might be in the event of trouble. The press attaché put his hand into his trouser pocket and withdrew his loose change.

The reporter watched in awe as he counted out seven shillings. 'I'd certainly give you all the change I have for the names', the Englishman confided. In fact the British got the information for nothing. The reporter went off to the local CIA agent and was paid 5,000 shillings—then worth £250. The Americans gave the names to the British. Shortly afterwards the luckless politicians were locked up.

Only rarely is a journalist unmasked for spying. In most cases, when the authorities become suspicious enough to warrant action but do not have enough evidence to stand up in court, the man in question has his work permit cancelled—in the case of Europeans—or, if he is a citizen, has it made clear that he had better get out of the country.

One such newspaperman was taken to court by the Smith regime. He was an Englishman, Roger Nicholson, financial editor of the *Rhodesia Herald* and the local correspondent of the London *Times*. At the end of October 1969, with Rhodesia an illegal state for almost four years, he was detained under the emergency powers. His desk at his office and his home were searched. At first it was thought that this was yet another case of the Smith regime making life uncomfortable for another newspaperman.

The *Herald* came out with an editorial, but as the emergency powers forbade the naming of anyone detained—there were already hundreds of Africans in detention—it was unable to be specific and referred in general terms to 'disquiet over the spiriting away of fellow citizens'.

Nicholson's trial, when it began in December, was in secret, though the charges, plea and part of the prosecution's opening statement were made known. Nicholson pleaded guilty to two charges accusing him of revealing information likely to assist the application of economic sanctions by foreign governments, and also revealing how the Rhodesian authorities were circumventing sanctions.

The court was told that Nicholson had been seen going into a Salisbury post office with a white envelope in his hand. He had opened a private *poste restante* box, put the envelope in, locked the box and left.

Shortly afterwards a watching policeman saw 'a person whom I shall call a foreign agent' go to the box and remove the envelope. Nicholson was then watched for five weeks; when he was arrested in his office at the *Herald,* a carbon copy of a six-page typewritten report was found which detailed how sanctions were being overcome. When Nicholson's home was searched, a three-page document was found containing instructions about gathering information for the use of the United Nations Sanctions Committee to show how goods were getting in and out of Rhodesia.

When Nicholson was sentenced to a total of eighteen months hard labour, the judge said that among his assets was listed about £9,000 with a bank 'in the foreign country concerned in the case'. The judge did not identify the country in question but said it was 'a Western nation'.

Nicholson told the court he had believed that 'it would be useful overall if a sound appreciation of the situation was received by the government in question as a corrective to the views held in other quarters'.

The report in the London *Times* of the judgement said it understood 'on sound authority' that the foreign agent for whom Nicholson had worked was not British.

The day after he was sentenced, the *Herald* announced in its leading article that Nicholson had been sacked. 'He betrayed those who entrusted him with special confidences', said the leader, 'so that he would be better equipped to do his job as a financial editor and betrayed this newspaper by breaking these confidences to (of all people) an agent of a foreign country. Thus, he broke in the most damaging way possible, the cardinal rule of newspaper ethics—that trust between informant and reporter must be preserved.'

After his release from prison, Nicholson returned to Britain and went into newspaper management with a Thomson paper in Wales.

Another celebrated court case involving a newspaperman in Rhodesia created a great deal of bitterness among Black newspapermen, and was used as a propaganda weapon by African nationalists to prove the double standards Britain applied in its dealing with the rebel regime.

Peter Niesewand was the best-known and most prolific freelance newspaperman in Rhodesia. Among his outlets were Britain's *Guardian*, the *BBC*, *Reuters*, *UPI*, *Agence France Presse*, the *Australian Broadcasting Commission* and a number of British and South African newspapers.

On 20 February 1973, he was detained under the emergency powers and in March he was brought to court at a secret trial and charged with contravening the Official Secrets Act. The director of public prosecutions, the same man who had prosecuted Nicholson, said that the charge was under a section dealing with publication of information 'calculated to be, or which might be useful, directly or indirectly to the enemy'. It was only revealed much later that what had prompted the charges were the stories and broadcasts Niesewand had sent out of the country which said that Rhodesian troops and 'planes were operating across the Moçambique border. By revealing this information, claimed the prosecution, Niesewand had endangered the security of the country.

Niesewand was sentenced to two years' imprisonment, but when he appealed, the High Court quashed the verdict. Chief Justice Hugh Beadle said that the reports Niesewand had sent out of the country had not damaged the state but merely embarrassed the Government.

But although he was now technically free, Niesewand was still detained under the emergency powers and went back to his prison cell.

From the day he had been detained under the emergency powers and all through the trial, a huge campaign had been mounted in Britain in support of Niesewand. The British National Union of Journalists launched a defence fund, and mobilised support among newspapermen in many other countries; ministers and members of parliament in the House of Commons spoke against his detention and trial; the Director General of the *BBC* made a public speech protesting at the 'conspiracy against the truth'.

The odium of the international campaign against Rhodesia convinced the Smith regime that it was not worth their while keeping Niesewand. After a total of seventy-three days in prison, he was released and deported to Britain where he joined the *Guardian.*

The hundreds of Africans who had been detained for years without trial in Rhodesia, among them journalists, learned of Niesewand's release in the handwritten underground newspaper which circulated in their internment camp at Gonakudzinwa, deep in the Rhodesian bush. The story was headlined THE WHITE WAY TO GET OUT.

The record of the Christian church—or any other church—in the African struggle for independence is not good. Although even before David Livingstone's time missionaries have performed excellent medical and educational roles throughout the Continent, to a great extent they have always been identified with the ruling establishment. Whether the authorities were the agents of Cecil Rhodes' British South Africa Company as it moved into Central Africa seeking further rich pickings, or the administrations of Britain, France, Germany, Portugal and Belgium as the colonial scramble carved tropical Africa into sections, missionaries have rarely made any significant stand against the abuses of the Europeans over Africans.

The religious press in Africa has been largely innocuous. Oddly, it has a better record of protest in the nineteenth and early twentieth century than during the years immediately following the Second World War when modern African nationalism came into its own and needed all the supporting voices it could find.

The explanation for the *sotto voce* of the religious press lies somewhere between the nervousness of the church hierarchy to get into the political arena, which forthright commentary on injustice would lead to, and the sheer inexperience of missionaries in running anything better than parish magazines. The result has been that while the conventional press has been persecuted by White and Black governments throughout Africa, the religious press has barely been looked at.

The outstanding exception to the servility of the religious press occurred in Rhodesia, where there was a church hierarchy which was not afraid to do battle with injustice, and a missionary who was not only courageous but also a first-class newspaperman.

Michael Traber was born in Switzerland and ordained as a Roman Catholic priest in 1956. He spent the next three years studying sociology and mass communication in the United States, and received a PhD in mass communication from New York University.

He went to Africa and became director of a Catholic-owned publishing house, the Mambo Press, in Gwelo, in the Midlands of Rhodesia. Mambo Press produces books in English and Shona, the language of the biggest tribe, the Mashona. Swiss nuns run all the machinery, from linotypes to printing presses, and the books are among the highest quality productions in Central Africa. Many are text-books in primary and secondary schools throughout the country.

When Traber arrived in Rhodesia in 1961, the mission also produced a conventional Catholic newsletter. He turned it into a monthly newspaper called *Moto*, which is Shona for Fire, and aimed at a much wider national readership than merely among churchgoers. UDI was still nearly four years off, but already the political boiling pot was simmering dangerously as White extremists provoked Black extremists.

Moto quickly caught on with Africans and a good many enlightened Europeans as well. The *Daily News* in Salisbury was still the main voice of the Africans, but as *Moto* began to speak on the turbulent issues, rapidly developing circulation grew from a few thousand to over 10,000, and with each copy being read by anything up to a dozen people its influence became considerable. Then Ian Smith closed the *Daily News*. Immediately *Moto* moved into the position of principal voice of African aspirations. Circulation soared: 15,000, 25,000, 30,000 and still upwards.

Traber had developed his small African staff into a highly competent and dedicated editorial team.

Menard Masvingise, who joined *Moto* in March 1965, after his 'O' levels and bookkeeping certificate had failed to get him a job digging ditches for the Water Department in Gwelo, remembers the moment when his bitterness at the world of the White man came to an end. Masvingise had been taken on by Traber for a trial. He was sitting at the production desk in the newsroom with the African sub-editors and Traber when the telephone rang. Traber answered it. 'Who is he?' he asked. 'Special Branch?' The three Africans looked up. 'Where is he?' asked Traber. 'In the reception? O.K., ask him to come to the window.'

Masvingise could hardly believe what he had heard. The conventional way for Africans to be received at many levels of White society in Rhodesia was at the window. Now here was a White man, and a police officer at that, being told to 'come to the window'.

Masvingise left the newsroom trembling with excitement and eavesdropped as Traber dealt with the White Special Branch man. 'That incident marked a turning point in my life', he said later. 'Here was a White man with courage and conviction and a missionary who practised what he preached.'

Masvingise was to go on to become sports reporter, political columnist and finally news editor of *Moto*. He was to follow his departed editor out of the country when the Smith government closed *Moto* down.

As well as voicing the aspirations of the Africans, Traber was concerned that *Moto* should function as a safety valve; when UDI was declared in November 1965, the intransigence of the Europeans convinced him that all the ingredients for a bloodbath between Black and White were at hand.

Although Traber had editorial control, the Bishop of Gwelo, Alois Haene, as representative of the Bethlehem Mission of Immensee, Switzerland, which owned Mambo Press, had laid down three principles on which *Moto* was to operate: to promote Christian principles in present-day conditions in the social, economic and political fields; to give a particular voice to African opinion and help the African people to assert their God-given rights according to Christian teaching; to be a fearless conscience of its readers, condemning evil and acknowledging good regardless of where they might be found.

Such principles inevitably clashed with the policies of the Smith regime. When upon the declaration of independence Smith said that '. . . it is indeed a blow for the preservation of justice, civilisation and Christianity', Traber wrote an editorial: 'It (UDI) is indeed a blow, not for the preservation of justice, civilisation and Christianity, but against it.' The censor banned the issue.

Pre-publication censorship lasted from the declaration of UDI to April 1968, and *Moto* had almost as many stories and editorials refused as it had passed. John Gaunt, himself a practising Catholic, boasted that he would reduce *Moto* 'to nothing more than a Bible tract', and with hundreds of African nationalists in detention and the rest of the Black population frightened and dispirited, circulation fell away badly.

But the ending of censorship, even though new laws had been brought in to deal with the press, saw the circulation rise again and by 1969 *Moto* was selling 36,000 copies. The *Rhodesia Herald* of 20 February 1970 said in an editorial that it 'expresses more than any other paper does now the aspirations of the African people'.

Traber planned each issue with the entire staff, always aware that with the best will in the world he was still a White man, and always anxious that *Moto* should reflect an African viewpoint. In June 1969 the regime proposed a new constitution. The pre-independence constitution, it said, contained a number of 'objectionable features'. The main objection was that under that constitution eventual majority rule was possible.

The White Paper announcing the changes read: 'The proposed new constitution will ensure that government will be retained in responsible hands.'

The Catholic Bishops of the country joined together in condemning the new constitutional proposals. 'No one should be deceived by them', said a pastoral letter. 'They offer a superficial but completely illusory hope of security for the future and can only breed violence. They have clearly been drafted with the deliberate intent of ensuring the permanent domination of one section of the population over the other.'

Traber got his editorial staff together to plan a special issue of

Moto featuring the Bishops' letter. Mordikayi Hamutyinei, a former schoolmaster who had spent eighteen months in a detention camp, suggested that to illustrate the Bishops' condemnation of the constitutional proposals, *Moto* should carry a cartoon depicting a pair of large White hands squeezing small, struggling Black bodies. The caption would be taken from the White Paper and read: 'The proposed new constitution will ensure that government will be retained in responsible hands.'

If the cartoon had been better drawn, it might have been more effective, but the draughtsmanship was so poor that it took a lot of studying to understand. But John Gaunt understood it all right. Traber was charged under the Law and Order Maintenance Act with 'Publishing a subversive statement'.

The case ran the normal course of such prosecutions in Rhodesia. Traber was found guilty by the Gwelo Magistrate, but on appeal to the High Court, the sentence of six months' imprisonment suspended for three years was quashed. Three days later, he was deported along with another priest who had written a column for *Moto* from Salisbury. The tally of expulsions of missionaries and journalists from Rhodesia in five years now read: journalists seventeen, missionaries thirteen.

There was a growing division between the liberal and the passive wings of the Roman Catholic church over the issue raised by the publication of the 'squeeze' cartoon. Prominent White lay Catholics protested to their priests and bishops. A prominent Bulawayo doctor, Charles Shee, wrote to Bishop Haene in Gwelo 'with all charity and restraint' to protest. 'The cartoon seemed to me to be a frank incitement to racial hatred, and I look forward to reading your public and unequïvocal condemnation of it', he said.

Bishop Haene replied that he had told Father Traber he strongly objected to the cartoon and condemned its publication, but that he did not think it was a frank incitement to racial hatred. Traber wrote to the doctor saying that it was not in the nature of cartoons to be 'balanced', as they were meant to be ironic or provocative.

The President of the Catholic Bishops' Conference, Donald Lamont, who was the pre-eminent liberal churchman in Rhodesia, said of the deportation of Father Traber: 'This is not the first time a priest has been removed because of his conscientious convictions. When I was a student in the nineteen

thirties my professor was given forty-eight hours to leave Italy
for criticising the Mussolini regime, and another friend of mine
who refused to spread Hitler's propaganda died in a dog kennel
in Dachau.'

Bishop Lamont said Father Traber's offence differed not in
essence but only in degree.

Nine years after arriving in Rhodesia, Michael Traber boarded
the aircraft at Salisbury to fly to Europe. A group of Black and
White friends and supporters saw him off, carefully listed by
Special Branch officers. As the 'plane taxied to the runway for
take-off, the crowd began to sing *Ishe komborera Afrika*—God Bless
Africa,—the national hymn of Africans all over Southern Africa.
Traber could not hear them. He read about it next day in exile.

It was not difficult to predict the aftermath of Traber's
deportation, and Bishop Lamont did so accurately. 'He will no
doubt be labelled a Communist' he said publicly.

There were still enough Europeans in the country to be
concerned that a priest who had just been cleared of criminal
charges by the High Court should be deported with no word of
explanation. The regime's watch-word throughout UDI was that
it was 'safeguarding civilised standards'. John Gaunt, now the
Chief Censor, set his officials to work on a campaign designed
to smear Traber and warn off booksellers handling *Moto*. The
psychological climate was ripe for rumours, and word was spread
that 'the real reason' Traber had been deported was because
Mambo Press had for years been used a centre for the importation
of 'subversive and pornographic literature' which had then been
distributed through the bookshops handling the output of the
publishing house. The Rhodesian Broadcasting Corporation
made constant reference on radio and television to both Traber
and the other deported priest in derogatory terms. A pro-
government magazine, *Illustrated Life,* ran an article entitled *The
Red Menace* which spoke about a certain mission station acting as
a post office for subversive and pornographic literature.

When a European businessman having a drink in Meikles'
Long Bar could no longer stand hearing John Gaunt holding
forth on the quantities of pornography which the mission had
imported during Traber's years, he asked 'Why the hell didn't
you seize it then and prosecute?'

Gaunt, not a man who liked to be questioned, shouted half
the length of the bar: 'There are plenty more 'planes leaving

the country.'

But Gaunt was yet to have his hour of triumph.

The staff of *Moto* was shattered by Traber's deportation, but under his editorship they had become a hardy, professional team and they set about producing the next issue. On its front page *Moto* announced: 'If the aim of this exercise was to frighten and demoralise us, it has failed. Government has massive powers. We do not know what will happen to us, to other people and to *Moto* in future. But we will not be silenced by 'phone-tapping, mail-searching, banning and deportation. We carry on.'

Another missionary priest, James Brandley of the same Swiss order, took over as editor. Traber had been full of energy, ingenuity and professionalism. Brandley was passive and happy to leave the production very largely in the hands of the Africans. At first the editorial staff was confused and uncertain, but when they began to appreciate that Brandley's motive was to let them carry the paper, they rose to the challenge.

There had always been obstacles put in the way of the paper but now these were intensified. When John Maposa, a reporter, went to report Ian Smith who was speaking in Gwelo, he was refused entry to the hall. '*Moto* has nothing to do with the Prime Minister', he was told by a policeman. No reporter was allowed into a government office; all interviews with ministers were refused; no *Moto* representative was admitted to press conferences of Smith's Rhodesian Front party. When press parties were taken on Ministry of Information tours of the districts where the guerrilla war was beginning to flare, *Moto* was excluded. The country's chiefs were under orders not to talk to 'Communists from the Mambo Press and *Moto*'. Pressure was put on advertisers not to use *Moto*. 'We are afraid to sign a contract with you', one sympathetic White manager told *Moto*. 'We are told your paper is against the Government.'

A number of White Catholic priests urged that the paper should drop politics altogether. They said their parishioners wanted a purely religious paper. They cited *Southern Cross*, the big Catholic newspaper published in Cape Town, as the model of a church newspaper.

But *Moto* did not temporise and the regime's efforts to squeeze it out were, if anything, counter-productive. By 1971 circulation was 40,000.

It was decided to go weekly. A modern off-set litho press was bought, and the Swiss nuns busied themselves learning to operate it. A number of new men of different religions were added to the editorial staff. On 3 September 1971, the first religious weekly in Central Africa appeared on the streets of Rhodesia.

In May 1972 six White and one Black CID policemen arrived at Mambo Press. They went through the whole complex of offices, print-shop and houses, and carried out several boxes of papers. In Salisbury the *Moto* office was also raided and the home of the Africa reporter in the capital searched.

Nothing happened for a month. Then Father Brandley came into the newsroom and told the staff: 'From tomorrow you will have a new editor.' He said he was resigning for personal reasons and that another Swiss priest, Albert Plangger, would be taking over Mambo Press.

On July 27 Brandley appeared in Gwelo Magistrate's Court, charged on two counts under the Law and Order (Maintenance) Act and three counts under the Censorship and Entertainments Control Act.

The first two charges referred to two issues of *Moto* headlined WHEN RHODESIA SAYS NO and RHODESIAN CHIEFS' FUTURE AS UNCERTAIN AS THAT OF WHITES. Both articles had been reprinted from *Tablet*, the British Catholic newspaper, which was freely available in Rhodesia.

But it was the three charges under the second Act which were to rock Mambo Press and *Moto* and undermine an enormous amount of the goodwill which the newspaper had won for itself over the years. In Brandley's room at the mission, the police had found a catalogue of sex magazines, an edition of *Man*, a girly magazine banned in Rhodesia, five photographs of a naked woman taken with a Polaroid camera, and the *Little Red Book* of quotations of Chairman Mao.

It was, as a White reporter on the *Rhodesia Herald* put it, 'Christmas for John Gaunt'.

Brandley was found guilty of all the charges except possession of the *Little Red Book*, which the Magistrate said was not contrary to the laws of public safety, and publication of one of the articles from the *Tablet*. He was fined a total of 225 Rhodesian dollars on the other counts. He left *Moto*, resigned from the priesthood and returned to Europe.

Menard Masvingise reported the case for *Moto* in the normal way. He wrote his story and handed it to Brandley's successor,

Father Albert Plangger. It did not appear in the paper. He did not ask why.

Plangger was an anthropologist, and although not lacking courage he did not have the professionalism of a newspaperman to rally the now badly shaken African editorial staff. But *Moto* continued to speak out as loudly as it dared under the new emergency laws.

In August 1972 Bishop Donald Lamont, who was now seen to be the outstanding voice of liberalism in the country, issued a Bishop's letter couched in scathing terms against the Smith regime.

'The African people detest now, and always have detested, the government of the Rhodesian Front', he wrote. 'Be they ordinary workers, minor civil servants, teachers, police, even chiefs, in their heart of hearts they regard the government as the oppressor and themselves as the oppressed.'

Masvingise knew it meant trouble if *Moto* published the letter as it stood. He made some changes, but Plangger said it must be printed as the Bishop had issued it—right down to the headline. 'A Catholic Bishop has the right to air his opinion in a Catholic newspaper without correction', he told Masvingise. Masvingise said he believed that if *Moto* published the letter as it stood they were likely to be taken to court yet again. But the priest was adamant and the letter duly appeared as Bishop Lamont had written it. Masvingise felt that his right to exercise his own judgment had been restricted. It was the first time since becoming chief sub-editor a year before that he had ever been told what to change and what not to change.

Later that month an entire edition of *Moto* was banned for publishing an article about the regime's 'provincialisation' measures which, said *Moto,* were a 'design of deepening apartheid'.

In November Plangger was summoned to appear at Gwelo Magistrate's Court over Bishop Lamont's letter. The charge, under the all-embracing Law and Maintenance Act, said that the letter constituted a subversive statement. The state prosecutor said that by publishing the Bishop's letter, *Moto* had exhorted the African people to 'stick to their guns'—a highly-loaded statement in the context of the times.

Plangger was sentenced to five months' imprisonment suspended for three years. Morale among the staff of the paper was now at rock bottom. With whole editions being seized after printing, pressure on advertisers not to buy space and the greatly increased costs since *Moto* had become a weekly, Plangger had to reduce staff. When in the general election of August 1974 John Maposa, a reporter, stood on the ticket of the African National Council and was elected to Parliament as one of the sixteen African members (against fifty Europeans), he was not replaced.

During the closing stages of the war in Moçambique between FRELIMO and the Portuguese Army, *Moto* gave extensive coverage to events just across the border. While the *Rhodesia Herald* and the *Bulawayo Chronicle* reflected the growing fear of Rhodesia's Europeans as yet another 'White' territory went Black, threatening its nearest access to the sea and providing a launching pad for the guerilla war that was already beginning from the Zambian border, *Moto's* coverage of Moçambique was altogether different. It proclaimed FRELIMO's victories and said of the Lisbon Army coup of April 1974: 'It is the best news we have had for a long time and we only hope that it will have a sobering effect in colonial and racist Rhodesia.'

This brought a call in Parliament from a European member to the Minister of Law and Order, Desmond Lardner-Burke, to 'take steps to bring this subversive paper under control'. Lardner-Burke was not long in answering the call.

Moto went to press on Thursday mornings. Menard Masvingise supervised the final page proofs for the issue of 21 September, 1974 and went home. When he arrived early the next morning, there was a crowd of young African newspaper sellers at the gate of the mission. 'There is no newspaper today', they told him.

Minutes after he had left the previous night, the CID had raided the mission and seized the page-proofs just before they were to be photographed for plate-making. At 10 o'clock that morning, the police returned to the mission and handed Plangger an order signed by the Commissioner of Police in Salisbury suspending *Moto* fo three months.

It was not made clear at the time why the banning had been ordered but it emerged later that it was because of a story about the African National Council congratulating Moçambique on attaining nationhood.

With no revenue for at least the three-month banning period, the Salisbury and Bulawayo editors had to be laid off. But

Plangger was determined to keep something coming off the *Moto* press, even if it was not *Moto*.

Mambo Magazine came out to fill the vacuum, but it was a shadow of the courageous, spirited newspaper it sought to replace. The regime had nearly doused the Fire.

On November 15 Parliament debated a motion to make the ban on *Moto* permanent.

One of the African MPs who opposed the motion was John Maposa, the former *Moto* reporter. The official Hansard Report of the debate contains this extract:

> *Maposa:* Two years ago *Moto* published a strong statement from a bishop in this country...
> *Interjector:* Which bishop?
> *Maposa:* Have you not been reading the newspapers?
> *Interjector:* We do not read the newspapers.

This is the Hansard extract of the speech by Mr I. P. Rees-Davies, MP for Bulawayo South:

> The Pope directed that any member of the clergy who was not a citizen should remain solidly out of the affairs of the state. As the Minister has pointed out, the past editor of *Moto* was not a citizen of this state. I believe he was a gentlemen belonging to Switzerland. One might extend this even further to certain bishops of the Catholic church and the support which *Moto* has given, particularly to Bishop Lamont and his stirring up of racial confrontation. I would add at this point that they are totally out of touch with their members. Lastly, I find it quite interesting in some reading I did in the parliamentary library that the late unlamented Reichsfuhrer SS Heinrich Himmler, had dreamt up a little scheme whereby members of the SS would infiltrate seminaries of the church with the idea of poisoning them with the virtues of Nazism. I wonder if Heinrich Himmler was the only person in this world who has thought of this when we consider the insidious poisonous, Mao-ist commentaries coming through media such as *Moto*.

The motion to make the ban permanent was put and carried. On November 18 the *Rhodesia Herald* carried an order signed by the President of the illegal regime, Clifford Dupont, formally promulgating the permanent ban as official and also forbidding publication of 'all other periodical publications consisting wholly or partly of political or other news or of articles relating thereto or to similar current topics'.

Thus the Smith regime had stamped on the last spark remaining from the flame lit by Michael Traber when he began *Moto* in 1961. The final edition of the paper had appeared just ten years and a month after the closure of the *Daily News*.

Menard Masvingise eventually found his way to Europe, to the headquarters of the Bethlehem Mission in Immensee. The International Press Institute in Zürich sent someone to see him. Masvingise asked if there was any chance of getting a job in Britain. The IPI man said it would be very difficult. He pointed out that newspapers were a contracting industry and that a lot of British journalists were out of work. Masvingise, whose entire career had been in opposition to the government of his country since he was little more than a schoolboy, had a final question for the IPI man.

'Perhaps there's a job on an underground paper?' he asked. He ended up at a polytechnic in an English provincial town waiting for the day when another Fire could be started in Rhodesia.

In its death throes, towards the end of 1976, the Smith regime sentenced Bishop Donald Lamont to ten years' imprisonment with hard labour for failing to report the presence of guerillas who had come to his mission near Umtali close by the Moçambique border seeking medicine.

Almost immediately he was deported.

10 Swaziland: The Light at the End of the Tunnel

On paper the odds against John Spicer making any mark—even surviving—in Swaziland were poor. Here was a White man from a White racist state moving into a key position in a Black state which had just achieved independence.

But Spicer's success as editor of the *Swaziland Times* provides the only example of a White editor in Black Africa who not only survived but who thrived. The credit must be shared between Spicer himself and the new Black rulers of the young state.

After the Gambia, Swaziland is Africa's smallest state, less than 7,000 square miles, bordered on three sides by South Africa and its eastern frontier facing Moçambique. Although a British protectorate before achieving independence in September 1968, it was almost a satellite of South Africa, as were Britain's other two protectorates in Southern Africa, Lesotho and Botswana.

The South African Argus Company had bought out the *Swaziland Times* before Spicer arrived in the country. It was the only newspaper in the country, a weekly, and even after independence still in the classic mould of the colonial publication owned by Europeans, run by Europeans and directed at a European readership.

Spicer quickly changed the paper's course. His target was the Black reader, and many a pink gin was downed angrily in 'the club' by local Whites as they contemplated the changed *Times*.

Part of the back-up service provided by the Argus from South

244

Africa was a pocket cartoon drawn by the cartoonist on the Durban *Daily News,* in which South Africa's 'ordinary little man' is portrayed making some observation about current events. As he is a South African 'ordinary little man', he is naturally White. When Spicer arrived in Swaziland the *Times* carried the cartoon. Spicer tossed the packet away and had a new stock set drawn of a Swazi. The first message in 'the bubble' coming from the little man's mouth was 'Wow! I've been localised!'

It was a clean, overnight sweep of the old order, but Spicer had enough experience of Black Africa—not to say his own White Rhodesia—to realise that more was likely to be accomplished in establishing a new readership by a steady chip-chipping than a bludgeoning, sledgehammer attack.

Racial tolerance was his theme. His message, stated time and time again, was that since it was bordered by South African apartheid on the one side and Portuguese colonial ruthlessness on the other, Swaziland could show by example that a Black state could run itself, rejecting both forms of oppression, and governing with decent, democratic standards. Faced with its geographic and economic facts of life, the *Times* said it was pointless for Swaziland to think about throwing petrol bombs across the border—even though apartheid was condemned out of hand.

During the run-up to independence, the opposition parties had joined in a coalition under the royal umbrella of the chief of the Swazis, King Sobhuza the Second, already an ageing though benevolent monarch. But in the first post-independent general election in April 1974, the opposition Ngwane Liberatory Congress won three of the thirty seats in Parliament from the ruling Mpokoso Party (the Grinding Stone) and this precipitated a state of emergency.

Even though the *Times* supported the ruling Mpokoso Party, Spicer argued that the Government should realise how lucky it was to command a substantial overriding majority, and yet be able to proclaim that Swaziland was a true multi-party democracy. But the Grinding Stone was set upon following the path taken by virtually every other state in Black Africa, and six weeks after the election a state of emergency banned the opposition. The constitution was suspended and the old King, then in his mid-seventies, ruled by decree. Thus democracy came to its short-lived end in Swaziland. The Government had been happy to allow an opposition but only up to the point where it found itself facing its representatives across the floor in Parliament.

Several—not more than half a dozen—political opponents of the Government Party were arrested, and the *Times* came out with a special edition and an editorial headed: 'It is wrong to detain people without trial.' Spicer made it his personal business to find out the names of those who had been detained, and as they were picked up by the police, he printed them. It was an unprecedented act for newspapers in Black Africa.

Although the state of emergency restricted what the *Times* could say on straight political matters, Spicer found plenty of other issues to air. The net of corruption was widening as politicians and civil servants at both the national level and in local authority found themselves for the first time in their lives near the purse strings of power. The *Times* exposed as much of it as it dared, and made many enemies—but also many friends—among the establishment and the great majority of decent, ordinary Swazis.

Inefficiency at all levels was another target. Spicer was slipped a confidential report on the Ministry of Information, and the *Times* ran its own investigation and published the findings under the headline: The Ministry of Concealed Information. This brought the Deputy Prime Minister, Zonkekhunalo Kumalo, who had considered that the *Times'* denunciation of the banning of the opposition party had been *lès majesté,* to the microphone of Swaziland Radio to warn Spicer to 'watch his qs and ps—a slight Africanisation of a very English admonition.

Spicer thought this was 'tickets'—the term which had come to mean the swift end of a White journalist in Black Africa. But he had a flash of inspiration, and in the next issue of the *Times* ran a picture on the front page showing the King shaking his hand. He reckoned that if the Deputy Prime Minister had considered it *lès majesté* of him to question the banning of the opposition, it might well be *lès majesté* to deport a man who had actually shaken the monarch's hand. It seemed to do the trick and Spicer survived.

The only way the King knew more of what was going on in the country than the political leaders chose to tell him was by reading the *Times,* and there is some evidence that this prevented the paper from being banned. The politicians Spicer upset used to try to use the King to frighten the *Times* off. A senior permanent secretary would come round to Spicer's office and say: 'His Majesty is very displeased with what he read in the paper this morning.'

Spicer would play these visits very cool.

He would counter: 'What exactly was His Majesty displeased about?'

Permanent Secretary: 'About what you said about the Immigration Department.'

Spicer: 'Was His Majesty displeased because he read it in the paper or because of what he found out about the bad things going on in the Department?'

If it reads amusingly, it was nonetheless poker with high stakes.

But though he had opponents at the centre of power, he also had many supporters. They would often slip into his office to wish him well.

Another subject on which the *Times* campaigned was the customs agreement with South Africa; it had been concluded by Lord Gladstone (son of British Prime Minister William Gladstone) in 1910 when he was High Commissioner for Swaziland, Basutoland and Bechuanaland. Under the terms of the agreement, the three Protectorates got the very thin end of the bargain, and the terms continued until well after independence.

Spicer had prepared a strong leading article attacking the agreement and calling for renegotiation with South Africa; but before the paper was printed, Zonkekhunalo Kumalo appeared in the office to object. One of the print-shop staff at the *Times* had slipped the Deputy Premier a proof of the leader. The Swazis, even as citizens in a free state, had been so indoctrinated by years of colonialism that when somebody urged them to seek a better deal for their country they became nervous and uncomfortable.

Spicer had another brush with Kumalo on a subject increasingly common in newly-independent Africa, but one rarely if ever commented upon by the press: the appointment of cabinet ministers to the directorships of big multi-national companies.

When the Coca-Cola company wrote a letter to the *Times* about its advertising, Spicer spotted that the name of Zonkekhunalo Kumalo was among the directors. The next issue of the *Times* appeared with the Deputy Premier's picture on the front page and the deadpan caption: 'The Deputy Prime Minister, who is now a director of Coca-Cola Swaziland Ltd.'

As soon as the *Times* appeared on the street, Kumalo was on the 'phone wanting to know why Spicer had printed his picture. Spicer played it cool again.

'Minister', he replied 'this is most unusual. I generally get asked by cabinet ministers to put their pictures in the paper.'

But why had he done it, demanded Kumalo.

Spicer said it was a matter of public interest. If the Deputy Prime Minister wished to complain, he would be happy to print a letter to the editor, an offer which was not accepted.

Spicer crossed another cabinet minister when he revealed abuses in the use of government transport. Official cars were being used to carry the produce from the farms of politicians and civil servants. As a result of the *Times* disclosures, the King set up an official enquiry.

The constant theme at which the *Times* hammered away was that while the old traditional tribal system of Swaziland had served its period well, with independence it was now essential that education, land reform and the teaching of people to make the best use of the soil be the paramount goals if the country was ever to break out of the poverty which gripped 95 per cent of the population.

But, of course, the people reading the *Times* were the other five per cent.

For his editorship of the *Times*, Spicer was awarded Britain's David Astor Award. The trophy was inscribed 'John Spicer, for his outstanding contribution to journalism and to Commonwealth understanding.'

What Spicer was doing in Swaziland was only what good small-town editors in the West had been doing for one hundred years—turning over stones to have a look at what crawled out, pointing a finger at corruption, suggesting new ways of doing old tricks.

But Swaziland was not the West. 'Can you imagine any other country in the world letting a foreigner come in, take over their only newspaper and start telling them what's what?', he asked at the end of his career in the young state.

In September 1975 the Argus Company sold the *Times*—to a Scotsman—and thus continued its policy of retrenchment from Black Africa back to the White South from which it had set out almost one hundred years earlier with Cecil Rhodes' pioneers.

Spicer left Swaziland with not an ounce of bitterness—indeed, the opposite, for all his time in the little Black state, at the very end of his career as a newspaperman, had been a final justification of his beliefs. More than any other White newspaperman in Southern Africa, he had seen all the drama, the comedy and the tragedy of Black Africa as a score or more of states struggled towards nationhood. There were many moments of despair as nuns were raped, mayors eaten alive and bloodbaths such as the ones in the Congo and Biafra reinforced all the prejudice of Europeans in Rhodesia and South Africa. But never for a moment did Spicer waver in his belief that this was an historical process, much the same as every other Continent had gone through, and that Black and White had no greater and no lesser right to share a life in Africa.

Spicer, a White African, son of White Africans, who had been born deep in the Rhodesian bushland, and who for the first five years of his life spoke better Sindebele than English, packed his bags for the last time but one and came to England. There was nowhere else to go until Rhodesia was free.

11 Unconquered Africa

LIBERIA: TAMMANY HALL IN THE TROPICS

If a large measure of the blame for the historical restraints of the press in Black Africa is to be laid at the door of the colonising powers—then handed over by them and further refined by the independent governments of Africa—then it should follow that the two states which avoided rule from Europe would have developed healthier newspaper industries.

They did not.

After one of the best beginnings of journalism anywhere in Black Africa, the story of the press in Liberia since Charles Force began turning out the *Liberia Herald* on the hand-operated press given to him by American missionaries in 1826 is one of steady decline. And across the other side of the Continent, where the sands of Arab Africa give way to the scrub and bushland of the tropics, newspapers in Ethiopia have seen the right-wing feudalism of rule by the Emperor replaced by ruthless left-wing regimentation from the Army which overthrew him.

Charles Force died a few months after the first issue of his four-page monthly appeared as the only regular reading matter in the little settlement the freed American slaves had established, and the *Herald* died with him. Another Black American, John B. Russwurm, who had worked on the first Negro weekly in the United States, *Freedom's Journal*, revived the *Herald* in 1830 and for the next thirty-two years the little monthly was an intelligent, literate and thought-provoking publication. On its mast-head the *Herald* declared 'Freedom is the Brilliant Gift of Heaven' and every issue hammered home the message of the abolitionists of slavery. Despite the anti-slavery laws of most European countries and the constant patrolling of the British Navy off the coast of West Africa, the slave trade not only continued but flourished. While the estimated export of slaves from West Africa alone was 100,000 a year at the end of the eighteenth century, by the time the *Herald* began publishing in 1826 it was more like 135,000.

There were plenty of apologists for the slave trade in Liberia, but the *Herald* gave them no quarter. It was particularly harsh on any missionary it found who was not prepared to condemn slavery unequivocally. The editorial in the issue of September 1830 said: '... fraud and violence have in almost every instance been the means by which our slaves were originally procured. Yet there are multitudes in our own enlightened country, in our boasted land of liberty, who, with the book of God in their hands, and a public profession of allegiance to the compassionate Saviour in their mouths, unblushingly stand forth as advocates of this cruel system.'

All the editors of the *Herald* during its life were educated men from either the United States or the West Indies. The last of the line was Wilmot Blyden, a West Indian writer and scholar who spoke and wrote Latin, Greek, Hebrew and Arabic. The *Herald* ceased when Blyden became a professor in Liberia College. Before it folded in 1862, the *Liberia Sentinel* had appeared in 1854 edited by Edward James Roye, the first pure Negro to become President of Liberia. The *Sentinel* marked the beginning of the Tammany Hall era of Liberian journalism from which it was never to break free. Roye was to be deposed as President by partisans of the True Whig Party who were dissatisfied with the terms of a British loan he had contracted.

The second half of the nineteenth century and the first half of the twentieth saw half a dozen new publications, *The Liberian Advocate* (1873) followed by the *Monrovia Observer*, *The Liberia Bulletin* and the *Whirlwind*. They all danced to varying political tunes as the new young Repulic settled down to building a nationhood closely modelled on the United States.

With slavery now a dead letter and with no glittering prize of independence to reach for like the newspapers of British west

Africa, the Liberian press was sucked into the insularity of
political life in the capital, Monrovia.

In 1939 the *Liberian Star* appeared as a weekly. This was to be
the only paper to survive the Second World War, the twenty-
eight year presidency of William Tubman, and the era of his
successor, William R. Tolbert. By the middle of the nineteen
seventies, of nineteen newspapers established since 1826, only
three, *The Star*, a daily, *The Age*, twice weekly and the *Sunday
Express*, were still publishing.

Newspapermen who can remember, point to the early Tubman
years as the period when the press of Liberia virtually threw
the towel in as anything more than mouthpieces for his True
Whig Party; a fairer verdict seems to be that they were beaten
into submission in much the same way as the newspapers of
many other Black States after independence had been achieved.

A Liberian newspaperman turned academic summarised
the situation thus: 'We were the first African state to attain
freedom, so we were the first state to have a sycophantic press.'

President Tubman was as colourful a figure, if lesser known,
as the ruler of Africa's other non-colonial state, Haile Selassie of
Ethiopia. Both had absolute power and wielded it absolutely.
While Haile Selassie assumed the mantle of religious mysticism
in a country where the Coptic Church had greater power than
any other faith in Black Africa, Tubman operated more in the
style of Haiti's Papa 'Doc' Duvalier, without the Carribean
dictator's bloody ruthlessness but with the same top-hatted,
spat-shoed, cigar-holder image.

It was said of Tubman: 'He hasn't exactly got his hand in the
till. He lives in it.' His presidential yacht cost one per cent of
the national budget. Over six per cent of the budget was
spent by him personally.

Tubman came to power in 1943 and it took the newspapers
a little while to get the message; although the political wheeling
and dealing of the True Whig Party had always made life
difficult for the press, it had not yet made it dangerous. Liberia's
first daily appeared in 1946, *The Daily Listener*, founded by
Charles Cecil Dennis, an MP. The same year Tubman's True
Whig Party started the *Liberian Age* as a bi-weekly, and it was to
remain bi-weekly thereafter. There are varying theories about
Tubman's view of the press, and the generally accepted one is
that he never really understood what editors who questioned

his policies meant.

'He just couldn't bring himself to believe that anyone was actually disagreeing with him' says a Monrovian politician who was close to Tubman in the early days of his rule. 'When something was printed which was a blatant criticism of government policy he used to shake his head and say 'This man must be mad.'

It was this disbelief that probably saved the day for the few journalists who took issue with authority. The first editor to overstep the mark in Tubman's eyes was a West Indian immigrant, Charles Frederick Taylor, who had started the weekly *African Nationalist* in 1940. He was convicted of libelling Tubman in 1947, and was to remain in prison for twenty-five years until Tubman's successor, President Tolbert, released him when he succeeded to the Presidency on Tubman's death. During the fifties and sixties, a number of journalists were locked up for terms ranging from twenty-four hours to, in a few cases, several years. The threat of incarceration was always there and Tubman never hesitated to voice it. At a presidential press conference in 1961, a reporter asked him a question which clearly embarrassed Tubman. 'Don't ask me stupid questions', he fumed, 'I jailed you before, and if I jail you this time you will never get out.'

But he also had other ways of dealing with errant pressmen. In 1951 Samuel Richards started *The Friend* as a bi-weekly supporting the opposition Independent True Whig Party. During the election campaign of 1955, Tubman sent a gang of toughs to break into the works at night and destroy the printing equipment. Richards was locked up and the *Friend* never appeared again.

In 1954, *The Independent Weekly* was started as another opposition voice by a naturalised Liberian from America, Mrs Bertha Corbin. The paper supported former President Edwin Barclay and his Independent True Whig and Reformation Party, which Tubman had ousted from power. Tubman gave the *Independent Weekly* just a year, then closed it. Mrs Corbin was held to be in contempt of the Legislature, and sent to prison together with the author of the offending article, Tuan Wreh.

Mrs Corbin will be remembered as the first non-African editor of a newspaper in Tropical Africa who was forced out of publishing and then forced out of Africa. She returned to

America. Tuan Wreh was later given a Government scholarship
to study in America. He took a course in journalism.

The Liberian Age, which had started as a private venture but
which was always financially supported by the Tubman
administration, eventually became the official voice of the True
Whig Party and was given a Government subsidy. When the
subsidy was announced, Tubman said it would also apply to
other newspapers. For a time the *Daily Listener* also benefited.
But even with the subsidy Charles Dennis, who had started the
Listener back in the middle forties and who was bold enough
to launch two more in 1970, the *Saturday Chronicle* and the *Sunday
Digest*, became so overstretched that the three papers folded
together in 1973.

The surviving daily, the *Liberian Star*, was managed for a brief
period in the mid-nineteen sixties by the British Thomson
organisation; it was never a satisfactory arrangement, and as the
Canadian Press lord's enchantment with Africa faded, he was
glad to end it. It duly collapsed in 1968, which left Tubman
with only the bi-weekly *Age* as the 'Presidential Trumpeter' as
it was known. The following year, therefore, the *Star* was
resuscitated.

But although the bi-weekly *Age* has always been the official
Party voice, this had not prevented successive editors falling
foul of Tubman. In 1959 Henry B. Cole was dismissed as
editor for criticising Government policies and his replacement,
Aston S. King, suffered the same fate for the same reason two
years later. In most African states, editors who have been
removed by Presidential order leave journalism altogether, but in
the peculiar world of Liberia, which is unlike anything in either
the former French or British colonies, and much more akin to the
sort of political incestuousness of the southern states of America
in the twenties and thirties, things are different.

Cole went on to become director-general of the Liberian
Information Services, and then editor of the *Liberian Star*. By
1969 he was back in favour with Tubman and serving as the
Presidential Press secretary. When President Tolbert succeeded
Tubman, Cole stayed on as Press secretary.

King is now public relations officer to the Government-
owned Electricity Corporation, and as an ordained clergyman
in the Episcopal Church, preaches much stronger sermons on
the socio-economic ills of Liberian society than he ever

published while editing the *Age*.

Even the present editor of the *Age*, Stanley B. Peabody (the names of many Liberians have a strong American ring about them), was jailed briefly along with a reporter, Berthram Walker, for describing a member of parliament as a radical. Moreover Peabody has frequently been warned by President Tolbert's brother, who is a senator and president *pro-tempore* of the Liberian Senate, for publishing letters criticising the Government. On one occasion Peabody was compelled to produce the writer of a letter to refute allegations that it had been written in the offices of the *Age*.

But these aberrations hardly effect the almost toadying line of all three of Liberia's newspapers, the *Star,* the *Age* and the *Sunday Express,* started in 1974 by a former *Star* editor, John Fitzgerald Scotland. The 7 October 1975 issue of the *Age* is a good example of the sort of Presidential coverage which is standard practice. The leading article enumerated and lauded the achievements of President Tolbert. On another page, a reporter wrote a similar piece citing the qualities of the President. Elsewhere a lawyer wrote an article entitled 'President Tolbert, The Man of Deeds and Positive Action', and yet another outside contributor had a piece headed 'VP (for vice president) Greene Extols 4 Year Achievement of President Tolbert'. The author of this was Vice-President Greene himself. Completing the quintet of praise was an article by a retired professor on 'President Tolbert's Total Involvement Policy'.

The inter-play between the press and the Government often leads to bizarre situations, even by African standards. In January 1975 the assistant editor of the *Star*, Rufus Darpoh, was summoned to the office of the chairman of the board of directors, a position held by Charles Cecil Dennis Jnr (son of the man who founded Liberia's first daily, the *Listener*), who was also the country's Foreign Minister. Also present at the meeting were the editorial and business directors of the *Star* and Darpoh's younger brother, Benjamin, chairman of the State Public Utilities Authority.

Rufus Darpoh had been a constant critic of many Government policies, both in the days of Tubman and also of Tolbert. Whenever he was able to, he put his views into print and had once been jailed for doing so. When he travelled abroad, he spoke and wrote scathingly about the curtailment of liberty in Liberia. In 1974 he wrote in the *African Journalist,* published by the

International Press Institute and circulated throughout the Continent: 'A few months ago the directors of the independent but pro-government *Liberian Star* called an editorial conference and announced that the order of the day was "survivalism and not journalism". The action of the directors was prompted by the fact that a powerful cabinet minister was reported as saying "We are going to see whether they (journalists) want to survive".'

Now as he stood before his Chairman and Foreign Minister, Darpoh was reminded that his brother occupied an important Government post. The two other directors of the *Star* present assured the chairman that they had constantly advised Darpoh to stop writing critical articles. Not long afterwards, Darpoh left the country to study journalism in Ghana. It seems more than probable that he will follow the same route as many other Liberian journalists who, after incurring presidential disfavour, vacated their editorial desks only to return after an appropriate cooling-off period.

ETHIOPIA: THE MIXTURE AS BEFORE

Shortly after the overthrow of Haile Selassie by the Ethiopian Army in 1974, Ato Mairegu Bezabih, one of the country's foremost newspapermen—in a land where foremost had never been able to mean more than educated and intelligent—wrote: 'The journalists of Ethiopia, oppressed and frustrated from time immemorial, are biting their nails waiting to see what life without the Emperor will mean.'

The journalists, and everybody else in the country, did not have long to wait.

'The only consolation newsmen have in this wait-and-see period is that things can hardly be any worse than they were under the Emperor', Ato Bezabih had written in the *African Journalist*.

After three years of military rule, and with every sign that government by gun will continue for the foreseeable future, that is a fair verdict on the press in Ethiopia: things are no worse under the soldiers than they were under Haile Selassie.

In any international table of travesties of the press, Ethiopia would come very near the top. In the era of the Emperor, the whole country's media were no more than a massive public relations exercise for Haile Selassie. Under the Army it is the worst form of Marxist mouthpiece on the Continent.

The principal daily is the *Ethiopian Herald,* the only newspaper published in English. Russell Braddon's biography of Roy Thomson suggests that he asked Haile Selassie to take over the *Herald.* James Coltart says it was the other way round; though run, as it was, virtually as a record of the Emperor's public life, it is difficult to believe that he wanted any foreign hand interfering with it. At all events the deal fell through, though Coltart's trip to Addis Ababa paid off in the shape of a contract to run Ethiopian television, an arrangement that continued long after the Army came to power.

It is almost literally true that every word printed in the Ethiopian press, or broadcast on the state radio, was angled to project the almighty image of the Emperor. Even when the news had nothing to do with him—for example, foreign news—it was selected for publication or broadcast in the light of how he would regard it. And certainly foreign news, no matter of what importance, was never allowed to interfere with the projection of the Emperor's image. The press followed him wherever he went on the basis that his every activity should be made known. Often the actual event he was engaged in was given scant attention; it was just that the Emperor was there. That was enough for pictures and full coverage of anything he said or did. Generally what he said would be the theme for the next day's leading articles.

One of the by-products of this state of affairs was that Ethiopia bred a school of journalists who never considered it their job to determine news priority on the basis of merit. As a matter of course, anything the Emperor said or did was the front-page lead.

The ultimate editor, not only of all the newspapers but also of all radio and television programmes, was the Minister of Information himself. He was not merely an influential cabinet minister, but he also had a special relationship with the monarch— a sort of super-PRO. The editors of the newspapers and the news programmes on radio and television were required to submit all their material to the minister. Often a group of editors would be summoned to the minister's office where an editorial would be dictated to them jointly. Needless to say, almost invariably, the monarch was the focal point of all editorial comment. On other occasions, the editors would be jointly instructed on how to treat the week's most significant government achievement.

It was not unusual for the editor of the *Ethiopian Herald* to see his paper to bed late at night, only to find when a copy was delivered to his breakfast table the next morning that the front page bore little resemblance to what he had locked up. The Minister of Information often called in at the print-shop at midnight and removed, changed or inserted stories.

Apart from the tremendous general restrictions under which the newspapers and the radio and television programmes operated, there were twenty-four specific 'taboos' (the official word). These were matters upon which no word at all could be published. This list was the brainchild of Tesfaye Gebre Egzi, Minister of Information under Haile Selassie, and it was approved by the Emperor himself.

The forbidden subjects—they became known as the forbidden fruits—were: unemployment, student disturbances, problems of tax collection, cost of living and inflation, salary increments, demonstrations and strikes, tribalism and religious differences, land tenure, tenancy and land tax, increases in taxes, price increases, proliferation of liquor and beer shops, increase in prostitution, misuse of development funds raised from voluntary contributions, the Southern Sudan question, the Eritrean problem, mineral resources, the administration of the city of Addis Ababa, facility problems and residential cards, illegal drugs, police activity, increase in the price of electricity, all activities of the military, slotting machines, church affairs, the bus company (owned by the Emperor).

A reporter on the *Ethiopian Herald* said that the list was designed one quarter to prevent comment on delicate political issues such as the Southern Sudanese and Eritrean questions, and three quarters to prevent exposure of the widespread corruption prevalent in all walks of life.

As if this control was not rigid enough, the Ethiopian News Agency was used to announce almost everything that happened in the country. All government announcements, declarations, denials, appointments, promotions and demotions, as well as visits by foreign guests, originated from the News Agency. Daily official coverage of all news of the Emperor, the Council of Ministers, and the meetings of Parliament itself came from the News Agency. There was no question of a reporter on a newspaper seeking out any news, or getting an idea for a story.

Every journalist had to be an authority on protocol. If the

Emperor left on a state visit abroad or an inspection tour at home, the list of officials on the entourage had to follow a strict protocol. Failure to comply with this rule was punishable.

Censorship in Ethiopia followed a curious form. Although the editor of a paper would bear the extravagant title of 'editor in chief', the real control within the office was a man with the title 'special adviser'. He was the Minister of Information's personal representative. If the editor and the special adviser disagreed about something, it was generally the adviser's decision that prevailed—although the editor could appeal to the minister.

Given the type of Government, these special advisers acted as a kind of safety valve which editors were glad to have. The adviser had the experience to point out that what might appear to be an innocuous story would put the paper in trouble because directly or indirectly it might offend the Emperor or his immediate satellites.

Besides this pre-publication censorship, which although carried on to an extreme degree in Ethiopia was only the ultimate refinement of a system followed to lesser extents in many African states, there was another form unknown in any other country. This was the post-publication scrutiny of all articles by a special official in the Ministry of Information. His job was to identify what was called 'unexpressed negative ideas'. As the Amharic language of Ethiopia is full of ambiguities and double meanings, the post-publication censor was kept very busy.

It was not merely threat of dismissal which kept Ethiopian journalists on a tight-rope; with the Government owning all the newspapers, dismissal meant the end of your career as a journalist, but a system of fines were imposed on any newspaperman who erred. And 'err' was something which in many instances could never have been anticipated as an error in any real sense.

Perhaps the classic example of such an 'error' was the fining of the editor of the *Herald* for publishing a picture of the prize-winning bull at the Addis Ababa agricultural show on the same page as that carrying a speech by a minister. This was alleged to demean the status of the minister.

Fines could be quite heavy, running to as much as a third of the monthly salary for a major error, to a day's pay for putting the name of the twelfth member of one of the Emperor's entourage above the eleventh member.

But if this was the whip there was also the carrot, for something called the 'award system' was introduced by the Emperor. Journalists were summoned to the Palace and commended by the Emperor when they had written something that had particularly caught his fancy. These occasions arose generally when the editors had coined some hitherto unused cliché of praise about the Lion of Judah. Such gifts could be very considerable, either in cash or kind land.

'When the Emperor speaks, his words ring in the hearts and minds of all mankind', was worth 250 acres of prime land.

On 23 July 1973, on the occasion of the Emperor's eightieth birthday—and the last he was to celebrate as ruler—three dozen journalists, including most of the editors in the country, and senior officials of the Ministry of Information were commanded to the Palace where the Emperor thanked them for the special coverage of the birthday anniversary. He told them they could keep the Government cars in their possession as a reward for the good job they had done.

While the Emperor's eightieth birthday celebrations were going on, at a tremendous cost to the country, Ethiopia was in the grip of one of the worst famines ever to afflict Africa. Oxfam, the British charity, estimated that something in the region of 200,000 people died and many times that number of cattle. At the peak of the disaster, a party of Ethiopian journalists went to the worst areas with senior Government officials and saw for themselves the mounting tragedy as thousands of dead and dying lay in their huts and all round the villages. When the party returned to the capital all their reports, pictures and films were taken by the Minister of Information. Not a word appeared in the newspapers and no mention was made of the disaster on Ethiopian radio or television. Had the stories been published and the pictures and films shown, thousands of those who died would have been saved, for news of the disaster would have been picked up much more quickly by the outside world and aid would have been available.

As it was, it was a British newspaperman, Tony Hall, who had worked with Frene Ginwala in Dar-es-Salaam and before that on Kenya's *Daily Nation,* who broke the story while working for Oxfam. He thus saved many more thousands of lives.

When the Emperor was overthrown at the beginning of 1974, the new regime set up a commission of inquiry into the famine. Journalists and information officials who had been on the visit to the disaster areas the previous year told the inquiry that they had been explicitly and repeatedly instructed by the Minister of Information that the famine story was taboo.

It is hardly surprising that the roll call of Ethiopian newspapermen who confronted the system and strove for something approaching professional and ethical standards during the Emperor's rule—there have been none so foolish since the Army took over—is a short one.

Their fate was remarkably similar to the Liberian journalists who offended President Tubman; removal, warning and occasional rehabilitation in another job. Haile Selassie, like William Tubman, did not like to see the white-collared classes killed. He was very conscious of his image in the West and anxious not to be bracketed with African leaders in the Amin and Bokassa class.

It is one of the great paradoxes of post-independence Africa that the Organisation of African Unity should have headquartered itself in Addis Ababa, capital of a country ruled under a despotic system compared with which colonialism from Europe was positively benevolent.

One newspaperman who deliberately stepped out of line was Ahadou Saboure, one-time editor of a weekly Amharic paper. Reporting the trial of the leader of the abortive 1963 coup, Saboure described the man, an army general, as an immaculate officer whose courage and intellectual qualities dominated the court trial. Immediately after publication, Saboure was picked up by officers of the Presidential guard and secretly exiled to a small town where he was placed under house arrest. Some years later he was appointed to a minor diplomatic post in another African state and told he would never be allowed leave to return to Ethiopia—probably the only diplomat in the world serving the government of a country from which he was exiled.

Another persecuted journalist was Berhanu Zerihun, editor of the biggest selling Amharic paper, *Addis Zemen*. He exposed the appalling conditions of ten thousand prisoners in the National Prison in Addis Ababa and was duly brought before the Council of Ministers. It was expected that he would lose his job or worse, but he was merely given a strict warning not to venture into criticism again. A little later he criticised a beauty contest, arguing that the country had more urgent matters to attend to.

For this he was suspended from his job. The end of his career as a newspaperman came when he printed an article by a freelance writer saying that Ethiopia's emperors should justify their rule by the good they did for people rather than by boasting of their descent from the legendary line of King Solomon and the Queen of Sheba. Many people thought that the publication of this article would cost Berhanu Zerihun not only his job but his life, for criticism of this sort was unheard of. It was probably because the article caused such a stir among the foreign ambassadors in Addis Ababa and became a talking point on the diplomatic cocktail circuit that Zerihun's life was not forfeited. After a period of unemployment, he was taken on by Radio Ethiopia as head of the script desk, a sure sign that the Emperor had given the royal nod of forgiveness.

A successor as editor of *Addis Zemen* was Negash G. Mariam, who had been trained in the United States. His offence was to print an article urging the Government and the public to intensify the campaign against cholera. For this he was summoned before the Council of Ministers and given a 'last warning'.

The most popular Ethiopian journalist for a generation from the fifties to the seventies was Assiminew Gebre Wold. He had a subtle touch to his writing that enabled him to survive not only the pre-publication censorship, but also the post-publication scrutiny for 'unexpressed negative ideas'. He achieved nationwide popularity among the educated classes, and though he was permanently in disfavour with the Emperor's court and constantly fined for stepping out of line, he refused to compromise beyond a point that he thought he could live with. The pressures on him mounted to an intolerable point during the early seventies. He never knew from one day to another whether he would be sacked, exiled or worse.

One day in late 1973 he was found dead at his home in Addis Ababa. It was claimed he had committed suicide, and he may well have done so, but many journalists believed that Haile Selassie had finally given orders to silence him for good.

A few months later, the Emperor himself was removed by the Army. Gebre Wold had lived all his professional life waiting for the day when he would be able to write and report freely. Had he even survived the era of Haile Selassie, he would still have been waiting.

12 Many Voices, Many Plans

Africa is the most multi-lingual area of the world if population is measured against languages. Nobody knows how many languages there are. A fairly small area of Cameroon, for example, contains more than one hundred languages, almost all of them unwritten. There are plenty of other similar examples. It is remarkable that history did not impose language patterns on Africa more specifically than it did.

Swahili in East Africa and Hausa in West Africa were on the way to achieving this and, given another century of uninterruption, they may well have taken root and spread over much bigger areas. But the coming of the Europeans and the imposition of colonial rule stunted them. The Roman influence in Europe brought Latin with it, and for a very long time it became the language of the towns, of commerce and of administration in precisely the same way as English, French and Portuguese did in colonial Africa.

Already there are signs that these European languages may go the same way as Latin did in Europe; if they do there will be profound changes in the press of Africa. Latin survived as a living language for many centuries. Whether French and English will is questionable; whether Portuguese will is doubtful. Arabic might have taken deeper root than it did in Black Africa had not the ending of the slave trade removed that particular form of colonialism.

When a country is governed by a limiting ruling class, it does not matter what languages the masses use so long as they learn to kow-tow. No colonial power made any real attempt to spread their language into the interior of the territories they seized. If the imposed languages of the colonialists in the capitals and big urban centres gave the rulers a common medium with the indigenous elite, it had at least the great benefit of allowing that elite to make it plain that colonialism was going to end one day.

A West African politician put it this way: 'Though English allowed the White man to tell us he was the boss, it also allowed us to tell him "Yes, but not for ever".'

Ironically, the spread of the independence movement throughout British Africa was not only hastened by the use of the English language but virtually dependent on it. It cut across tribal languages, and thus to a large extent also across tribal differences. The same is true today in the struggle of Black Africa against 'White' Africa (Rhodesia and South Africa). For when the leaders of Independent Africa get together to plot the overthrow of remaining White rule, it is English they use in their deliberations.

But a new generation of Independent Africans is beginning to question the use of foreign languages. It is not yet a major issue nor a loud voice, but we may yet have the final irony of post-colonial Africa with newspapers which were in the vanguard of the independence struggle calling for the abandonment of the old imperial languages and the use of 'African' languages.

The voices beginning to speak this message are using English.

One of the most persuasive voices for 'national' languages is that of Doctor Kwasi Ampene of the Institute of Adult Education at the University of Ghana. In Ghana, a small country, there are nine languages, plus English, in general use. 'This is not compatible with our status as an independent nation', he told a meeting of West African journalists in 1974. 'We must start now to look for a Ghanaian national language which every Ghanaian can speak and can read and write in.'

On the whole Africa's newspapermen are uneasy about any change from English or French, or even Portuguese, as the medium for reporting. The *African Journalist* has said of the language issue in so far as it concerns the press: 'Be wary. Of the enormous list of things that Africa needs "national" languages must be very near the bottom . . . like it or not, the common denominator is English or French, dependent upon colonial history. It is wrong to put national pride at stake merely because something non-African is being used by Africans. If you do that there is no end to the list—all the way from trousers to traffic lights.'

And the *African Journalist* echoed the thoughts of many African newspapermen on the language issue when it concluded: 'Such a move would threaten the very existence of the press.'

But the *African Journalist* was a White edited publication.

Even if national pride wins the day and 'national' languages become the pattern of the media, it is highly unlikely that English, French and Portuguese will ever totally disappear from the press. Ethiopia's experience suggests that some sort of bastardisation may come about. Apart from its brief encounter with Mussolini's dream of an Empire—from 1935 to 1940—Ethiopia has never been ruled by outsiders. And though the press has always been one of the most pitiable on the Continent, Ethiopia at least has something of the superstructure of a vernacular press.

All the Amharic newspapers borrow heavily from English and French (once the language of the old Imperial Court). Italian never really caught on. And it is not only words of Western technology and concepts outside of the experience of Ethiopia that are used. There are perfectly good Amharic equivalents for the following words, but you will still find them in Ethiopian newspapers and magazines:

matematiks
medisin
sekuriti (security)
kallektiv (collective)
resposabiliti (responsibility)
maritaym (maritime)
layberari (library)

All this is bad enough for those newspaper readers with enough English to understand such words, but the great majority of Amharic newspaper readers have no English. Why does the press do this—and it is not confined to Ethiopia? Since knowledge of a European language is a prestige symbol, it is simply a question of the reporter writing the story and demonstrating what a clever chap he is.

This question of language and style by reporters is the constant bugbear of most African editors. Boaz Omori, who before his death in 1973 was editor-in-chief of the East African *Nation* Group, and who before that had been editor of the *Voice of Kenya* Broadcasting Station, told a gathering of journalists in April 1972: 'African journalists have to avoid at all costs running the risk of becoming so clever that when they report or interpret news of development the public never understands a thing. The African journalist must speak the language of the people if he hopes to be effective.'

Some of the blame for the wordiness of African journalists is due to the mission education many received. Education in the modern sense was founded by Victorian missionaries, and the style of English taught still has the characteristics of that age. This is even more true of the journalists from French-speaking Africa, where educationalists are proud of the 'classical' French learned at senior school level.

An applicant for one of the journalists' training courses run by the International Press Institute from 1963 to 1968 in Nairobi and Lagos urged that he should be accepted 'so that I might learn to write like Charles Lamb and Charles Dickens'.

MANY PLANS

Rolled up and somewhat yellowing, there lies in the cupboard of a government ministry in Accra the architect's plans for an all-African news agency. They are part of Kwame Nkrumah's dream of Pan-Africanism. Though Nkrumah is long gone from the African scene, this part of his dream remains, to be taken out, dusted off and mulled over from time to time, not just in Ghana but in many other parts of the Continent.

The African case for an ending of the monopoly of the international news agencies—principally Reuters, Agence France Presse, and Associated Press—is simply stated. K. B. Brown, general manager of the Ghana News Agency, by far the best national news agency in Independent Africa, summarises it thus: 'However much they claim to be impartial and accurate they are not—in fact, cannot be. Their selection of news and choice of words do not serve African interests.'

Even though in recent years Tass, Ceteka (Czech) and the New China News Agency have begun operating in Africa, there is no question that the big three Western agencies still have the lion's share of the market, and given the historical past of English-speaking and French-speaking Africa, plus the language issue itself, it is difficult to see the Russians, the Chinese or the Czechs making much of an inroad.

The knowledge that all the international news carried in their newspapers is served to them by foreigners—and in the case of Reuters and AFP, their erstwhile colonial masters—sticks in the throats of many Africans, though more so in the case of African politicians than African newspapermen.

The daily transmission from Reuters in London and AFP in Paris are seen by some politicians as the very manifestation of the neo-colonialism they claim has replaced the genuine article. Even more invidious is the fact that the foreign agencies enjoy a monopoly of African news both in Africa and abroad. At the root of the argument is the realisation that the big international agencies are not just foreign, or even Western, but White. This is not put forward as a racial argument, but to support the claim, which is undeniable, that both the news received of the outside world and the news of Africa sent by the agencies to their customers outside the Continent is predominantly the work of non-Africans.

How, ask the critics of the foreign news agencies and the champions of a pan-African agency, can British, American or French journalists whose backgrounds, culture, history and aspirations which are rooted in the industrialised world (some come right off the fence and say capitalistic world) either understand the sort of news Africans want of the outside world in their newspapers or, in so far as the agencies bureaux in the Continent are concerned, how can such journalists intelligently and accurately project the image of Africa abroad?

Such critics have a much stronger argument for the first half of their case than they have for the second half. A substantial amount of the service provided by all foreign news agencies to African newspapers seems not merely remote from the world of the average African but often irrelevant to him. And as television has spread through the urban centres of Africa, the irrelevance of much of the news material obtained from foreign agencies supplying African broadcasting stations has been underlined.

Visnews, the Continent's biggest supplier of television news film, which is partly owned by Reuters and the BBC, frequently gives wide distribution to material which by any standards seems difficult to justify. Ivory Coast viewers, for example, were being treated in September 1976 to the debates of the British Labour Party at its annual conference in Blackpool, and the same item was presumably sent to all *Visnews'* other African customers.

It is certainly not the Western agencies which supply the most obtuse items to Africa. Tass has been operating in some parts of the Continent for more than a decade. Its local correspondents today are a very different brand of journalist from the political heavies who opened their bureaux in many English-speaking countries immediately upon independence, but they can still perpetrate transmissions which are calculated to set even the most avowed African Marxist sub-editor groaning with dismay.

On independence, the Kenya government had two distinct political wings; the one that leaned to the East was in the control of the Ministry of Information with Achieng Oneko as Minister. When Oneko announced the setting up of the Kenya News Agency, the *East African Standard* was asked to give up the exclusive rights it had had for more than sixty years to the Reuter service. The *Standard* management agreed, too hastily in the view of most of the editorial staff, and immediately found it was no longer getting the twenty-four hour in-depth Reuter service beamed to Southern Africa, but a specially tailored service little more than half the old wordage and including many fillers on the comings and goings of ministers in West and North Africa.

Worse was to come. The Russians offered the Tass service free to the Government, and Oneko devised a system whereby the Ministry of Information would put out to Kenya's newspapers an amalgam of what it thought ought to be used from Reuters, Tass and other sources. In an attempt at ideological objectivity, the Ministry began to transmit 50 per cent from Tass and 50 per cent from Reuters. On one memorable day still talked about by Kenya's newspapermen, the Kenya News Agency began to transmit at 9.30 a.m. the full text of a letter from the Soviet Communist Party Secretary to his Chinese counterpart. It was still running at 2.30 p.m. and many yards of telex copy were spread around the editorial offices of the *Standard* and its competing *Nation*. Sub-editors trying to fill early news pages with usable foreign copy were bewildered. When Eric Marsden, deputy-editor of the *Standard*, telephoned the Kenya News Agency to protest, he was told he was showing bias to the capitalist West.

Kenya provides a rare—probably the only—example of how the newspapermen of a Black African state were able to take on the government on a major issue concerning the press and emerge not only unscathed but victorious.

It was not long after the creation of the Kenya News Agency that two forms of censorship began to operate, wittingly or otherwise. Apart from the delays in the Reuters service when it was taken over by Government, the newspapermen found they were only receiving about half of the full service. Long delays were caused by the selection and editing of the service as it was received from London by the mostly inexperienced staff of the Kenya News Agency. The Kenya Union of Journalists protested at the new arrangement and passed a resolution condemning the agreement between the Government and Reuters which, it said, 'made censorship possible'. A Reuters spokesman commented: 'It is utterly untrue to suggest that Reuters can bear responsibility for the imposition of censorship or the restrictions on the flow of information in any country.'

Nevertheless, there certainly were restrictions on the flow of the news and censorship now that Reuters was doing business exclusively with the Kenya Government.

A few days after the agreement was signed, an item critical of Ghana was deliberately withheld on orders from the Ministry of Information. It was disclosed that KNA staff had been instructed to submit certain types of stories for approval by the Director of Information.

Things came to a head at the height of the Congo crisis when for a day and a half the KNA withheld all items about the Congo. This naked censorship had the opposite effect from that intended. Since the newspapers were unable to get the Reuter reports they wanted, they were more than willing to accept the handouts of the United States Information Service in Nairobi. The pointlessness of the Government's action was demonstrated by the fact that throughout the crisis the *Standard*'s competitor, the *Nation*, continued to receive the service of Associated Press direct into its office.

A footnote to this series of incidents was the detention without trial not long afterwards of the Information Minister, Achieng Oneko, who during the years of Mau Mau had served a long term of imprisonment with Jomo Kenyatta at the hands of the British authorities. Now his independence jailer was his old colonial cellmate.

Kenya was one of a number of states who expelled representatives of foreign news agencies—both East and West—and there is hardly a country in the Continent which has not barried, banned or deported the foreign correspondents of the international press, with South Africa topping the table.

Nairobi's *Daily Nation*, commenting on 11 March 1966 on the expulsion of a dozen Communist diplomats, including two Soviet news-agency correspondents, a Soviet film-maker and a Czech news agency representative, said:

> Here is a method of spying, subversion and espionage which has now become fashionable in Africa. People from various countries come under the banner of 'journalists', employees of news agencies or just 'clerks' in the embassies without diplomatic protection. While in Africa these people deny any association with their own governments. Yet it is known that these newspapers and agencies are owned and run by governments. It is no secret that some of these men who pose as newspapermen are high officials in the intelligence network of their governments.

It is not always Western-inclined states expelling Eastern correspondents. In February 1976 Reuters' office in Nigeria was summarily closed and its chief correspondent, Colin Fox, expelled after he had reported the abortive coup by Lieutenant-Colonel Dimka. The Reuter office was in the same building as the British High Commission in Lagos from where, in the first hours of the coup attempt, Dimka tried to telephone the former Head of State, General Gowon, in exile in London.

But the overriding impression of the long list of expulsions of foreign newsmen from all over Africa is simply that they were beyond the control of the local authorities; that if they also worked for international news agencies, they were further tainted by being part of some unknown Eastern or Western animal with innumerable tentacles.

Peter Webb, for many years the Africa bureau chief for *Newsweek* magazine, told the IPI world assembly meeting in Nairobi in June 1968 that some African states had a rooted belief in 'the conspiracy theory of history'.

Said Webb : 'Under this, foreign correspondents were "lackeys" or "puppets" of their capitalist master.' But while the great majority of foreign newsmen operating in Africa are bona-fide journalists, there have been and continue to be enough of them either using newspapers or news agencies as fronts for other activities or just being simply 'bought' by one side or the other in the cold use of intelligence gathering.

It is with this knowledge that the call for a pan-African news agency is increasingly heard—presupposing that Black journalists are less corruptible than White. Chris Asher, editor/owned of Ghana's *Palaver*, is one of a good number of African journalists who do not think so. 'In Ghana today any diplomat can tell the story of some journalists who frequent diplomatic homes soliciting for money', he wrote in his paper.

But the greatest hurdle facing the planners of an all-African news agency is not the corruptibility or otherwise of its news gathering staff, nor even the enormous physical difficulties of creating a communications network between Africa's states; it is the diffuse and widely differing political systems of the individual states. There are a score of friction points between many of Africa's states. In countries like Nigeria there are a good many within the different regions of the countries themselves.

What sort of coverage would the Uganda bureau of an all-African news agency be able to send out of the country? How would capitalist Kenya react to the flow of pronouncements on the evils of Western imperialism from the Marxist government of Moçambique? What would the attitude of the Sudan be to the speeches of Libya's Colonel Gadaffi, whom it constantly accuses of trying to undermine it?

The emotional appeal of such a project seems to have blinded its planners to the realities that would surely be faced by every correspondent in every bureau of a pan-African news agency almost every time he put a piece of copy paper into his type-writer.

The international news agencies are constantly accused of not employing local correspondents, and in recent years some of them have yielded to these pressures and taken on nationals of the countries in which they operate, though none as bureau head. However strong the arguments of the politicians that foreign reporters do not understand us, the record of intimidation against

Africa's journalists in virtually every State is sufficiently daunting to suggest that a local journalist in charge of a news agency's office would be subjected to pressures much greater than those carried by an expatriate bureau chief.

This consideration is likely to be magnified under a pan-African news agency system. However authoritarian government rule may be, a foreign bureau chief is still able to decide which of the government announcements issued in profusion every day by African ministries of information he will send to his London, Paris, New York, Peking or Moscow head office, and also which parts of those statements he will send. Very few African states would allow a local journalist in charge of a foreign news agency bureau this freedom of choice; Kenya, perhaps—but only perhaps; Tanzania, possibly—but possibly not.

Nigeria, with the most complex media network of any state in Independent Africa, is a significant example of those few countries without a news agency. After years of discussion, as government changed hands four times, the military junta finally issued a decree early in 1976 establishing a news agency and setting out its objectives. The military decree provided for an eight-member board of directors to run the day-to-day affairs, controlled by a trustee council drawn from the Nigerian Bar Association, the Newspaper Proprietors Association, the Nigerian Union of Journalists, the Nigerian Guild of Editors and three other people appointed by the Federal Commissioner for Information.

The announcement was received with mixed feelings by journalists. They saw it as just one more government hand in the control of news. But at the eleventh hour, in October 1976, the military had second thoughts about the whole idea and postponed the project for two years. A contributing factor to the delay was the rupture between the government and Reuters, which had been closely involved in the planning for years, caused by the closure of their office over the Dimka incident.

Nigeria's cautionary attitude to even a national news agency is a major stumbling block in the creation of a pan-African agency, for its oil wealth was expected to be a major source of the finance needed to bring such a project into being. Estimates of the capital and running costs vary enormously every time a meeting is held to discuss plans. In fact the Union of African News Agencies was founded in Tunis as far back as 1963, but though it had a membership of twenty national news agencies, it never made any significant impact on the creation of a news gathering and distribution agency for the Continent, or at least the Black section of it.

During the early seventies, a number of Arab states were active in trying to get a pan-African agency off the ground; but, as in almost every other field, Black Africa has been wary of the Arabs. With the Organisation of African Unity embracing both parts of Africa, it is a delicate operation to fend off the Arabs. At an international conference of journalists in Lagos in May 1975, although no delegate raised the point, it was in the minds of all, and some suggested that the various zones of the Continent should each have their own agency. Yet another meeting was held in November 1976, this time in Abidjan, Ivory Coast, and an unresolved question was where the head-quarters of such an agency should be situated—with the political sensitivities of Africa perhaps the most vital decision of all.

There appear to be five contenders: Cairo and Algiers, which it is difficult to see Black Africa accepting; Kinshasa and Abidjan, which are expected to be opposed by many English-speaking countries, and Ghana, which because of its long established and excellently run national news agency, has a strong claim but which may run into trouble with its big neighbour Nigeria, almost traditionally opposed to anything coming out of Ghana.

The odds seem long against those yellowing architect's plans being taken from their cupboard in Accra for a long time yet.

13 Freedom—and After

There are as many definitions of freedom inside Africa—of the press and everything else—as there are out of it. It is just that in Africa they talk about it a lot more.

It was Western culture that produced the notion of a 'free press' and a fundamental concept of freedom was that anyone with money enough to start a newspaper should be able to do so. Whether the newspaper he produced was just or unjust was part of that freedom. Fairness and balance were a long time coming in the West, and whether they have yet arrived is still a great debate. What freedom there is in the Western press is related very much to the openness of society, in the sense of the plurality of the political systems, the trade unions and the hundred and one other bodies, each with their own axes to grind and not afraid to grind them in public.

This freedom is becoming less and less possible in most of Africa. In some states it has disappeared altogether. What axe-grinding goes on is more of a sharpening of the instrument of revolution designed to cut down the prevailing authority, and it is carried on secretly. There is no government in Africa, from Cape Town to Cairo, that feels itself to be entirely secure; and the less secure it feels itself, the greater the strictures it puts on the press, for an independent press is the only instrument of possible dissent *it can get at*. And whether civilian or military, Africa's rulers are united in the belief that an independent press is more likely than not to be associated with any forces seeking to change the *status quo*.

It does not bode well for a press in terms acceptable in the West. But Africa is not the West. Nor is it the East. Though a few Black States, noticeably Ethiopia, Angola, Moçambique and Somalia, appear to have moved nearer the East than the West, this may prove to be a transitory thing, as it did in Guinea.

Peter Enahoro believes that the future of the press of Africa cannot be considered in isolation from the future of political development. He thinks military rule will come to an end in 'domino style'.

'It will just go out of fashion in Africa', he says. 'There is a lot of imitation in Africa—the knock-on theory. There will come a new group of military men who will believe that a return to civilian rule is a revolutionary act.'

Though this happened in Ghana, when the military handed over the government to Kofi Busia's Progress Party, it was not long before the soldiers returned to office. But Enahoro prefers to draw his analogy of what will happen from Greece and Portugal.

'People are getting tired of military rule. There was a time when they welcomed it. It cleared up the mess the civilians had made. Now we are going through the disillusionment and awe at the enormity of the military machine. The ordinary man sees it everywhere and asks himself "How can I deal with this?" '

Enahoro does not believe that there will be anything like an uprising against military rule, but that it will end through that mysterious bush telegraph that works in all societies. The message will get through that soldier power is no longer tenable. As for the press, he believes that at this juncture of African history it makes little difference whether you have civilian or military rule; it will still be shackled. The shackles of military rule are marginally heavier than civilian rule, but there are exceptions: the press of Nigeria is better off than the press of Liberia. Ghana is no worse off than Zambia.

The best hope for the press, though, he believes, must be with democratically elected governments. 'With civilian governments there will be political parties. They will want a voice over and above their parliamentary spokesmen, and so newspapers will be started. This may at least solve some of the economic problems of the press in as much as political parties are likely to be able to raise the money that pure speculators would not look at.'

On top of this, the African public is becoming more and more a reading public and there is precious little to read other than newspapers. As education spreads and intelligence levels rise, the public will want more than the sycophantic messages of so much of the African press today.

As the states of Africa cast around for a suitable way to govern themselves—in exactly the same way as the states of Europe did in an earlier age—so will the fortunes and the freedoms of the press ebb and flow. Only when the forms of government are set will the pattern of the press become clearer, and that pattern is bound to be a patchwork. Where military fanatics like Uganda's Idi Amin and the Central African Empire's Jean-Bedel Bokassa rule, the press will function almost as a joke, in total servility. Where men like Tanzania's Julius Nyerere survive, the press, though an agency of government, will continue to play a significant role as a nation-builder. And anyone who knows something about the character of the people of Nigeria will believe that whatever soldiers come and go, newspapers there will somehow keep putting their toe, then their feet, then their shoulder over the line drawn for them.

There is no unified voice about the role of the press coming out of Africa. There used to be. In the immediate post-independence years, Africa's new leaders spoke about the press with an unanimity almost as solid as the voices that had been raised in the struggles for independence from the colonialists. That same 'Freedom!' that had been roared from millions of throats at the midnight ceremonies on independence was, presumably, to include freedom of the press.

But gradually the realities of nation-building, the frailties of human nature, the abuses of responsibility by both politicians and pressmen, have brought as many different interpretations of the place of the press in the society they serve as there are forms of government itself in Africa.

Although there are some states in Africa which have strong similarities with the closed societies of Communism and Fascism, this is true in only a handful of cases. The majority of African countries are somewhere between the closed societies of totalitarianism and the open societies of the West, and their newspapers reflect this.

Zambia's President, Kenneth Kaunda, who spends more time talking about the press, worrying about its deficiencies and trying to convince his country's newspapermen what they should be writing than anyone else on the Continent (in 1972 he made three speeches in twenty-four hours, each more than an hour long, about newspapers) has tried to find the right path between East and West for his press. 'The news media everywhere in the world reflect the interests and values of the society they are serving', he told what was billed as an 'eyeball to eyeball' meeting between Government and newsmen. 'I want you to study very closely the news media in the capitalist, the Communist and colonial societies and you will find the truth about the nature, objectives and operations of the news media.'

And he put this to the journalists: 'I therefore now ask you; Where do you belong? Which society are you serving? Our news media must reflect the nature of our society, project and defend our philosophy, our values and our interests as a sovereign state. If you do not, you are not with us as a nation.'

Then he got down to specifics—and left the journalists in no doubt about what he expected, and what they could expect if they did not deliver.

'I know some of you have always wanted to project an image of disunity in the party and the nation', he said. 'The facts you have been gathering, the preparation of facts in a distorted manner, the expressions of terminology used in all news media, the choice of items for the front page stories, the choice of headlines and the emphasis given to negative aspects of the Party and the Government and life in Zambia in general all indicate the intentions of some of our newsmen. Some of you have been the instruments of our enemies bent on the destruction of Zambia.'

Having waved his big stick at Zambia's journalists, he had this to say about the freedom of the Press: 'You know that the Press in this country as a pillar of democracy enjoys unparalleled freedom. You cannot doubt this. But freedom does not exist in a vacuum. The freedom of the press is based on the right of the people, the public to know, to have access to information.'

Item by item he listed the sort of stories the newspapers had been printing that he found 'disgusting': housebreaking, rape, arson, conflicts between chiefs.

Success was to be the watchword, the success of Zambian development. 'Some of you have been pre-occupied with the failures of some of our development programmes', he said.

He ended: 'You must stop it before other measures are taken.'

President Kaunda is an emotional man and his speeches often reflect this. But he is also a highly intelligent man and that speech was a watershed for the press of Zambia.

At almost the same time as Kaunda was making that speech, 1,000 miles to the north, one of Kenya's most profound thinkers was also talking about the press and press freedom. Mwai Kibaki was then Minister of Finance. He is often seen as a future president of Kenya.

He didn't pretend to like the idea of a free press, but he had come down on the side of it because it was part of the democratic idea. 'You agree only because you are committed to a greater principle of democracy', he told a meeting of East African journalists. 'If one is committed to democracy, then you cannot but be committed to a free press.'

He was full of trepidation. 'But then, if you want a free press, if you want an independent press—and *we* want it—I have been asking myself in what sense is a press free, in what sense is a press meant to be free? Can it be free? Can you really have an independent press when the people in charge of it, like everyone of us, have their own likes and dislikes, have their own ideas of what they would like to see happen in a given country?'

In a country where the three daily newspapers and virtually all the others are owned by foreign interests, it was a highly pertinent question.

'They'—he meant the owners and managers of the papers— 'have their own circle of friends in these small countries which tend to be very small circles. They have their own shareholders. The people who own these companies have their own views on what should be going on, and more important everybody who is in the press is orientated in a given manner, and insists that independence means the right to publish what they decide at their own discretion should be published and the right to decide what should be given prominence; what is important news and what is unimportant news and the right to decide whether to publish certain material or whether not to publish certain material.'

This is an argument carried on in societies much more advanced than any in Africa; but in states where you often only have one or two newspapers, and where the number of people who can read them are a tiny if important proportion of the population, the point is far more relevant than in developed societies.

But the final choice whether in Zambia (where the press is owned or controlled by the government) or in Kenya (where it is owned and controlled by private and foreign interests) has to be made between giving the press an element of independence or not.

Mwai Kibaki does not hedge his bets. 'I think maybe that it is the lesser of two evils to tolerate a press which claims or pretends to independence, although one knows it is subject to influences which make it hardly independent in a meaningful sense.'

There is often much less double-talk in Africa from its soldier rulers than its politicians, though it is noticeable how this changes as they acquire a taste for power and adopt the postures and the platitudes of the men they overthrew. A few weeks after the military coup in Ghana that ousted the civilian government of Kofi Busia, Major A. H. Selormey, the new regime's Commissioner for Information announced: 'A military government by its very nature is certainly inconsistent with any pretensions to subscribing fully to the concept of freedom of the press.' Major Selormey had a straight message for any newspapermen who did not like the idea of the Government taking control of the press: 'He should feel free or be honest enough to advise himself as to what steps he considers it best for him to take.'

An aspect of the press freedom debate little voiced in Africa is the incompetence of many reporters. 'When I see what the average newspaperman who reports my speeches—even when they are given to him in a handout—does to them in print it sorely tests my belief in press freedom', the late Tom Mboya, one of the Continent's most able politicians, said shortly before his death by an assassin's bullet in 1969. His fellow cabinet minister, Mwai Kibaki, was saying much the same thing to a meeting of East African journalists in 1972. 'I am appalled by the level of information of the majority of the men and women who run our press in East Africa', he said. 'The level of information compared with the rest of the world is incredibly low.' Mwai Kibaki said that time and time when cabinet ministers were being interviewed, it was patently obvious that the reporters had just 'not done their homework' and that questions rarely rose above the gossip level.

Adamu Ciroma, managing director of the *New Nigerian*, told the world assembly of the International Press Institute in Munich in 1972 that incompetent journalists were one of the main threats to a free press in under-developed countries.

'Where journalists have an insufficient knowledge of their craft and where their reports and coverage of events are demonstrably incorrect or where they misuse their freedom and privilage by pursuing selfish or sectional interests, they leave themselves wide open to criticisms and governmental actions which can whittle away the freedom of the press.'

Ghana's Chris Asher, editor/owner of *Palaver*, put it more succinctly in a leading article headed 'Ghana's Punk Journalists'. 'Even people who can hardly write their own name claim to be journalists. You have all kinds of punks and muggerfackers parading in the name of journalists.'

But though the role of newspapers is differently defined according to the dictates of Africa's leaders—in or out of uniform— the place of newspapermen is much more universally accepted; they are part of the nation-building process. Just what part they should play varies widely according to the tradition of journalism in a particular state and often the standard of professionalism inherited from colonial times. In Nigeria, for example, where the press can rightly claim to have played a major part in the struggle for independence, even though the country's leading newspapers are now Government-owned, there is a deep-rooted belief among journalists that they have a special right to play a special role.

At the other end of the spectrum, in Tanzania, where the press was seen to be both an agent of colonialism and thus an obstacle to independence, even the country's best journalists have no quarrel with the new role defined for the press; national service.

Ben Mkapa, who moved from the managing editor's desk of the *Daily News* to be President Nyerere's Press secretary in State House, and thence to Foreign Minister, did not even raise an eyebrow among Tanzanian journalists when at a seminar in Dar-es-Salaam he told them: 'I do not look upon journalists as a class of workers who are fundamentally different from other workers and therefore entitled to fundamentally special status. They are nation-builders. At least they should be nation-builders just like any other workers in society.'

Ben Mkapa is one of the relatively few journalists in Africa who look beyond the city-limits of the capitals where most of Africa's newspapers are produced—produced for the peoples of those capitals who are often a whole life-style away from the ninety-five per cent of peasants in the small towns and villages of the Continent.

Whether you read a newspaper in Africa—or anything else—depends upon where you live. Percentages vary from country to country, but *every* form of communication—newspapers, television, telephones, even mail and roads—is restricted to a minority, generally a tiny minority, of city dwellers. The so-called national newspapers are a mouthpiece of the urban elite talking to the urban elite.

There is thus a two-way traffic in ignorance; the urban elite knows nothing and cares even less about the rural peoples and their problems, and the peasants have no more than the haziest idea of what is going on at the centre of the nation.

Ben Mkapa told Tanzania's pressmen: 'Is this the way things should be? Should the continuation of this state of affairs be considered the fulfilment of the nation-building role of the press? The urban population is a largely unproductive community, the industrial and service workers notwithstanding. In East Africa the people who work on the land, a staggering 90 per cent and over, are the true producers. The urban community is distinguished by its consumption of a disproportionate slice of the national cake. Has not the press given this section of society an inordinate importance in national development?'

President Nyerere has summarised the dilemma of the urban-peasant gulf thus: 'While other nations try to reach the moon we are trying to reach the village.'

The 'national' newspapers of Africa can never hope to bridge this gulf. Indeed, if they ever tried to, they would be in danger of putting themselves in an even more parlous economic position than they now face, for that life-style of difference between the townsman and the villager mitigates against producing newspapers with an appeal to both, and even if a magic formula could be found to editionalise the city newspapers for the rural areas, distribution costs would rule such a plan out.

Gradually, but much too slowly, it is becoming clear to the governments of Africa that the peasants of their nations will only be reached, if at all, by a press which is tailored specifically to peasant needs and produced in the rural areas.

It is something of a commentary on the urban-orientated leaders of so many of Africa's new states that they have not long since tackled the problem of providing a rural press. In terms of the many almost insoluble problems facing Africa, this is something that could be achieved with relatively little trouble or expense. The failure of so many governments to do anything about producing newspapers for the rural areas indicates that Africa's leaders, though constantly paying lip-service to the needs of 'the people', have fallen into the same trap as the city dwellers and grown apart from their roots in the hinterlands of their nations.

Inseparable everywhere in the world are illiteracy and high birthrates, illiteracy and poor health, illiteracy and poverty. Three quarters of African men cannot read. For African women the figure is even higher. Conventional education is losing the battle. Many children do not go to school; many more leave school before they are literate in any real sense. Therefore there is nothing to sustain the little literacy they have—no books, no magazines, no newspapers.

A hundred years ago Western Europe and the United States were in much the same position. The great leap forward to literacy coincided with the spread of the local community newspaper, the so-called 'penny Press', Russia made the leap in half the time, from an agrarian, peasant community at the beginning of the century to a highly literate society. Under Lenin the state-ownership of paper factories and printing houses provided every group of citizens of a certain size with an equal right to the use of newsprint and printing machinery. As a result newspaper circulations skyrocketed and literacy moved up to match.

Where rural press schemes do exist in Africa, they have often been the creation of non-Africans, men who with no axes to grind have seen at once the enormity of the gulf between town and country and the opportunities there are for a new-style press to help bridge it.

Neff Smart began his missionary work for the Mormon Church of Salt Lake City in the working-class sprawl of Britain's Gravesend on the borders of London. Forty years later it is just possible that he has laid the groundwork for the most important press development in the Third World.

Smart is no longer a missionary for the Mormons. After his youthful evangelising, he became a small-town newspaperman in the United States and then moved into teaching journalism at the University of Utah.

He is still at Utah, but during the sixties and the seventies he spent several years in Ethiopia, Nigeria and finally in Ghana.

It is in Ghana that he has launched two little publications which have twin aims: to help spread literacy and encourage the newspaper reading habit.

Smart launched his *Densu Times* in Eastern Ghana in October 1974. He had previously done a thorough survey among forty-four schools in the area with children in the thirteen–fifteen bracket, measuring reading skills and literacy levels.

The Ministry of Information pays for the printing of the *Densu Times,* and two research students at the Ghana University's School of Journalism are the editors. Three full-time reporters work in the area covered by Smart's survey. Twenty-four of the forty-four schools in the survey have newspapers delivered to them, and the remaining twenty do not. The idea is to see what difference, if any, develops over a period between the newspaper schools and the non-newspaper schools.

Because the *Densu Times* is very much a community newspaper dealing with issues and personalities known and understood in the area, it is eagerly awaited and as eagerly read and studied. Even among those students whose literacy is very low, it has provided a great spur to becoming literate.

This is the basic idea behind the project, but in addition there is an attempt to measure the impact of the newspaper on the whole community, as many of the students take the paper home. The school children read the paper to their mainly illiterate parents, and some of the schools use the paper intensively in the class-rooms.

A continuing stream of letters, poems, stories and news stories written by local people flow back to the production centre at the School of Journalism in Accra.

The newspaper, sometimes four and sometimes six pages, is produced by photo off-set and in 1976 a sister publication, the *Akora New Era,* serving another part of Ghana, was launched.

Forty per cent of Ghana's population is under fifteen years of age and before 1980 this figure will rise to over 50 per cent. The same sort of thing is true of almost all African countries.

If young teenagers can be captured into the newspaper reading habit, they will be weaned on to something which hopefully will endure for the rest of their lives.

The success or failure of ventures like these almost always depend on the driving force of a single individual. In Ghana this is Neff Smart, though he is now back at Utah and tries to nurture the operation from there, realising that its ultimate success must depend on the will of the Ghanaians themselves.

If UNESCO had its priorities right, they would be pouring resources into the creation of a rural press in Africa. In fact they have only one full-time officer concerned with such ventures. Fortunately he could hardly be a better choice.

Roland Schryer is a French-speaking-Swiss. Of all the countries of Europe, Switzerland, for all its affluence, has the most primitive local papers. Schryer's background is thus much more relevant to Africa than someone's from a sophisticated press would be.

Schryer has been, and continues to be, an enormous driving force in the development of newspapers serving the peasant peoples of French-speaking Africa.

Mali, Togo and the Congo are among the states he has helped create papers. These little publications are all packed with the sort of information which peasants need to have; news about insecticides, hygiene, how to be a better carpenter or mason, advice on what fish to breed, how to bring up baby, how the local administration works, advice on local geography, what the current prices for foodstuffs in the market should be.

There are strip cartoons that tell of the adventures of a peasant couple, people the rural areas can identify with.

One of the best of these rural papers is the Congo's *Sengo*. Its style is simple and direct. One issue discussed literacy this way:

> Because you know how to read you have had good luck that others have not had; that's all.
> So you are not obliged:
> to wear two or three ballpoint pens in your pocket to show that you know how to use them;
> to wear a suit every day because you think it is the uniform for those who work with their heads;
> to let your nails grow long like a film actor's to show that you do not work with your hands.

But you should assist those who do not know how to read:
by helping them to learn to read, write and do sums;
by explaining to them what you read.
When you have finished reading this newspaper let other
villagers profit from it.

Almost all the rural papers in France's former colonies are
published in French, and this makes good sense as in all these
states French is the language of the decision makers.

The editors of rural newspapers in six West African states,
Gabon, Mali, Niger, Senegal, Togo and the Congo have formed
the African Association of Rural Journalists. There is nothing
like the effort being made in the former British colonies to
create a rural press, though Tanzania, Kenya and Zambia are
making some attempt.

It seems inevitable that such papers must be government
ventures. The danger is not that they will then push an
establishment line; in the rural areas no 'line' other than keeping
above starvation level is really relevant. Rather that governments
will lack the dedication of individuals like Neff Smart and
Roland Schryer to ensure that the papers continue not only to
be published but to reach their destinations.

In many countries in Africa, as elsewhere in the Third World
where governments are anxious to window-dress their attempts
to 'reach the people', a huge range of literature is being churned
out from government presses. Much of it is very useful, but
any visitor to African Ministries of Information in a score of
states knows only too well, after picking his way round the
bundles littering the corridors, that a great deal of this material
remains in bundles, undelivered and unopened. For the annual
reports of the government ministries which produce them, it is
enough to report that they came off the printing presses.

But if the idea of a rural press catches on and flourishes,
bringing some form of newspaper to the vast hinterlands of
Africa now virtually untouched by the written word, though the
message of such a media may not have anything to do with
the freedom of the press, it may bring something arguably much
more important—basic literacy and with it the beginnings of
freedom from the abject poverty of most of Africa's peoples.

Selected Bibliography

I have deliberately avoided footnotes to prevent interuption of the text. Research material on the press in Africa is still scarce, most of it being confined to articles from magazines or academic journals so I have included a selection of the more important of these.

Professor William A. Hachten, Professor of Journalism at the University of Wisconsin and the leading United States authority on mass communications in Africa, has compiled an annotated bibliography, *Mass Communication in Africa*, published by the Centre for International Communication Studies, University of Wisconsin in 1971. This is an invaluable work for anyone doing research into the subject, and contains descriptions of virtually everything of importance written about all forms of media in Africa since modern communications began.

The library of the International Press Institute, at the City University, London, has the most extensive collection of newspaper cuttings and other material on the African press in Europe particularly concerning restrictions of press freedom. It also contains the reports of the many meetings and seminars on the press in Africa, organised under its training programme for African journalists, and run for all the English-speaking African states in Nairobi, Kenya, and Lagos, Nigeria. The monthly bulletin of the Institute, *IPI Report*, going back some twenty-five years, contain innumerable articles of the press in Africa.

The African Journalist was a quarterly publication issued by the

Internation Press Institute from September 1971 to March 1975 as part of the consultancy service provided to the African press. Each of the fifteen issues contains articles on the African press, many of them written by African journalists themselves.

Bibliography

Books
Africa South of the Sahara 1975, (Europa Publications, 1975)
Ainslie, Rosalynde, *The Press in Africa* (Gollancz 1966)
Ajayi, J. F., and Espie, Ian (eds.), *A Thousand Years of West African History* (Ibadan University Press and Nelson, 1965)
Apter, David E., *Ghana in Transition* (Princeton University Press, 1972)
Braddon, Russell, *Roy Thomson of Fleet Street* (Collins, 1965)
Broughton, Morris, *Press and Politics of South Africa* (Purnell, 1961)
Clapham, Christopher S., *Haile Selassie's Government* (Praeger, 1970)
Coker, Increase, *Landmarks of the Nigerian Press* (Nigerian National Press, undated)
Cultural Engineering and Nation Building (Northwestern University Press, 1972)
Curtin, Philip D., *The Image of Africa* (Macmillan, 1965)
Doob, Leonard W., *Communication in Africa* (Yale University Press, 1966)
Dumont, Rene, *False Start in Africa* (André Deutsch, 1966)
Enahoro, Anthony, *Fugitive Offender* (Cassell, 1965)
Europa Year Book, (London Europa Publications)
Fyfe, Christopher, *A History of Sierra Leone* (Oxford University Press, 1966)
Hachten, William A., *Muffled Drums* (Iowa State University Press, 1971)

Hatch, John, *A History of Postwar Africa* (André Deutsch, 1965)
Hepple, Alexander, *Verwoerd* (Penguin Books, 1967)
Jones-Quartey, K. A. B., *A Life of Azikiwe* (Penguin Books, 1965)
Keatley, Patrick, *The Politics of Partnership: the Federation of Rhodesia and Nyasaland* (Penguin African Library, 1963)
King, Cecil, *Strictly Personal* (Weidenfeld & Nicolson, 1969)
Laurence, John, *Seeds of Disaster* (Gollancz, 1968)
Lindsay-Smith, H., *Behind the Press in South Africa* (Stewart, 1946)
L'Information en Afrique, Affaires Extérieures et de la Coopération and *Office de Radiodiffusion Télévision Française*, Paris
Oliver, Roland and Atmore, Anthony, *Africa Since 1800*, (Cambridge University Press: 1967)
Parker, John *Little White Island* (Pitman, 1972)
Potter, Elaine, *The Press as Opposition: the Political Role of South African Newspapers* (Chatto and Windus, 1975)
The Press in West Africa: Report of a Seminar at the University of Dakar, 1960
Rosberg, Carl G. Jnr. and Nottingham, John, *The Myth of Mau Mau* (Praeger, 1966)
Sanger, Clyde, *Central African Emergency* (William Heinemann, 1960)
Schwarz, Frederick R. O., *Nigeria: The Tribes, the Nation or the Race* (M.I.T. Press, 1965)
Sommerlad, Lloyd, *The Press in Developing Countries* (Sydney University Press, 1966)
Spencer, John (ed.), *Language in Africa* (Cambridge University Press, 1963)
Stokke, Olav (ed.), *Reporting Africa* (Scandinavian Institute of African Studies, 1971)
Wilcox, Dennis L., *Mass Media in Black Africa* (Praeger, 1975)
World Communications, (UNESCO and Gower Press, 1975)
Articles
Aloba, Abiodun, 'Journalism in Africa: Nigeria', *Gazette* V, No. 2
Aloba, Abiodun, 'Journalism in Africa: Tabloid Revolution', *Gazette* V, No. 4
Azikiwe, Nnamdi, 'Journalism in West Africa', 22 articles appearing between 18 May and 13 June in *West African Pilot* Lagos, 1945
'The Battle of the Newspapers', *Weekly Review*, Kenya, 18 October 1976
'Lord High Everything' (President Bokassa, Central African

Republic), *Time* 4 March 1974

Carter, Felice, 'The Asian Press in Kenya', *East African Journal*, October 1969

Edeani, David Omazo, 'Ownership and Control of the Press in Africa, *Gazette* XV No. 1, 1955

Enahoro, Peter, 'Why I Left Nigeria', *Transition* No. 36, July 1968

Epelle, Sam, 'Communicating with the New Africa', *Communique*, February 1967

'Freedom of the Press: An Empirical Analysis of One Aspect of the Concept', *Gazette* XVIII, No. 2, 1972

Ginwala, Frene, 'The Press in South Africa', *Index*, Autumn 1973

Jones-Quartey, K. A. B., 'Press Nationalism in Ghana', *United Asia*, February 1957

Hachten, William A., 'Newspapers in Africa: Change or Decay' *African Report*, December 1970

Hall, Tony, 'Liberalism....the toughest creed there is, (Rajat Neogy interviewed'), *Sunday Nation*, Nairobi, 11 June 1967

Hall Richard, 'The Press in Black Africa—How Free is it?', *Optima*, March 1968

'The Influence of Newspapers and Television in Africa,' *Journal of African Affairs*, July 1963

'Kaunda in Command,' *Time*, 9 October 1973

Kleu, Sebastian, 'The Afrikaans Press: Voice of Nationalism', *Nieman Reports*, October 1961

Howe, Russell Warren, 'Reporting from Africa: A Correspondent's View', *Journalism Quarterly*, Summer 1966

Mukupo, Titus, 'What Role for the Government in the Development of an African Press?', *Africa Report*, January 1966

Nelson, Daniel, 'Africa: Why the Newspaper Boom has not Arrived', *U.K. Press Gazette*, 12 May 1969

'Nkrumah and the Guinea Press', *West Africa*, 11 April 1970

Omu, Fred, 'The Nigerian Press and the Great War', *Nigerian Magazine*, March/May 1968

Paterson, Adolphus, 'Why Africa Needs a Free Press', *Africa Report*, April 1971

UNESCO Report on Meeting of Experts on Mass Communication and Society, Montreal, June 1969

Van den Berge, Pierre, 'Africa's Language Problem—Too Many, Too Late', *Trans-Action*, November 1969

Index